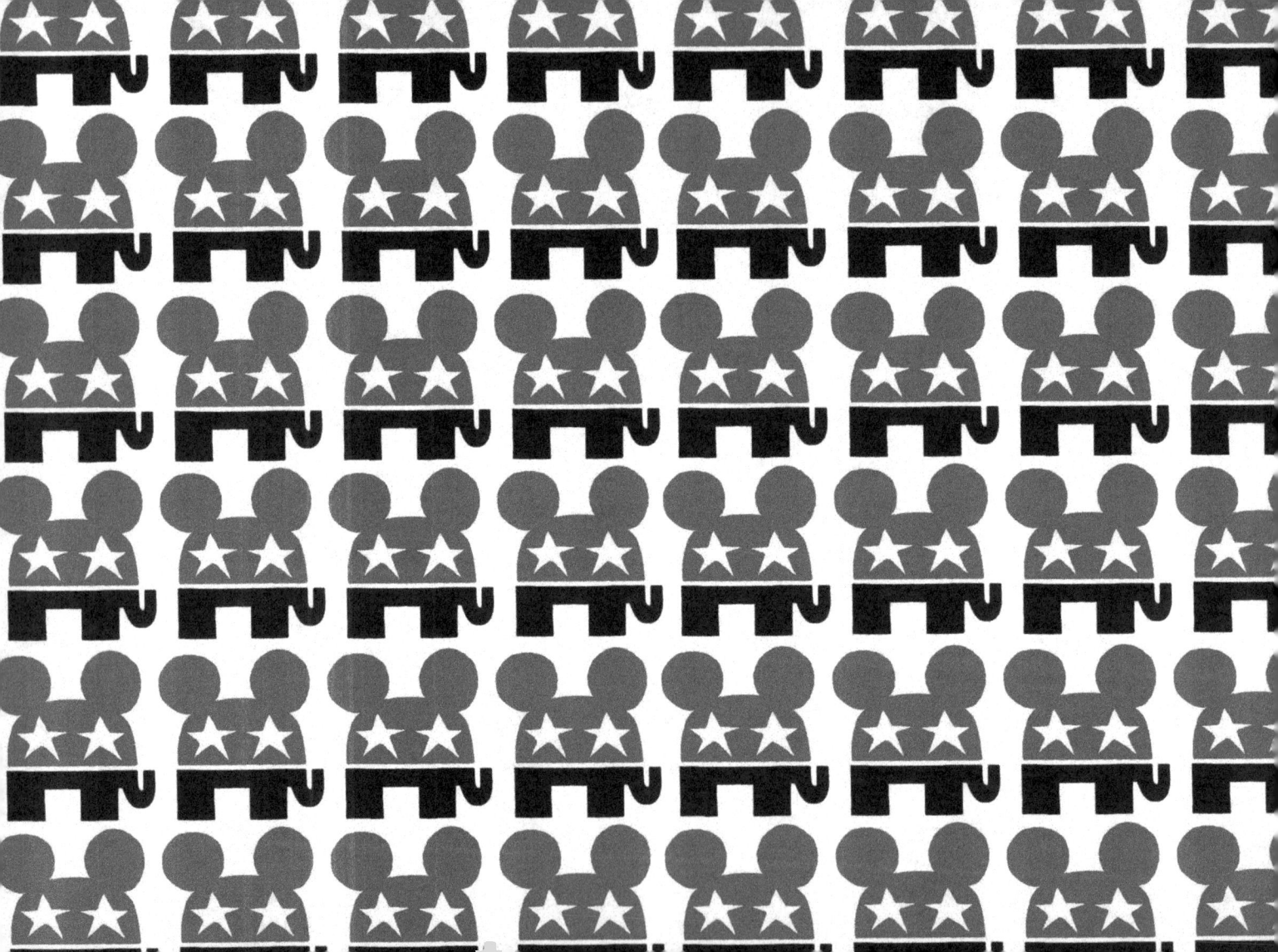

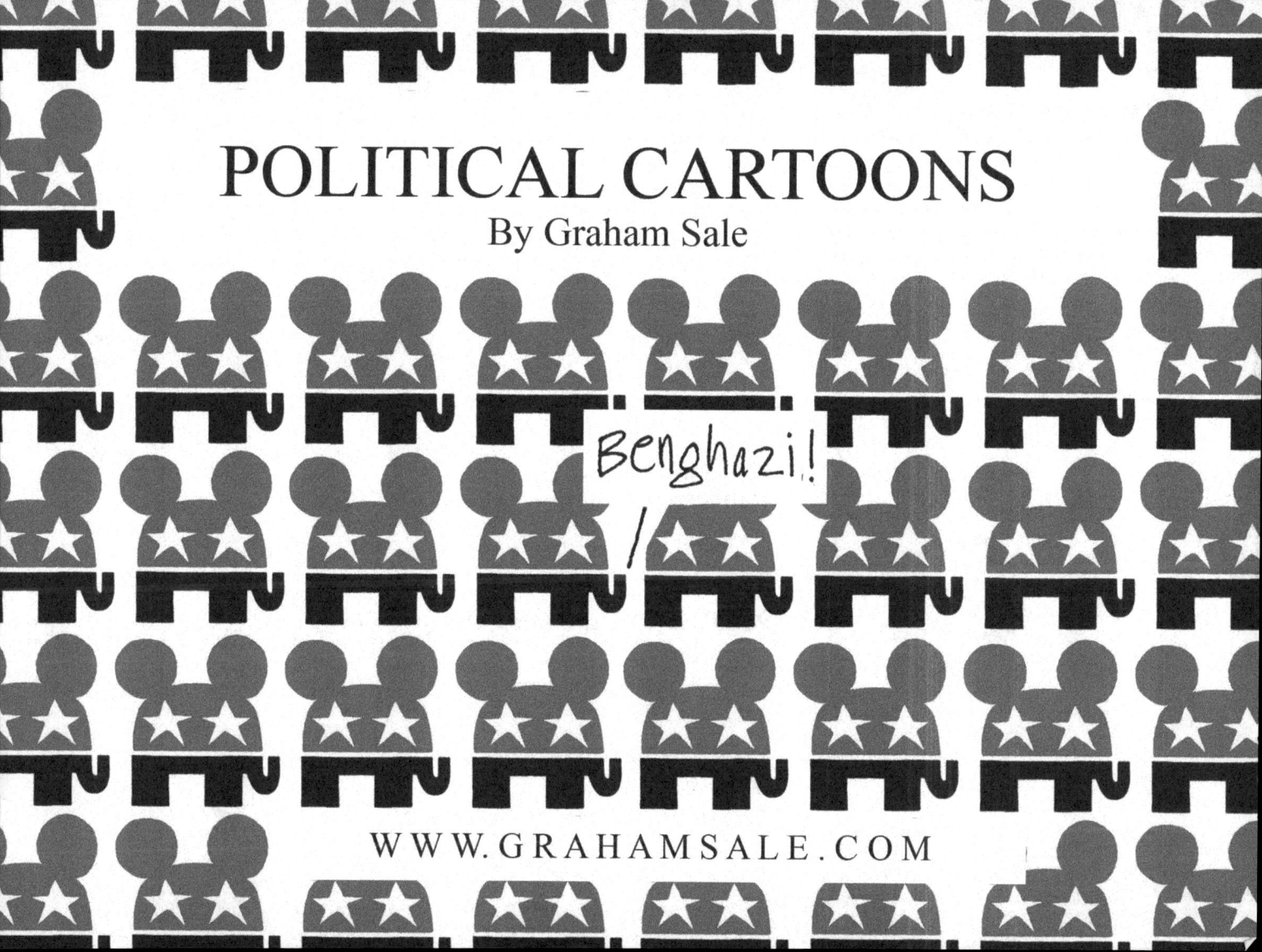

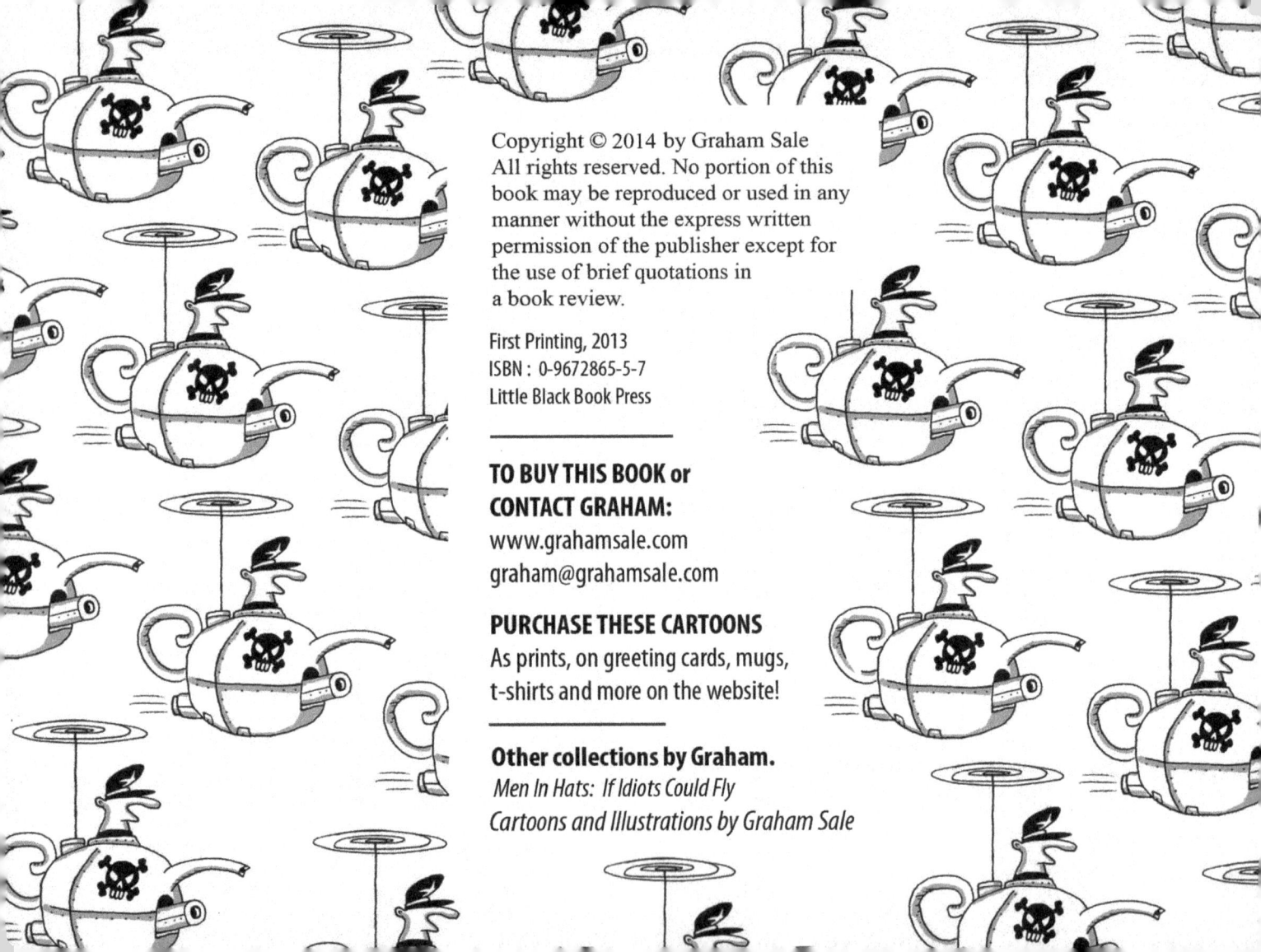

First Printing, 2013
ISBN : 0-9672865-5-7
Little Black Book Press

_____

**TO BUY THIS BOOK or
CONTACT GRAHAM:**
www.grahamsale.com
graham@grahamsale.com

PURCHASE THESE CARTOONS
As prints, on greeting cards, mugs,
t-shirts and more on the website!

_____

Other collections by Graham.
Men In Hats: If Idiots Could Fly
Cartoons and Illustrations by Graham Sale

"Graham has a different take on political cartooning. His cartoons feel fresh and original.
Graham doesn't come from the traditional school of political cartooning, so you won't find the often over-used
elephant and donkey icons of old. His work can take a minute to fully comprehend, but it is worth the wait.
Graham's cartoons wickedly point out the hypocrisy spewed by many politicians these days."
- Chris Peck, Editor, *The Commercial Appeal*, Memphis, TN

"Graham Sale's cartoons
are crispy, pithy, surprising,
elegant, tasty, sophisticated,
stylish, clever, beautiful,
provocative, pertinent,
outrageous, timely,
perceptive, revolutionary,
and above all, absolutely
hilarious!"
- Randall Enos,
Reknowned illustrator

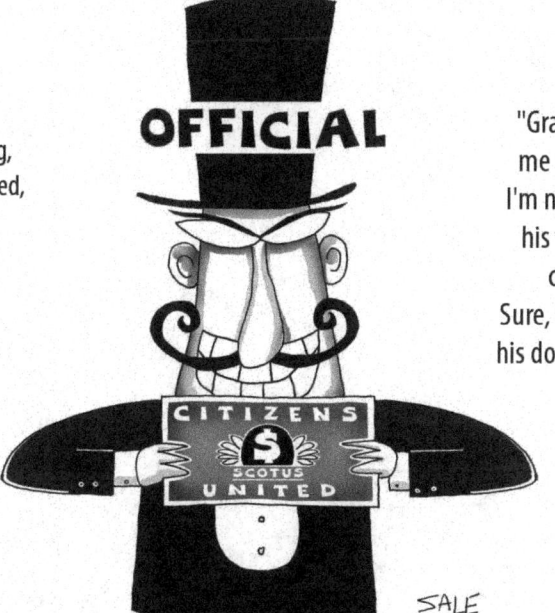

"Graham's cartoons and wit make
me grin, wince, groan and giggle.
I'm never sure what to expect from
his twisted, sardonic mind except
coffee-spitting entertainment.
Sure, he has light moments, but it's
his down and dirty satire that keeps
me coming back for more!"
- Sandee Beyerle,
Managing Editor,
Funny Times

W W W . G R A H A M S A L E . C O M

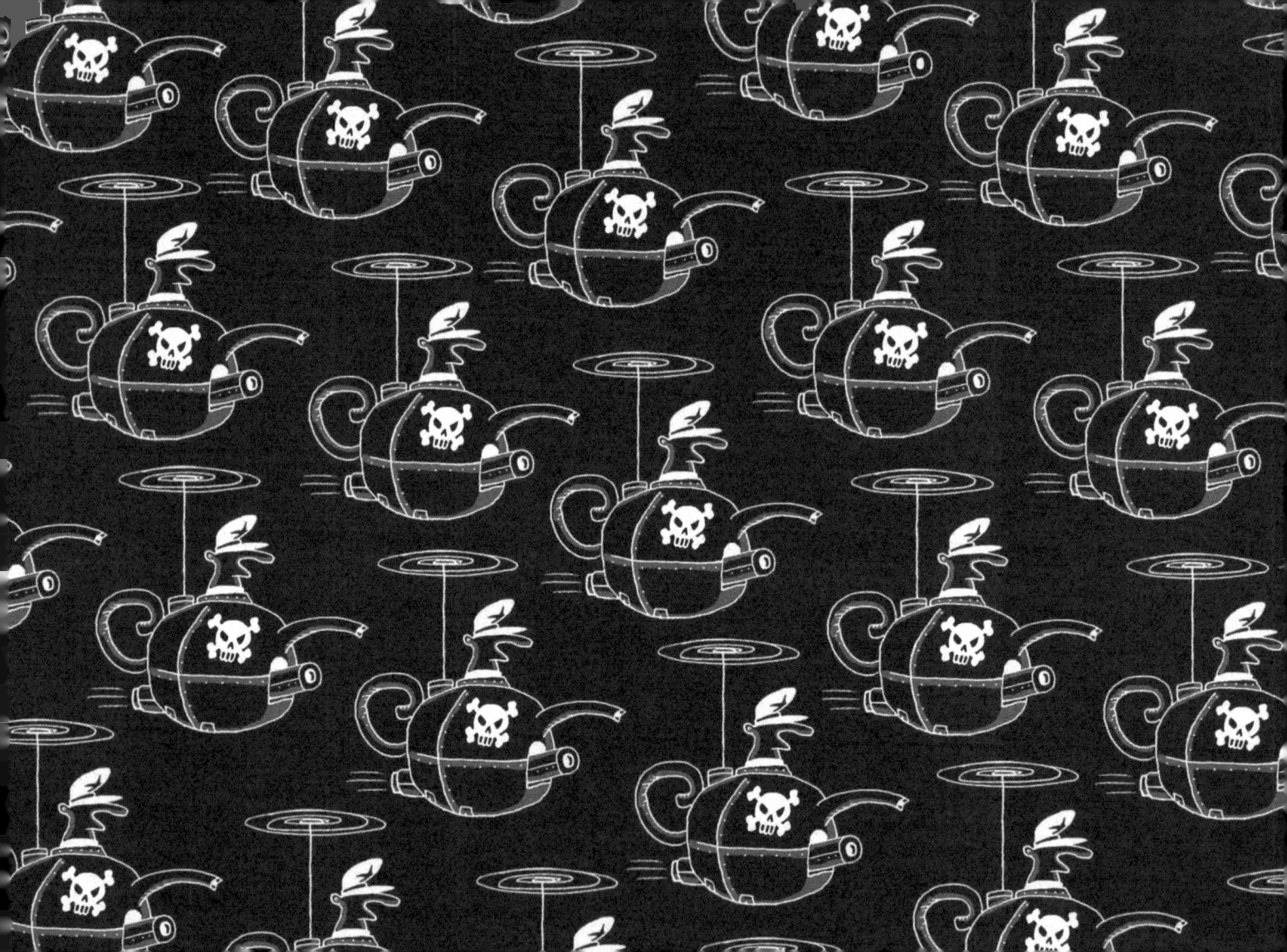

About This Book...

Through a series of events in 2010, I found myself in Memphis, TN, sitting in the office of Chris Peck, the editor of the *Commercial Appeal*, one of the nation's oldest newspapers. The paper had a long history of publishing award-winning editorial cartoonists, both conservative and liberal, including a Pulitzer Prize winner. But, slashing budget cuts forced the paper to lay off its last staff cartoonist a few years earlier.

America was already steeped in the upcoming 2012 presidential primaries, and Chris wanted the paper represented in the national debate by a local cartoonist. He learned that I'd just moved to the area from Los Angeles and hired me to create cartoons for the paper.

Hw also wanted to feature my fledgling cartoon, *Men In Hats*, every Saturday in the editorial section. I was stunned and excited. During one of the most pivotal times in the country's history, when editorial cartoonists were being purged from newspapers, I was being hired to participate in the national political conversation - *and* asked to develop a new cartoon series. Wow.

This book is a compilation of those efforts and contains cartoons from 2010-2013, including never-before-seen works.

I've also included some *Men In Hats* cartoons in the bonus section of this book. Their book, *Men In Hats: If Idiots Could Fly*, can be purchased on the website: **www.grahamsale.com.**

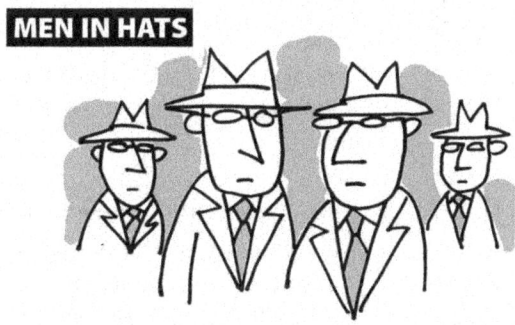

MEN IN HATS

I Need to Talk to a Man About A Cartoon.

I was thrilled at the opportunity, but I had a concern. I told Chris that my cartoons would not look like the traditional political cartoons that readers were accustomed to seeing.

My drawing style is completely different, and I wouldn't be using the usual iconography of donkeys, elephants, and buses going off cliffs with "Economy" written on their side. I'm a humorist and satirist whose point of view is similar to Bill Maher, John Stewart and Stephen Colbert. My work was likely to be very pointed. I asked if this would be a problem especially in the deep South.

He said, absolutely not. Unlike some editors, he felt humor had a place in editorial cartoons and my unique perspective was an asset that would make the cartoons fresh and original. *Whew.*

"Graham has a different take on political cartooning. Not the same old gags. Not the worn formats of old. I saw the difference the first day we met....

He doesn't come from the traditional school of political cartooning, so you won't find the often over-used elephant and donkey icons of old...

His work can take a minute to fully comprehend, but the wait is worth it. Graham mixes sharp humor and intelligence with great effect."

Chris Peck, Editor
Commercial Appeal
Memphis, TN

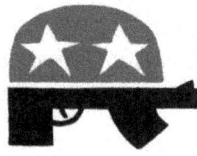

The Job.
The Challenges.

**Editorial cartooning is a tough business.
I have a deep respect for those who do it.**

The daily grind to educate yourself on a new issue, boil it down to its essence, find a unique way to present it, then illustrate and make it to the press on time, is several jobs in one. Sometimes the topic you're working on all day is no longer in the news at the end of that day. You also find yourself in competition with technology, social media, cable TV shows and late night comedians to get your original ideas out.

As a freelance commercial artist, my deadlines ranged from several days to several weeks, depending on the project. Having daily deadlines took some getting used to.

I also had to create *Men In Hats* for the weekend edition - which was a totally different type of cartoon. I hadn't drawn so much in my life.

I also encountered an unexpected by-product from watching the news all day, every day - it made me angry and depressed. I shouldn't have been surprised.

Being a compassionate person and a fan of the truth, I could only watch Fox News in brief spurts for fear of breaking my TV. I often woke up in the middle of the night, pounding my fists on the bed while dreaming I was arguing with a politician I'd seen on the news that day. Watching bold-faced liars go unchallenged by media pundits is infuriating, and it took many months before I could separate my feelings from the things I heard and read during the day. I'm still not too good at it.

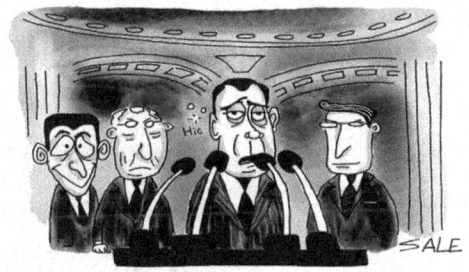

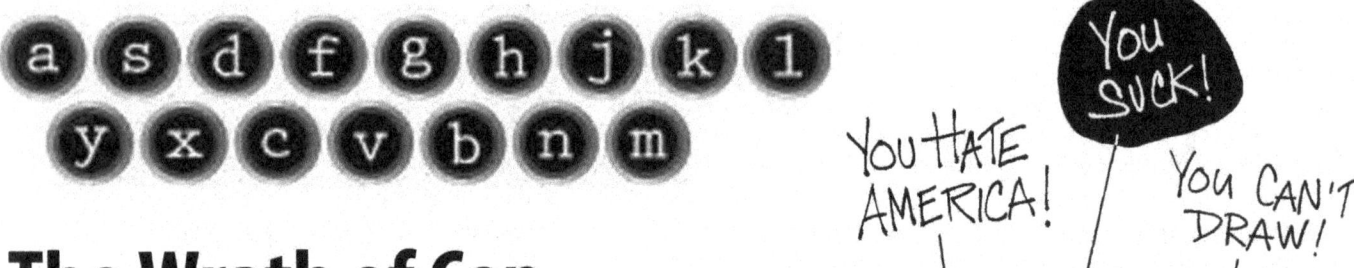

The Wrath of Con.

One thing I wasn't prepared for was the hate mail I received from right wing republicans and tea party nuts - over *a cartoon!* It wasn't as if I'd mentioned them personally or insulted their sister. Yet, people felt free to insult and even threaten me. One reader called me a child molester. Huh? Many of the letters were printed in the paper.

I couldn't imagine taking the time to respond to a drawing you look at for ten seconds and then turn the page. Yet, some people went ballistic and wrote three page letters - usually men. Others, typically women, prayed for me.

A friend and fellow cartoonist told me he was confronted by a menacing man who demanded to know, "Are you Graham Sale?" When he said, no, the man asked if he knew me or how to find me. My friend was pretty shaken. Ironically, these sorts of people react in the same intolerant way as the fundamentalist groups they hate so much. But that observation is lost on them.

My new business cards had just arrived, but after hearing about this incident they went straight in the trash. Initially, I was thin-skinned and responded in kind to these letters. But, I soon realized it was a waste of energy. So instead, I found pleasure in getting under their skin.

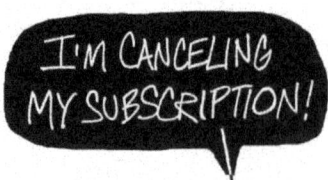

COMMENT

"I'm appalled that you would criticize Mitt Romney for being a liar, when the current President isn't even an American citizen. His birth certificate is a fake. No one even remembers going to college with him. He went to college on a Fulbright scholarship, which means he is a foreigner. When he lived in Indonesia, he was considered Indonesian. This election is over America continuing to be America or becoming a socialist country. The current President said he wishes we didn't have a constitution, so he could do what he wants. He is the puppet of people who want to destroy our country. Is that what you want too?"
- *MV, Memphis*

"You have a sick depraved mind and need counseling. I know a Christian Counseling Center that can help you. I'll be praying for you. There is a day of accountability and you need to prepare for it, Mr. Sale." - *DM*

"I have spent the last thirty years studying and teaching the word of God. Your cartoon portraying the Lord Jesus Christ as a dark-skinned, foreign-born, anti-war liberal socialist who wants to give away health care and food to the masses, in no way represents the Christ of the Bible. It is offensive. Socialism attempts to make government play the part of the Holy Spirit. There is not a single word in the Bible allowing charitable use of tax dollars. Socialism is anti-biblical."
- *Pastor F Washington*

MY FAVORITE CON-MENTS:

I won't print the vilest letters I've received. But, these appeared in the newspaper. They'll make you feel smart.

"You are an idiot. All you do is lie. You lefties have destroyed this country. And you have a sick mind."-DK

"Your cartoons are so stupid. How can you accept money for them?" - TM

11

COMMENT

POSITIVE LETTERS from folks who let me know that my contributions made a difference. These were wonderfully uplifting especially during particularly negative news cycles.

"Dear Chris (Peck):

...I know that all too often you are bombarded with criticisms of things your readers wish were different in your paper.

I just thought you might appreciate hearing about something that one of your long-time readers enjoys.

I am especially partial to Graham Sale's political cartoons. His work is not only humorous, but also intelligent and insightful. I've ordered several of his prints and am ordering another."

- Roy B. Herron, *State Senator,* TN

Dear CA Editor,

I want to express my gratitude for your printing the spot on cartooning of Graham Sale. He is one of the very best observers of the national political scene that I've witnessed in your pages going back to Draper Hill in the 70's.

Is he controversial? Is he provocative? Is he doing his part to "comfort the afflicted" and "afflict the comfortable?" You bet he is, in spades. Guilty on all three counts. How great is that?!

He is one of the much needed Liberal voices that this city needs, almost every minute of every day, if it is to totally overcome its moral and social foot dragging.

Jim Palmer, Memphis, TN

A FEW MORE...

COMMENT

...Let me be among the "few and proud" to let you know how much I appreciate your work. It represents a point of view sadly out of favor in thies area. We need more of you given the prevailing political winds. Give 'em hell!" - JS

"Your cartoons have been spot on lately. I look forward to your thoughts and wit and applaud your courage to present ideas that are clearly unpopular in this part of the country." - J Huffman, *retired banker (from the days when banks were honest and provided real service.)*

"Finally, the Commercial Appeal has a cartoonist with courage and an editor with the courage to let him tell the truth. There are many of us who appreciate the fact that someone at the CA has the cajones to stand up to the wing nuts who preach love and family, but actually spew hatred and venom. Mr. Sale's cartoons are a breath of fresh air amidst a swamp of paranoid bible/gun nuts." - Roy G

"My wife and I look forward to your cartoons in each edition of the paper. They speak truthfully and with the force of a thousand words. Your messages speak loudly and clearly. Your work is excellent. Thank you." Ralph S

"My political views are definitely to the right of yours, but you do have some very smart and clever cartoons. And believe it or not, every now and then you draw something that makes me wonder if my view is correct. You do a great job of getting under my skin, which goes to show you how good you are since this is the first time I've ever responded to a cartoon. Good luck." - David

"On behalf of teachers everywhere, thanks for your right-on-target cartoon. It is now hanging in our faculty lounge and causing quite a stir! Thanks again." - S Barnett, Elementary School Teacher.

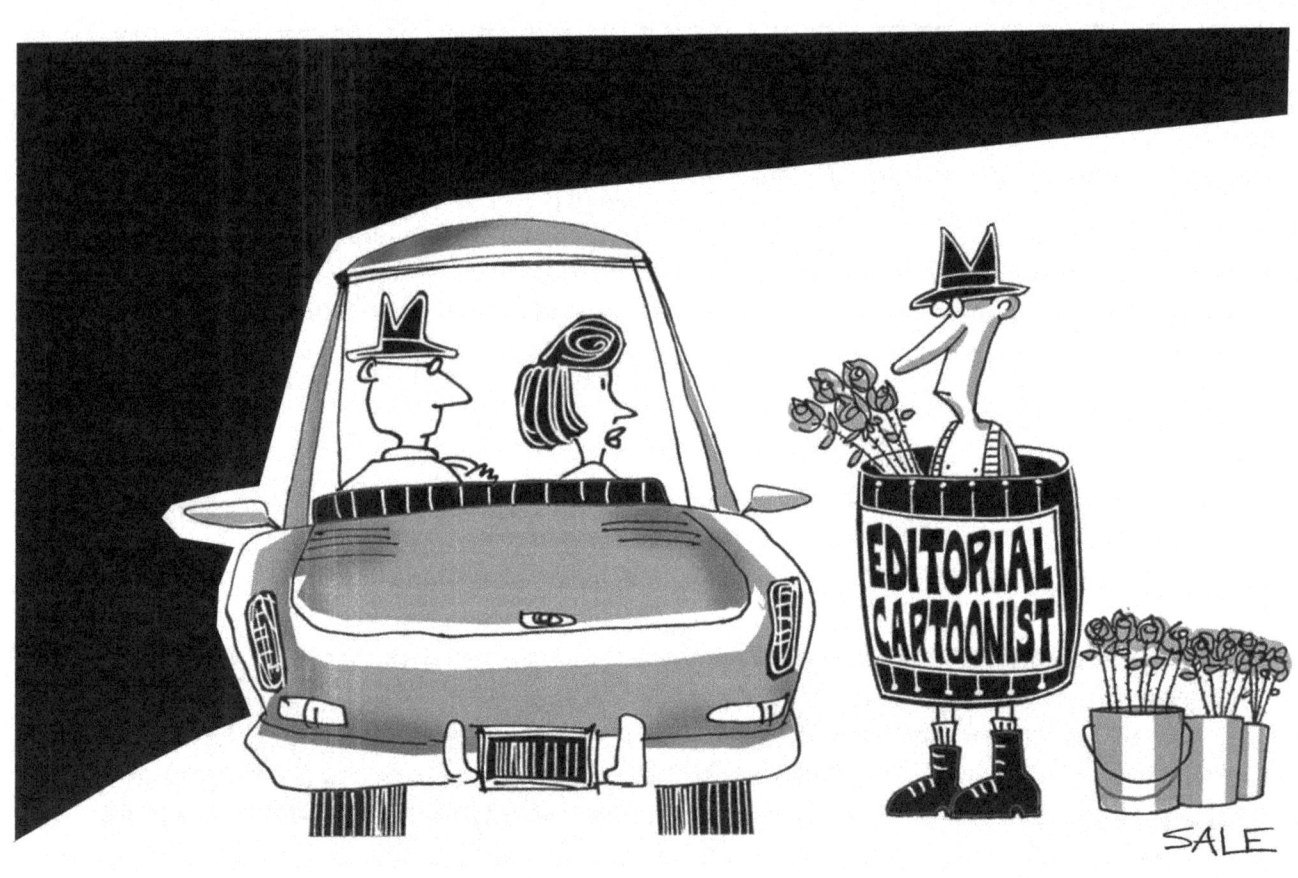

Disappearing Ink. The Editorial State of The Union.

Editorial cartoonists were once a staple in American print journalism and a rich part of our country's history. Last century about 2000 cartoonists worked for newspapers. Traditionally, cartoonists worked on staff, were syndicated or both. Today, there are only a few dozen full-time staff cartoonists.

The position has disappeared as newspapers downsize, merge or fold. Salaried cartoonists (with benefits) have been dropped in favor of syndicated cartoons, which cost less. But even syndicated cartoonists find they can't make ends meet as they once could.

A syndication company is basically an agent who represents cartoonists they think have broad appeal to as many newspapers and news outlets as possible. A newspaper pays a monthly amount to choose from the various cartoonists' work and pays a fee for each cartoon they use. A cartoonist is paid a portion of that amount. The fees are very low so it's a numbers game.

How low is low? A cartoonist's cut can be as little as $12 to $35. Some cartoonists report being paid as low as $3 a cartoon. It has always been a numbers game, but the payouts have dropped with fewer outlets to sell to. Those facing low circulation and budgets cuts often ask for a discount, which comes out of the cartoonist's pocket.

Today, being popular doesn't equate with being profitable. It is tragic, and it is not going to get better. Making a living as an editorial cartoonist has become difficult, if not impossible. Even Pulitzer Prize winning cartoonists are unemployed, working other jobs and/or drawing on the side.

The internet has changed publishing forever. The speed of technology, cable TV, talk radio, memes, and social media directly compete with cartoonists making it difficult to get their messages out to the public quickly. Who knows what the new face of political cartooning will look like, but as of today, Internet websites are not known for paying artists fairly - if at all.

15

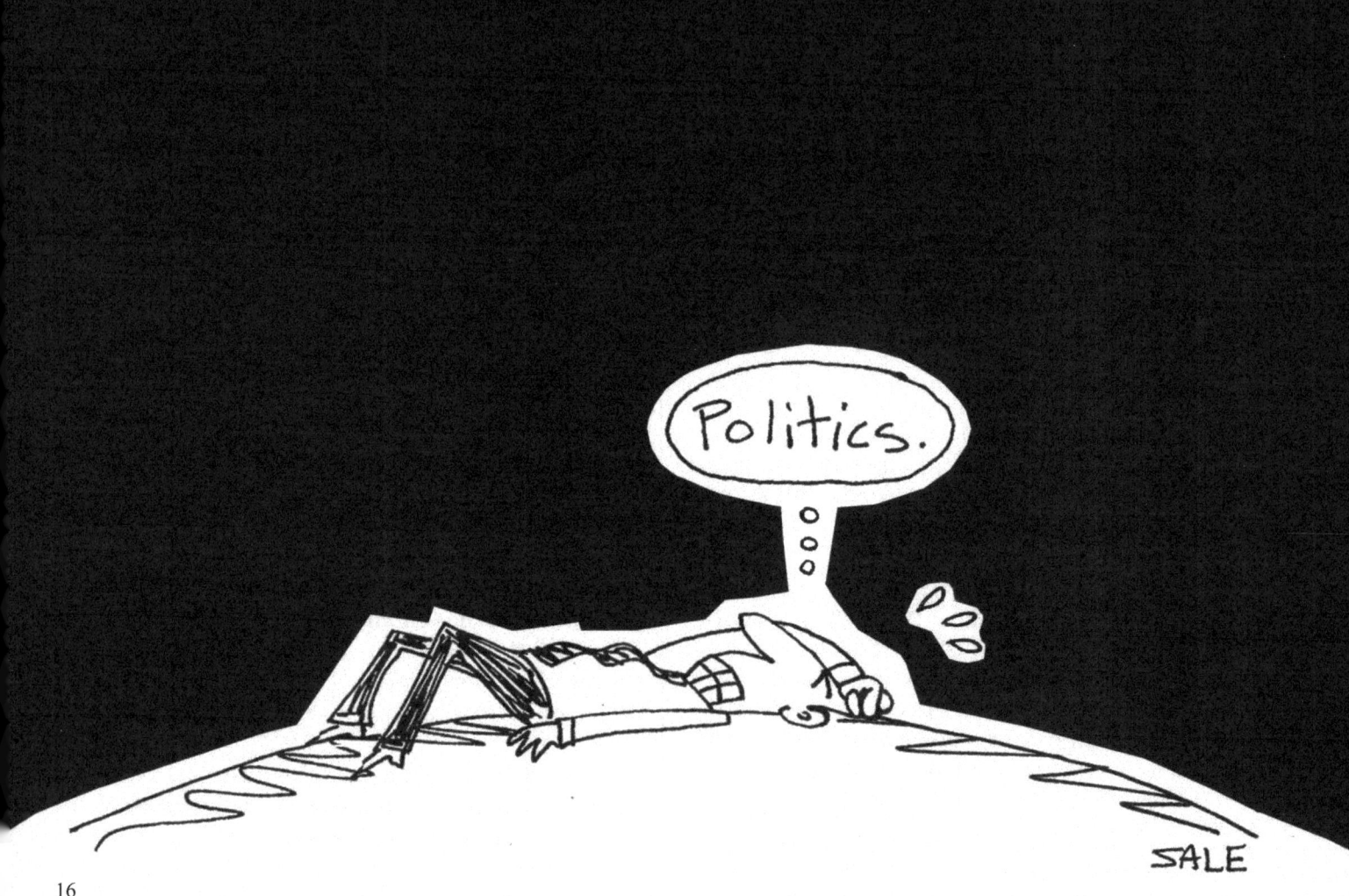

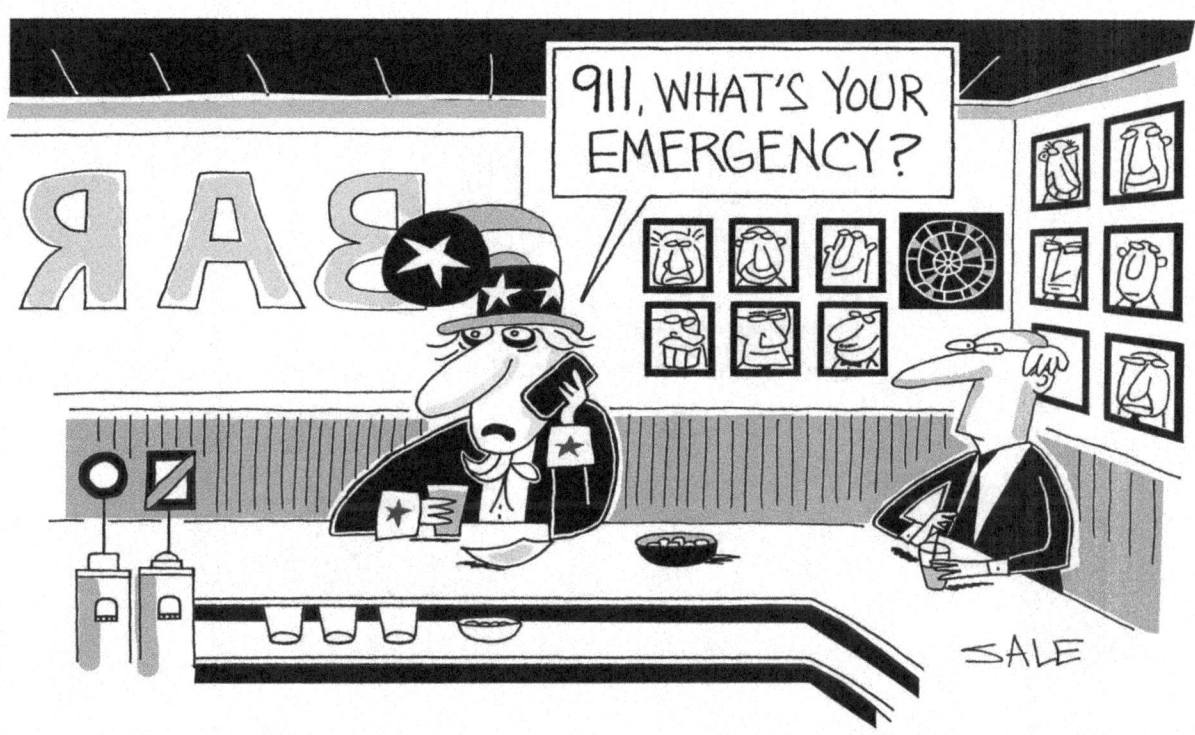

"I've been experiencing an election lasting more than four years."

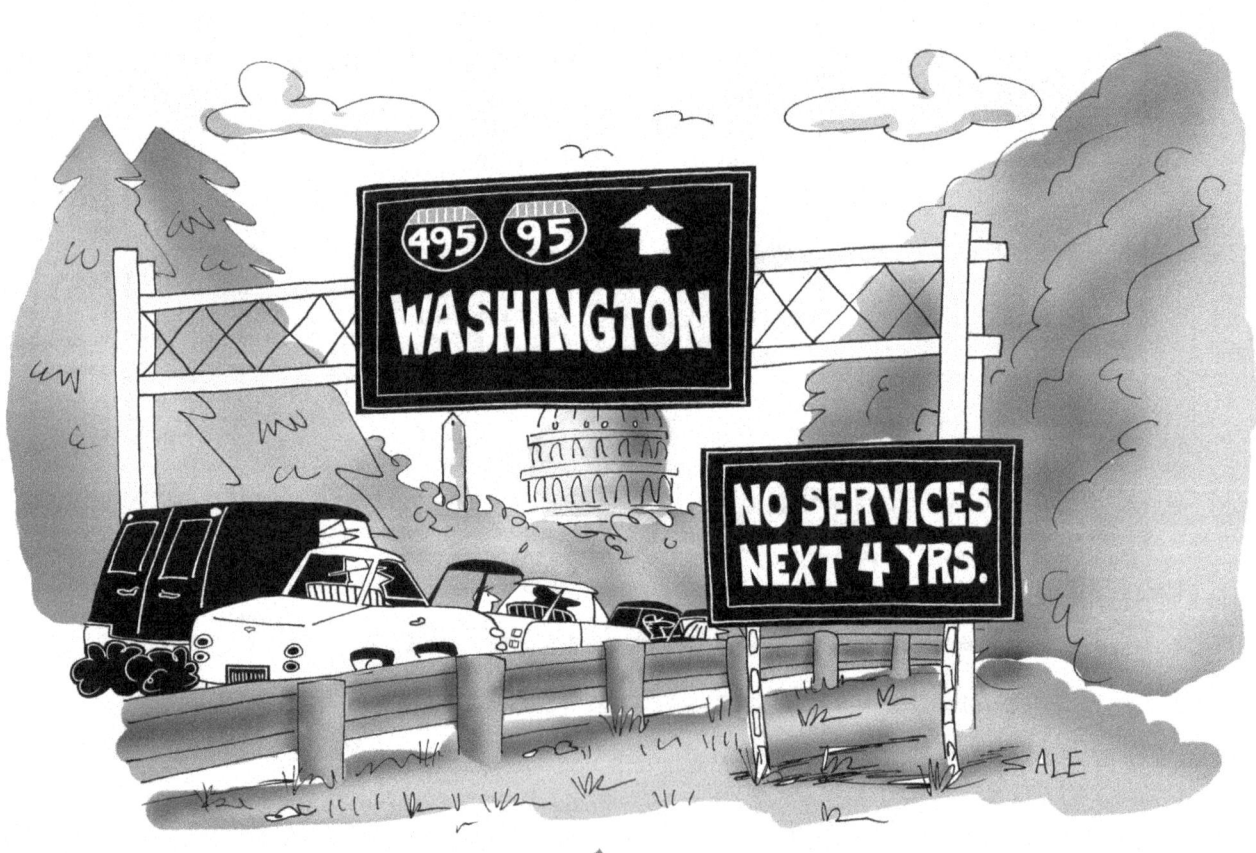

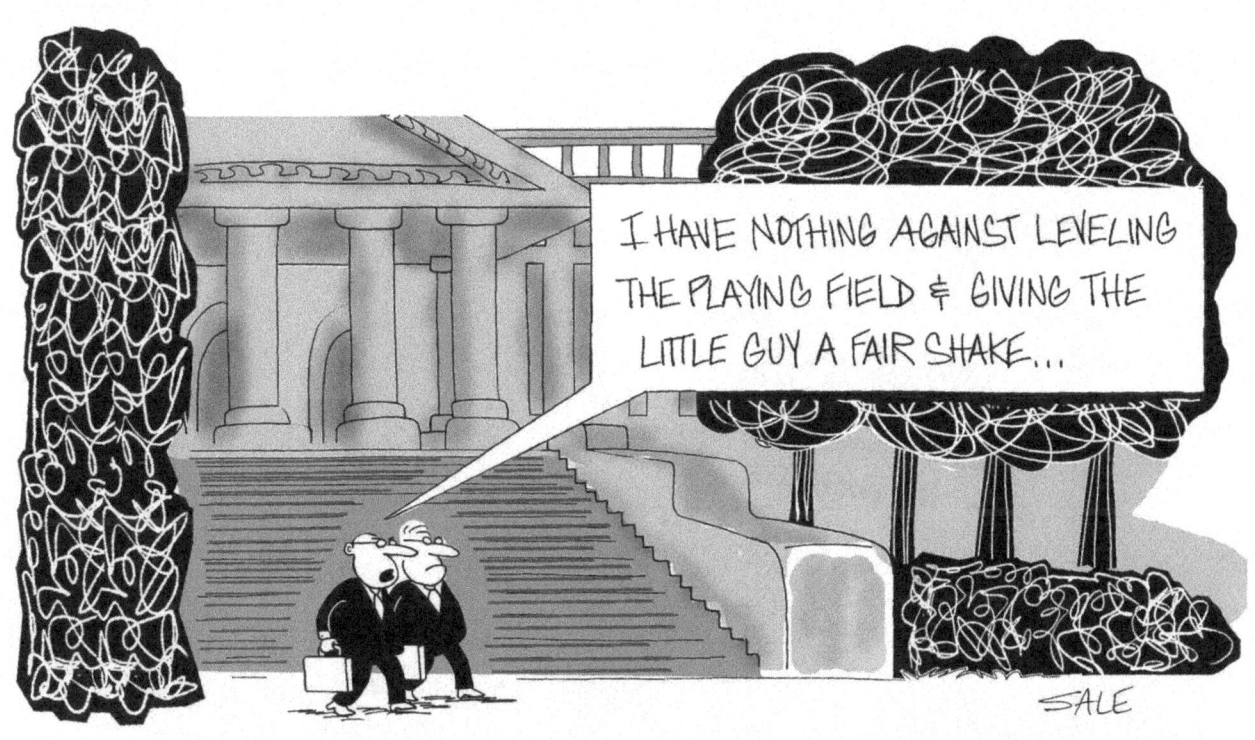

"But I fail to see how that sort of 20th century thinking will benefit me."

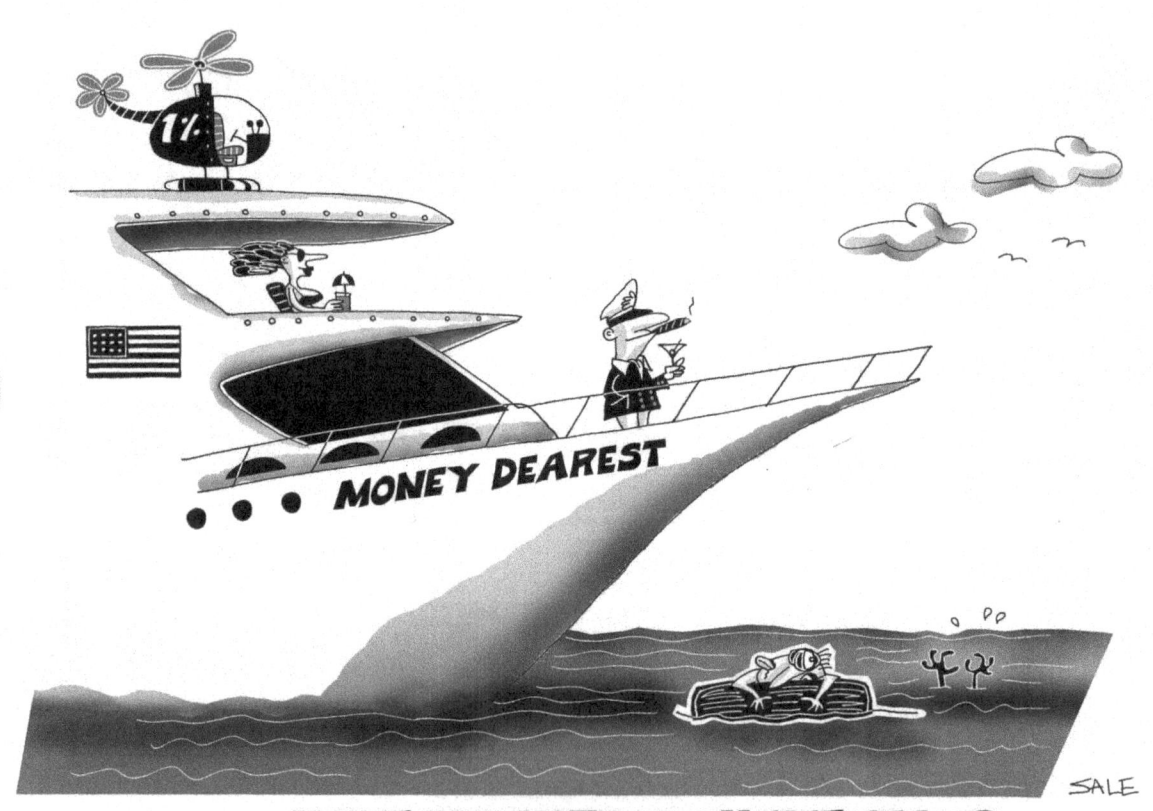

HAVE YACHTS vs. HAVE NOTS

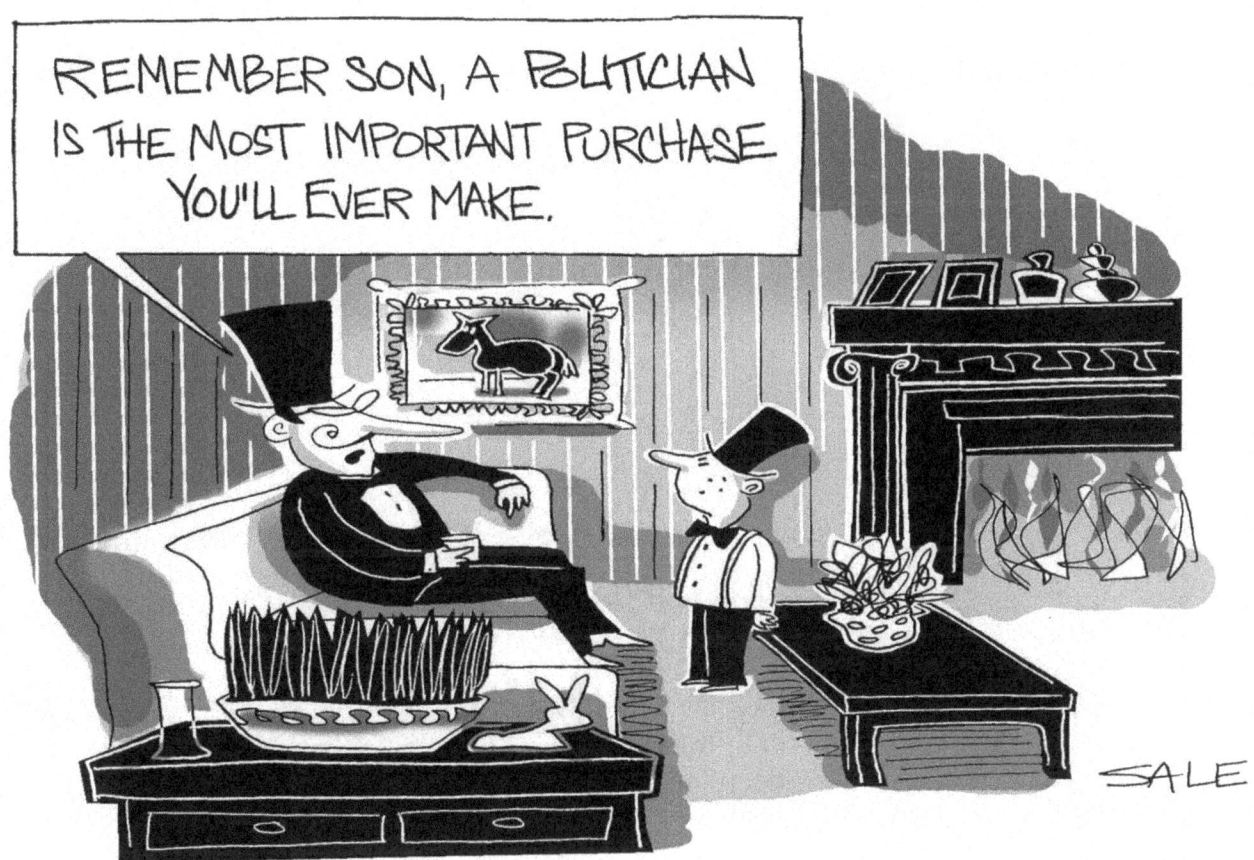

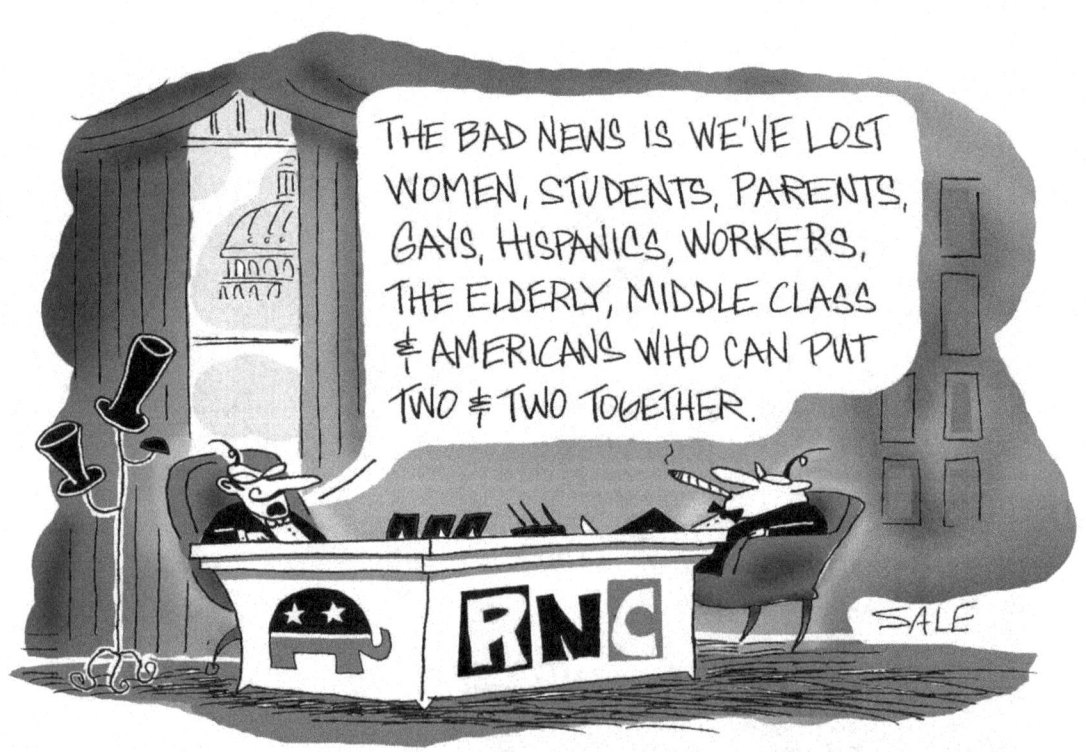

"The good news is we still have our base, the people you can fool all of the time."

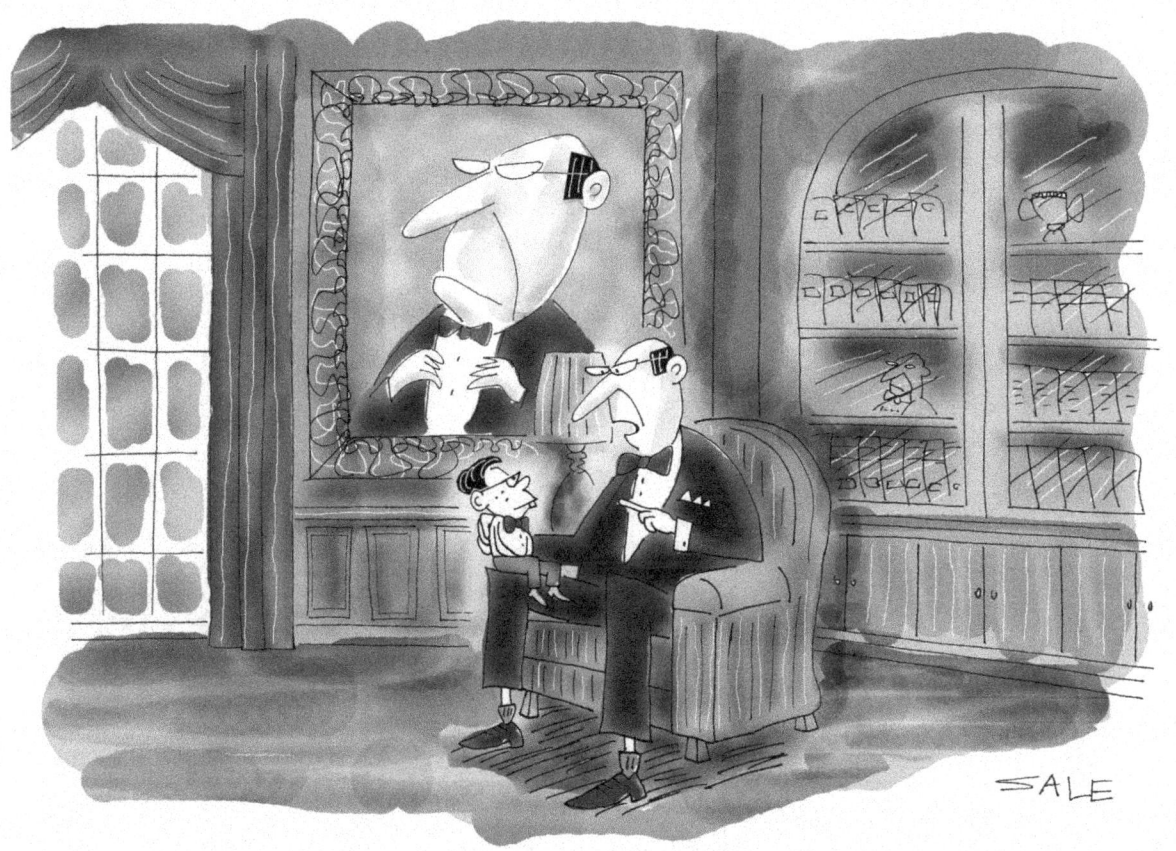

"Always remember you get the government you gerrymander."

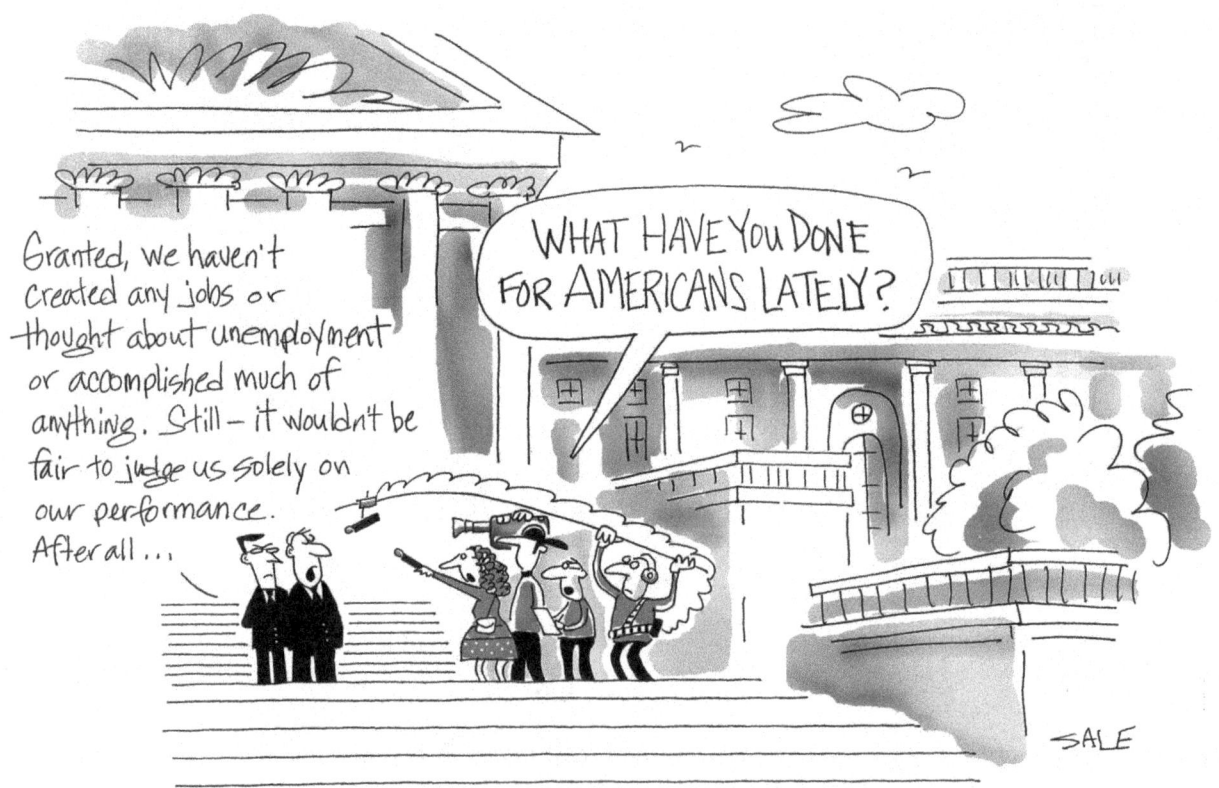

"We are politicians, and we didn't come to Washington to be treated like teachers."

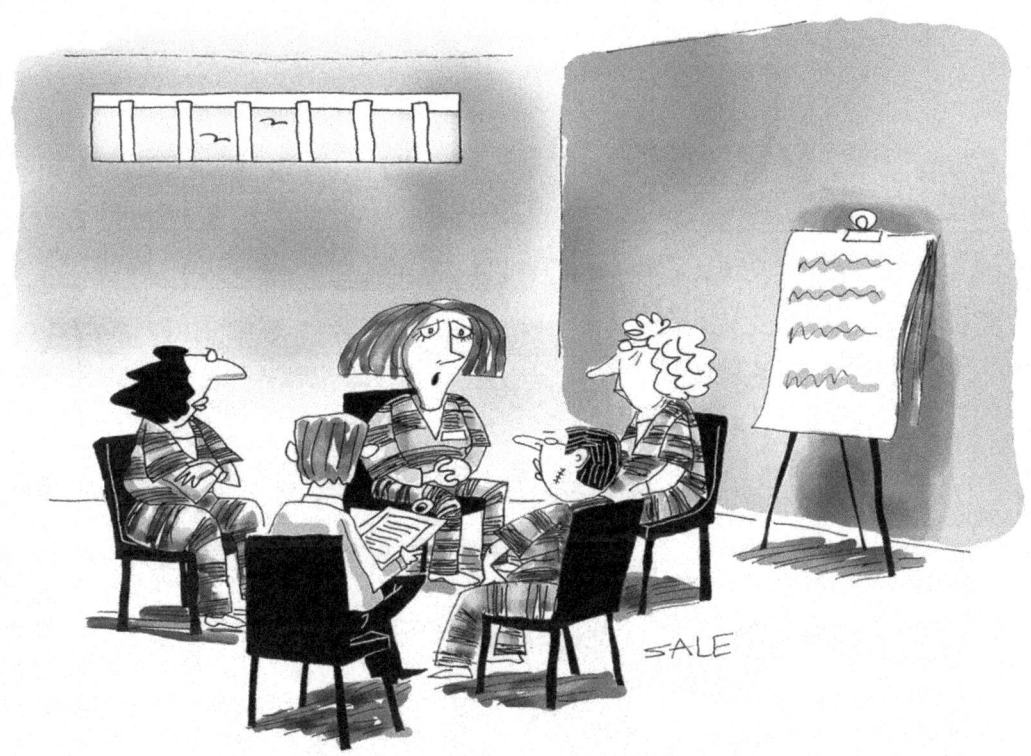

"Hello, my name is Ms. Dunbar. I'm a school teacher, and
I stole supplies from my home to bring to class."

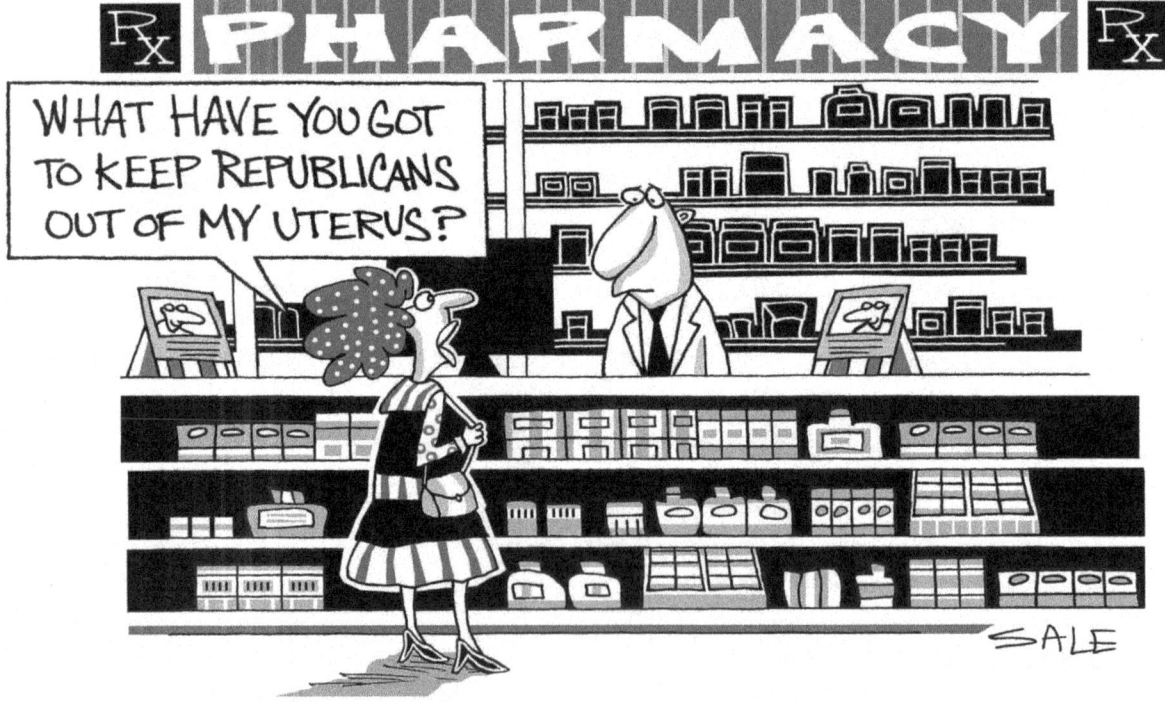

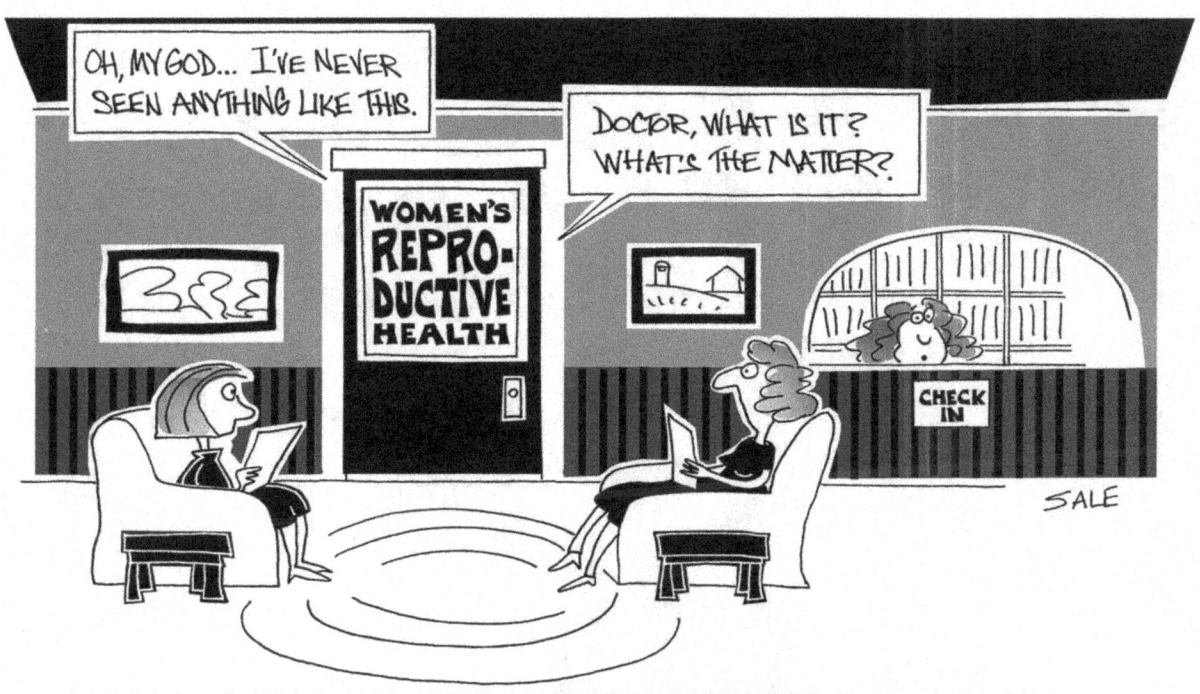

"*This is quite shocking, Mrs. Pearlman. If you lie perfectly still...*
I can see Washington from here."

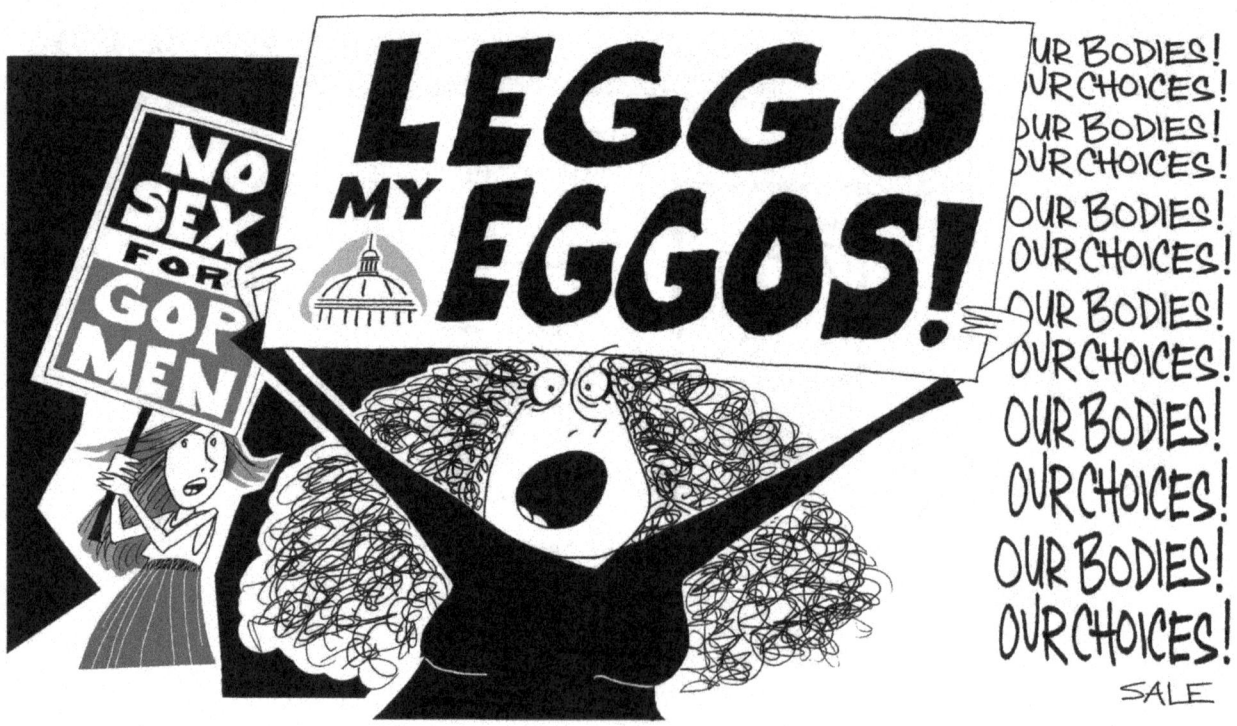

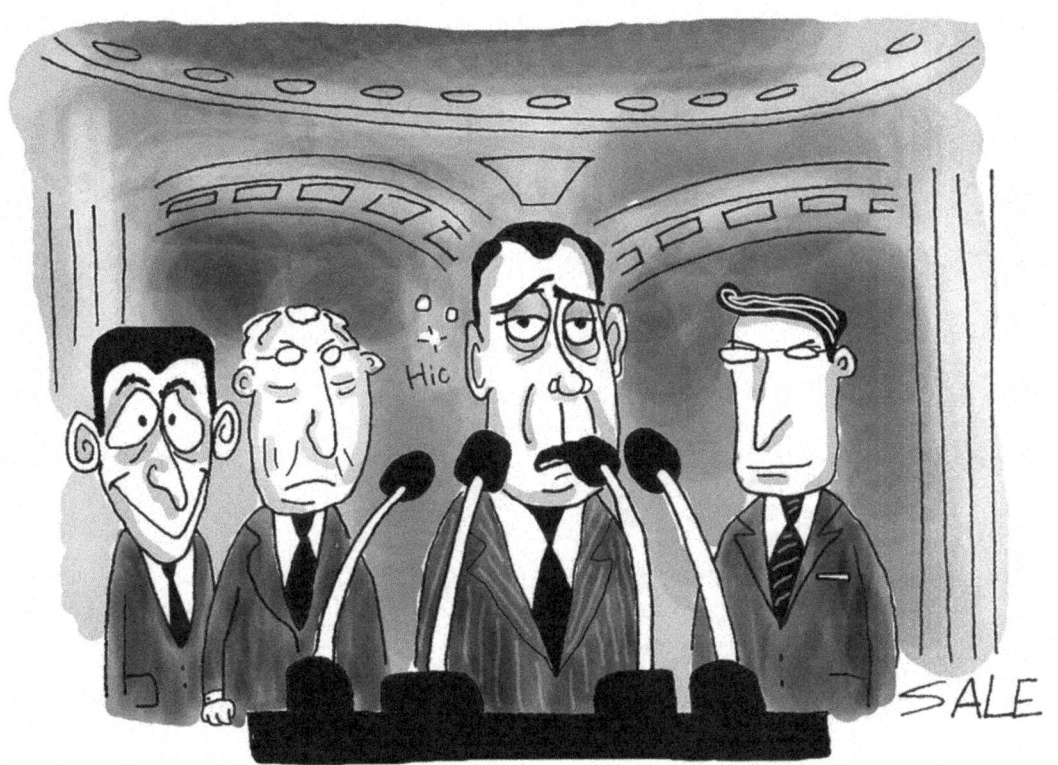

"We're not gynecologists or obstetricians,
but we play ones in congress."

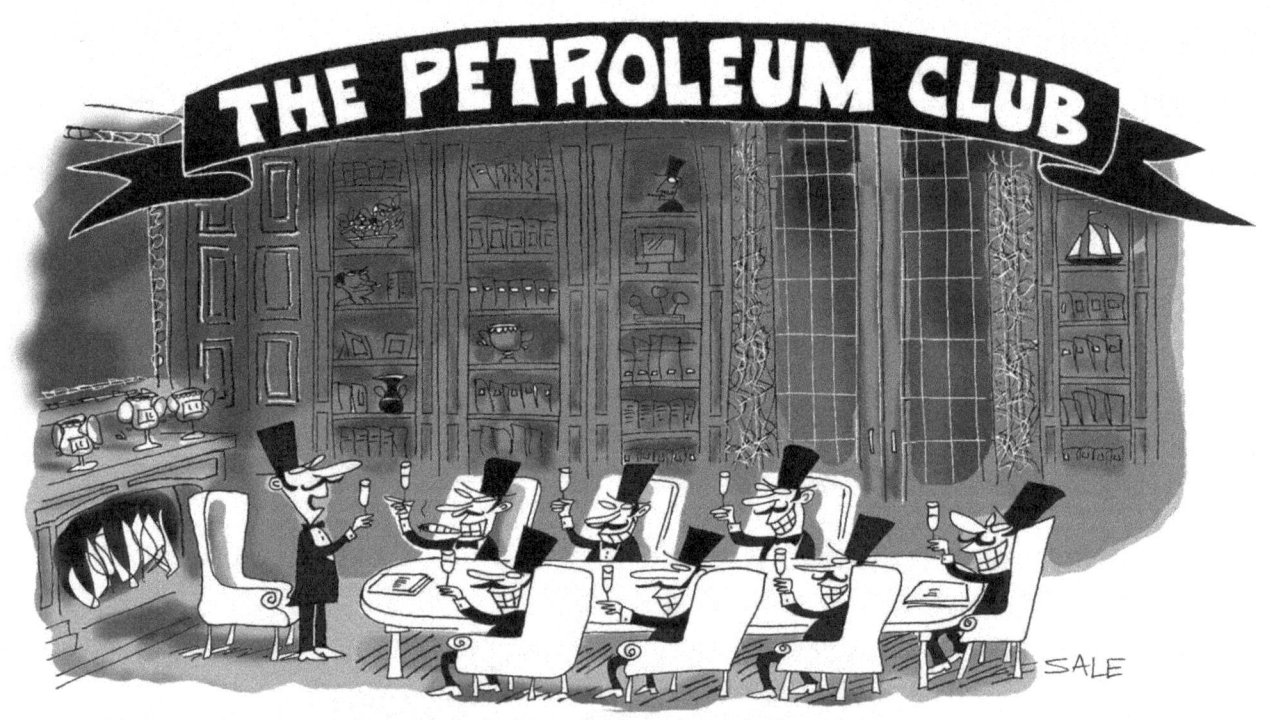

"Let us toast that wonderful law of supply and demand.
When you control the supply you can demand whatever the hell you want."

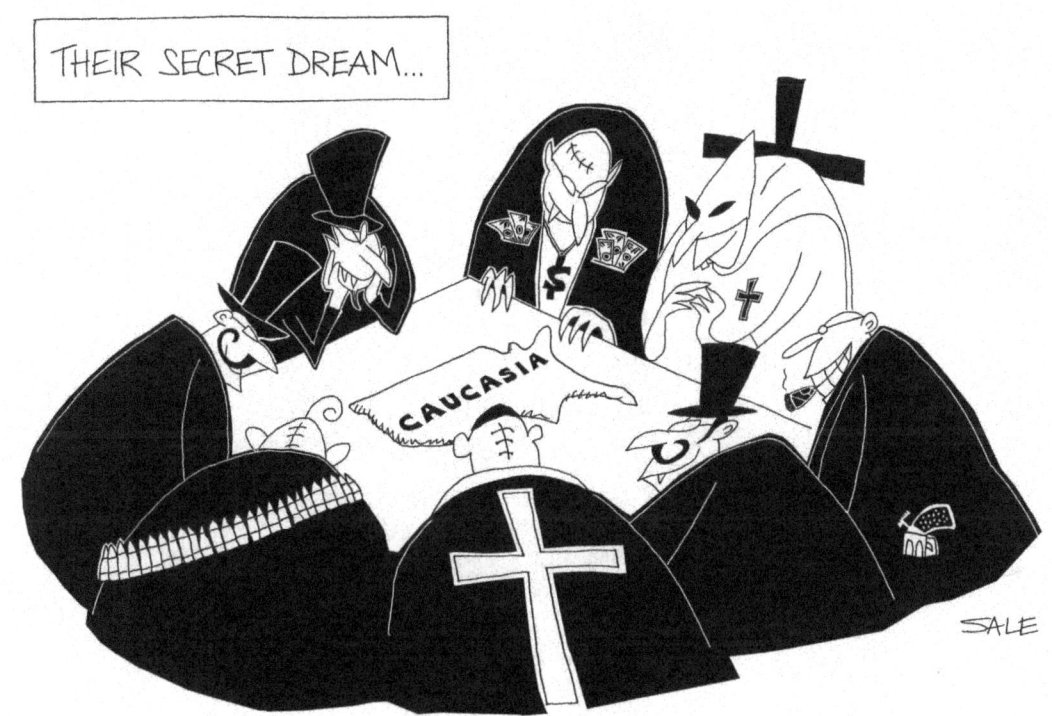

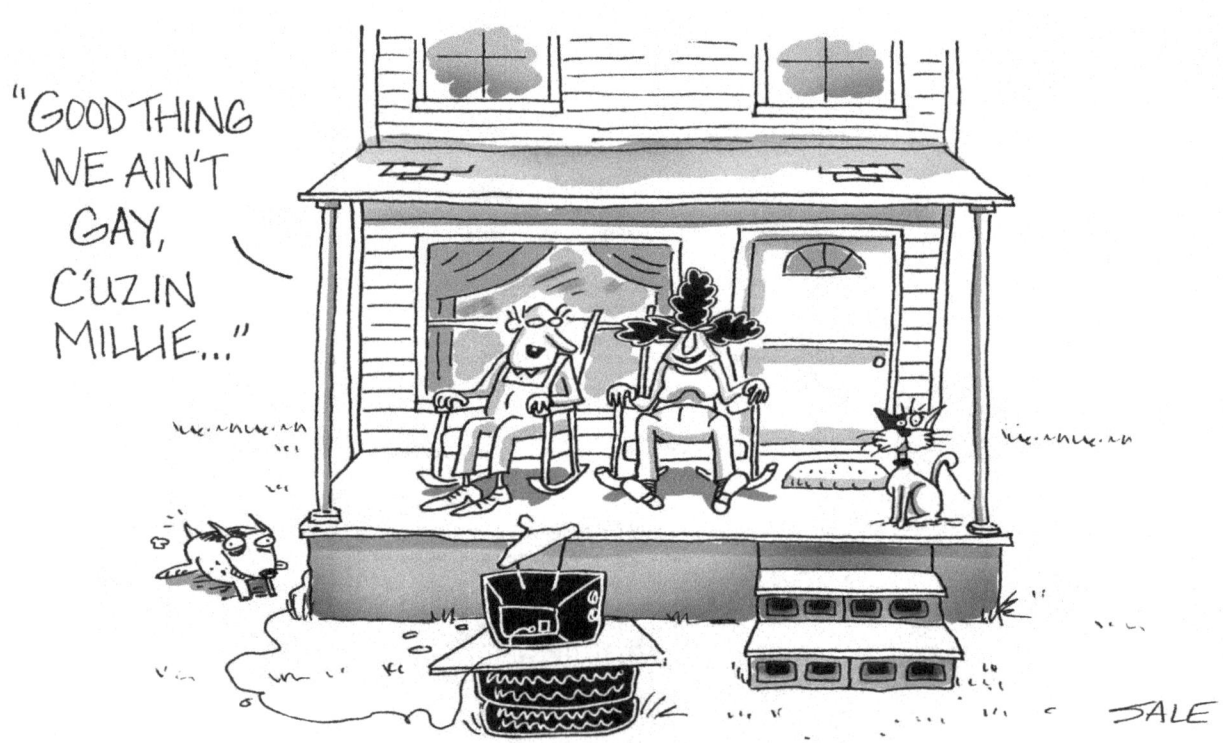

"Or we couldn't a got married."

THE GAYS.

HI, WE'RE YOUR TYPICAL LIBERAL, ATHEIST, GAYS.

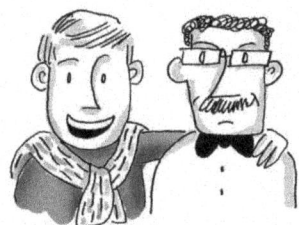

AND WHEN WE AREN'T CHANGING THE CLIMATE & CAUSING APOCALYPTIC WEATHER EVENTS...

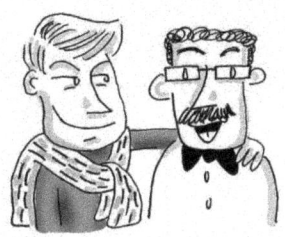

...TURNING PEOPLE GAY, OR CAUSING RANDOM ACTS OF HORRIFIC VIOLENCE...

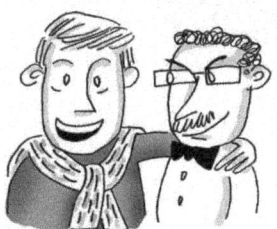

WE ENJOY LOTS OF ANONYMOUS SEX, PROJECT RUNWAY & **BEING FABULOUS!**

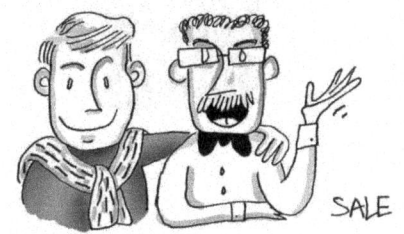

SALE

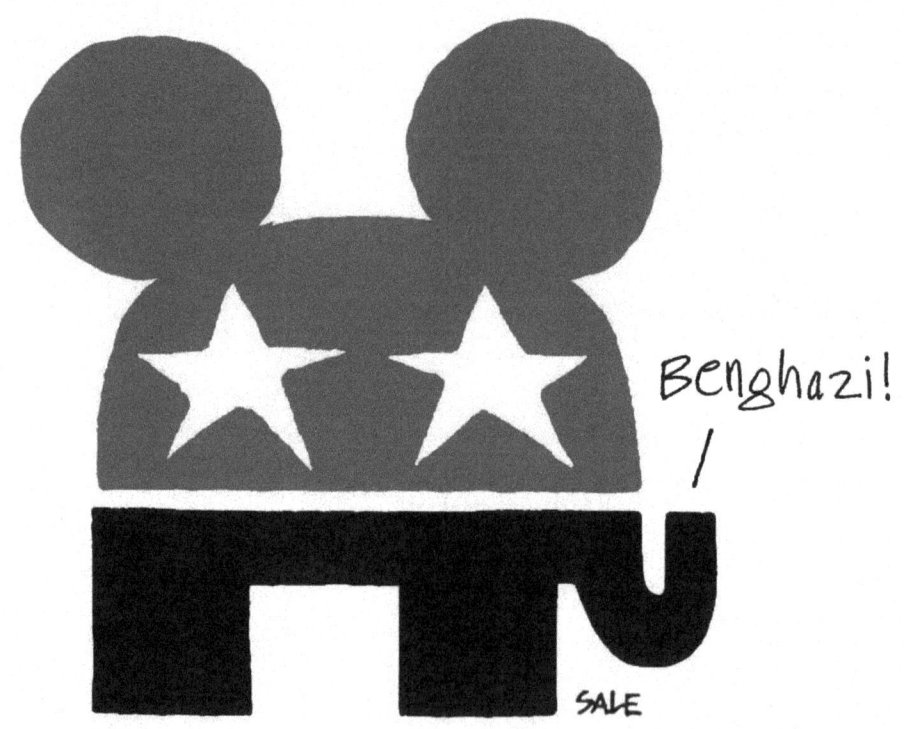

34

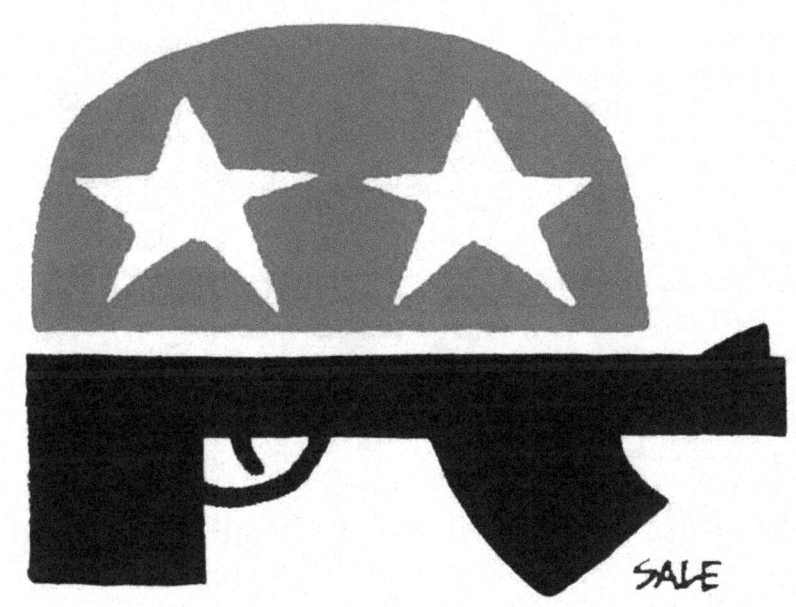

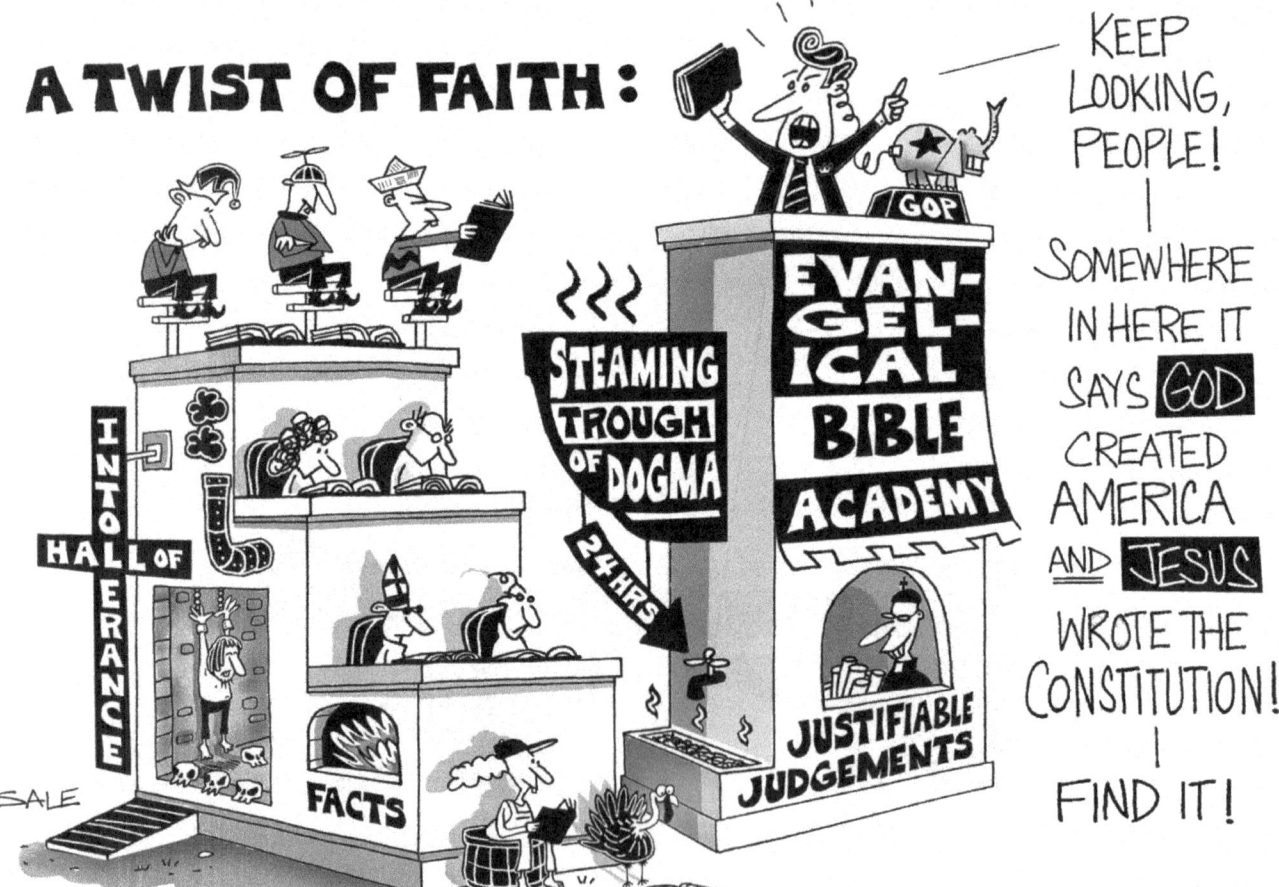

THIS IS OUR COUNTRY - NOT YOUR CHURCH.

INTERVIEW w/GOD: GOD REVEALS WHY POPE LEFT...

YOU'LL LOVE THIS, JIMMY...
AS THE POPE WAS PRAYING
THE GAYS AWAY...

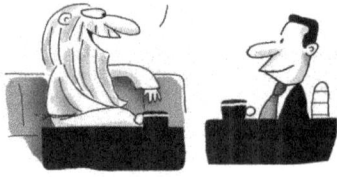

THEY WERE PRAYING
HIM AWAY!

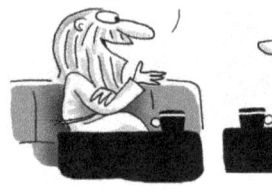

MY PRAYER LINES
WERE ON FIRE!

I BET.

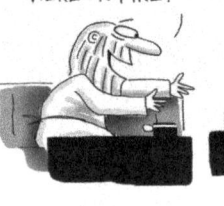

I'M FAMOUS FOR HYPOCRICY,
BUT EVEN I COULDN'T IGNORE THIS.
PLUS, THE NAZI THING HAD BEEN NAGGING
AT ME.

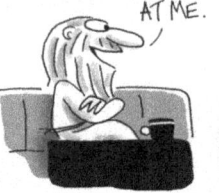
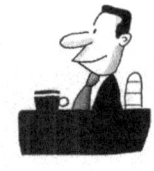

SOME FOLKS WILL FEEL
I STOPPED SHORT & SHOULD'VE
ENDED THE PAPACY ENTIRELY.

THAT'S
UNDERSTANDABLE.

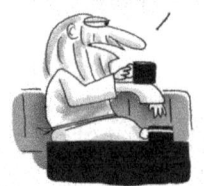

SO, AS A COMPROMISE I RECALLED
HUGO CHAVEZ & I'M GOING TO
BRING BACK THE McRIB.

BOTH
REAL
CROWD
PLEASERS.

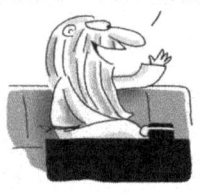
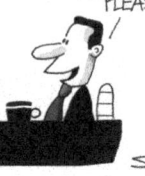

SALE

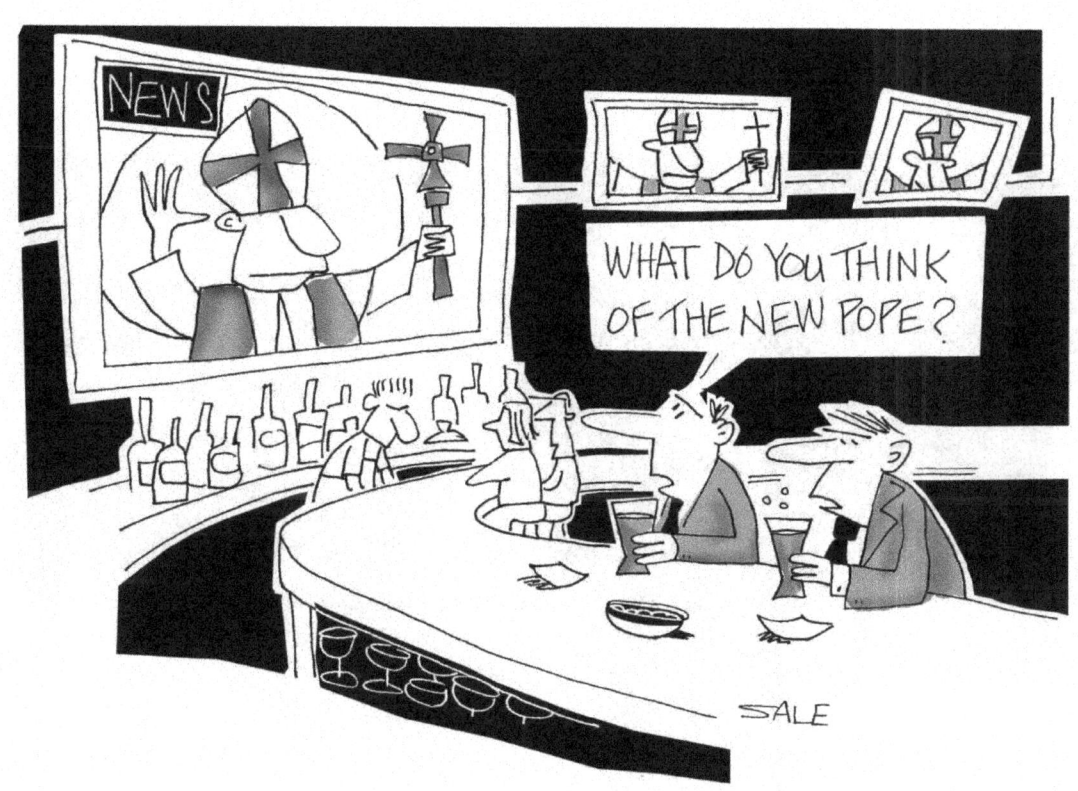

"Different pope. Same poop."

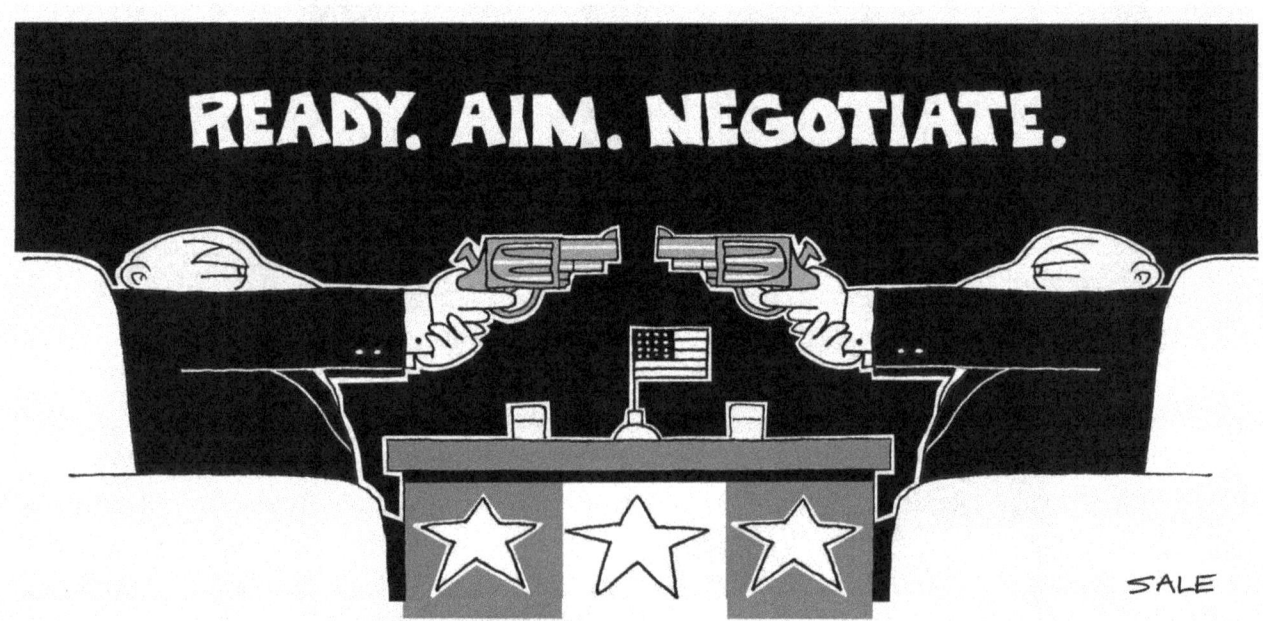

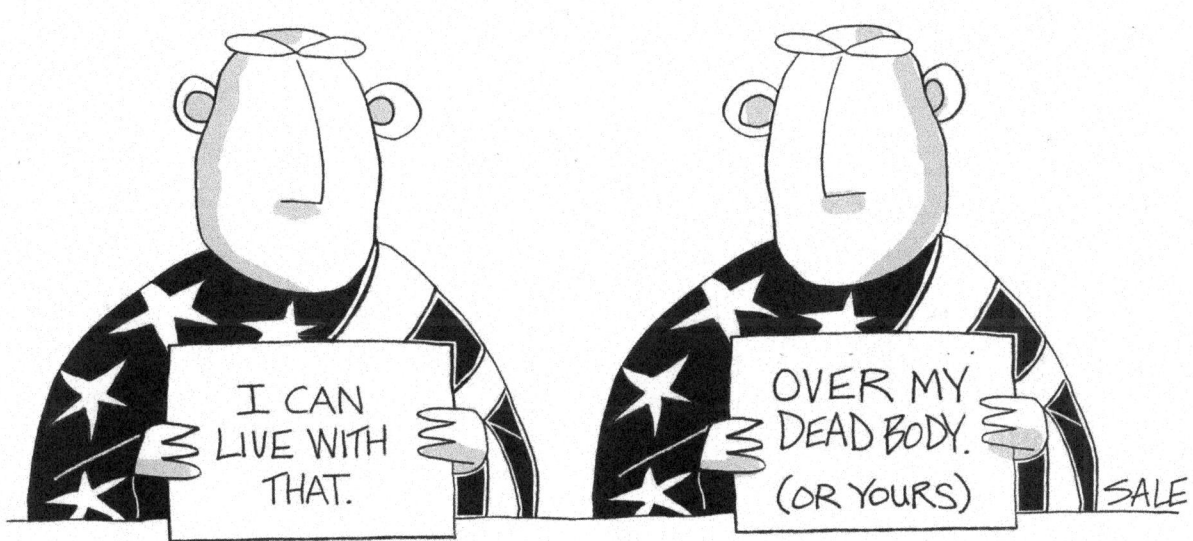

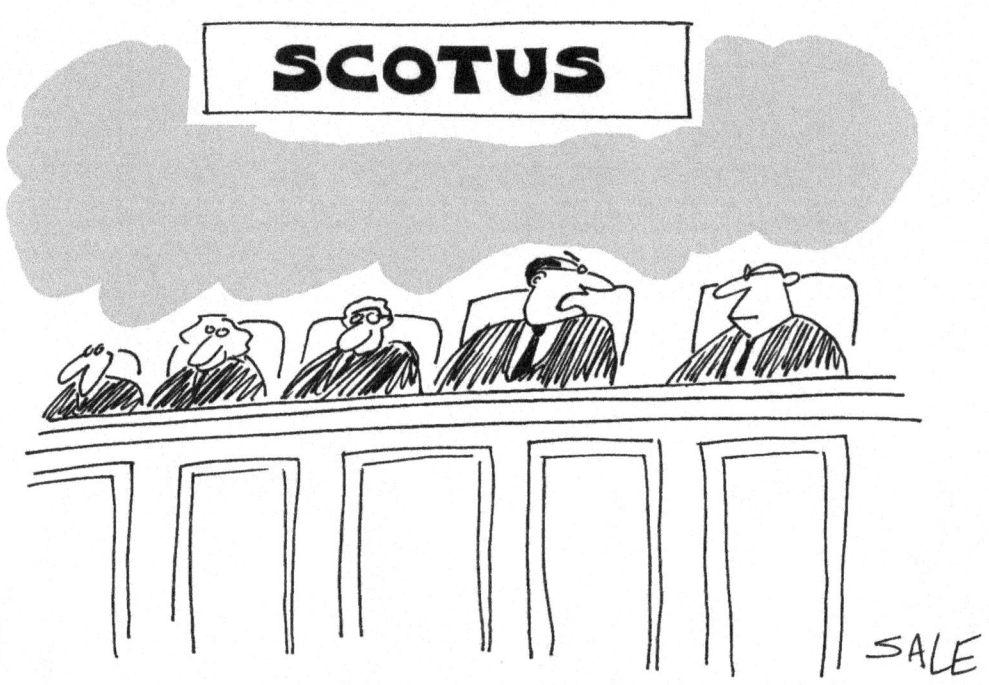

"*For cying out loud, everyone knows justice is blind, so why are they always so damn surprised that it isn't fair?*"

LIBERTY & JUSTICE FOR ALL

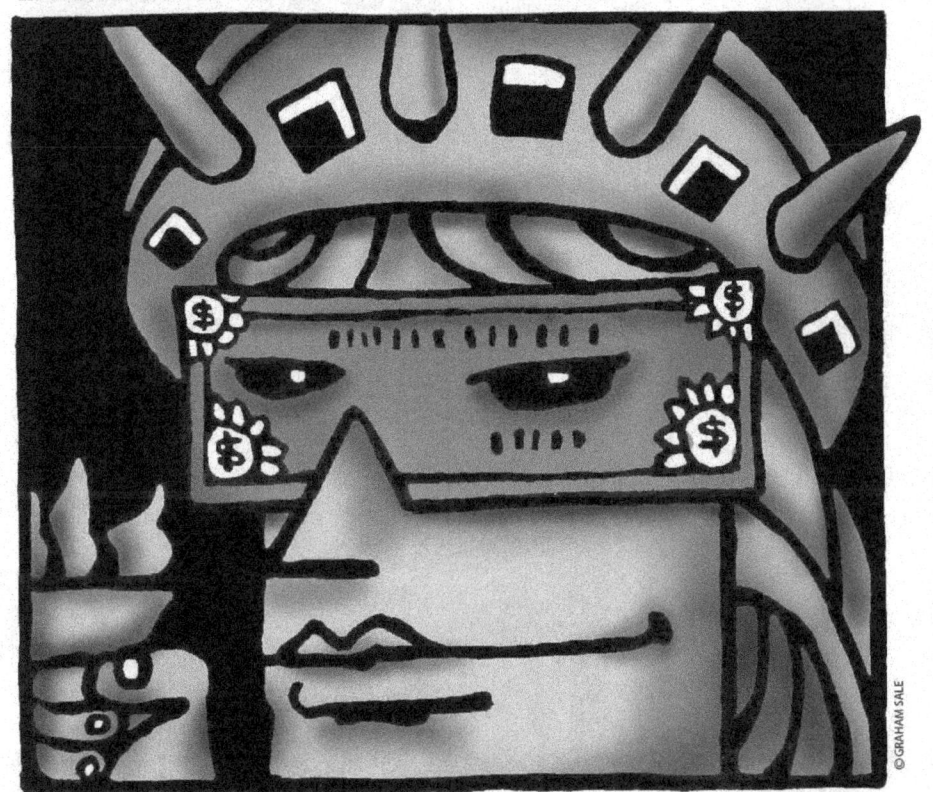

©GRAHAM SALE

WHO CAN AFFORD IT.

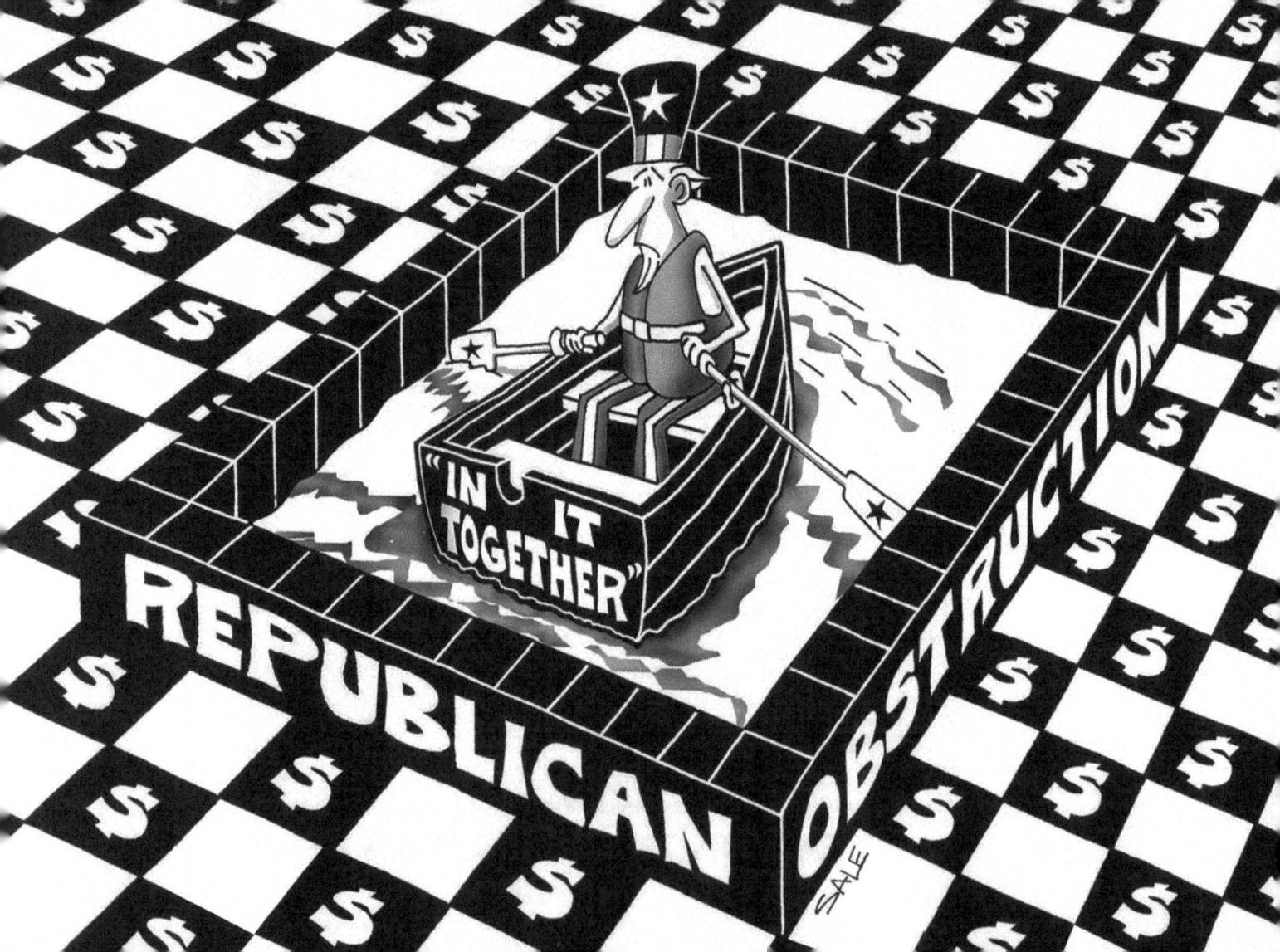

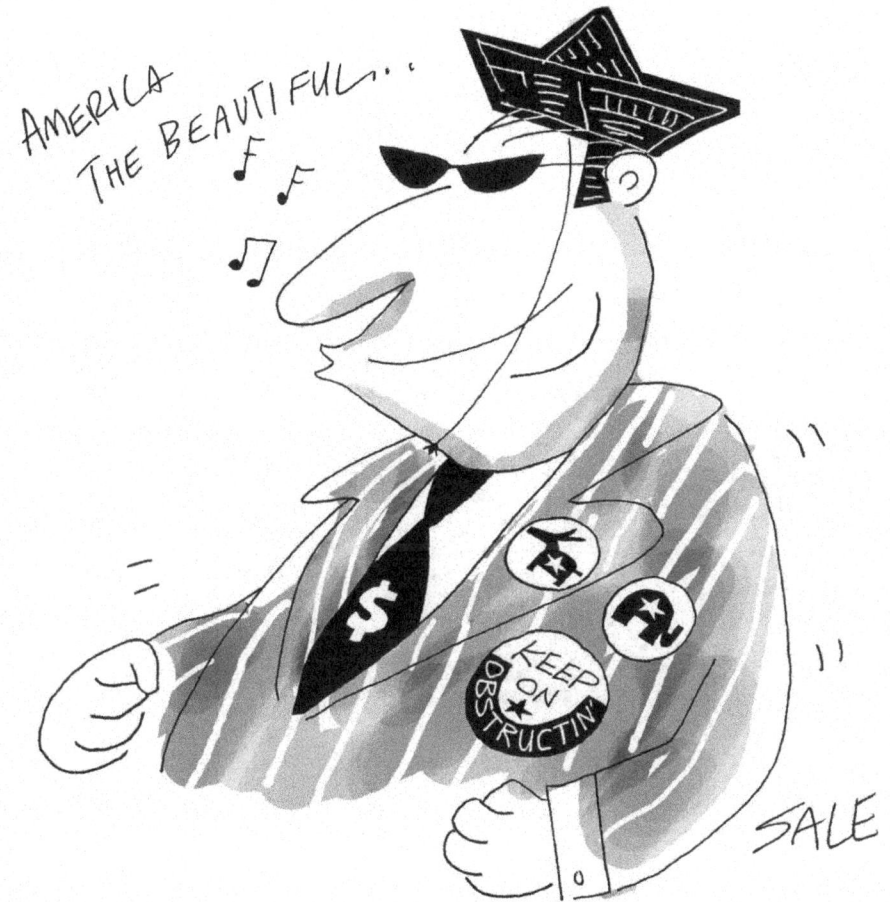

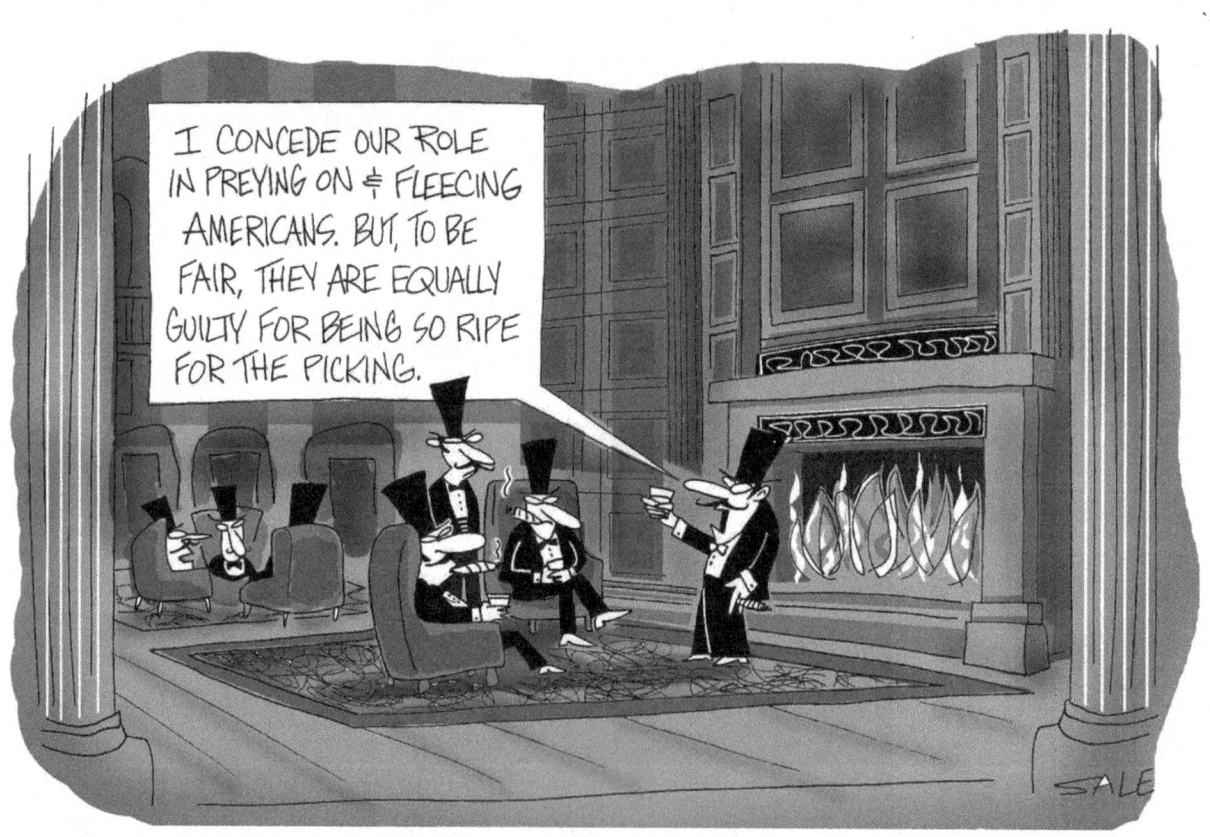

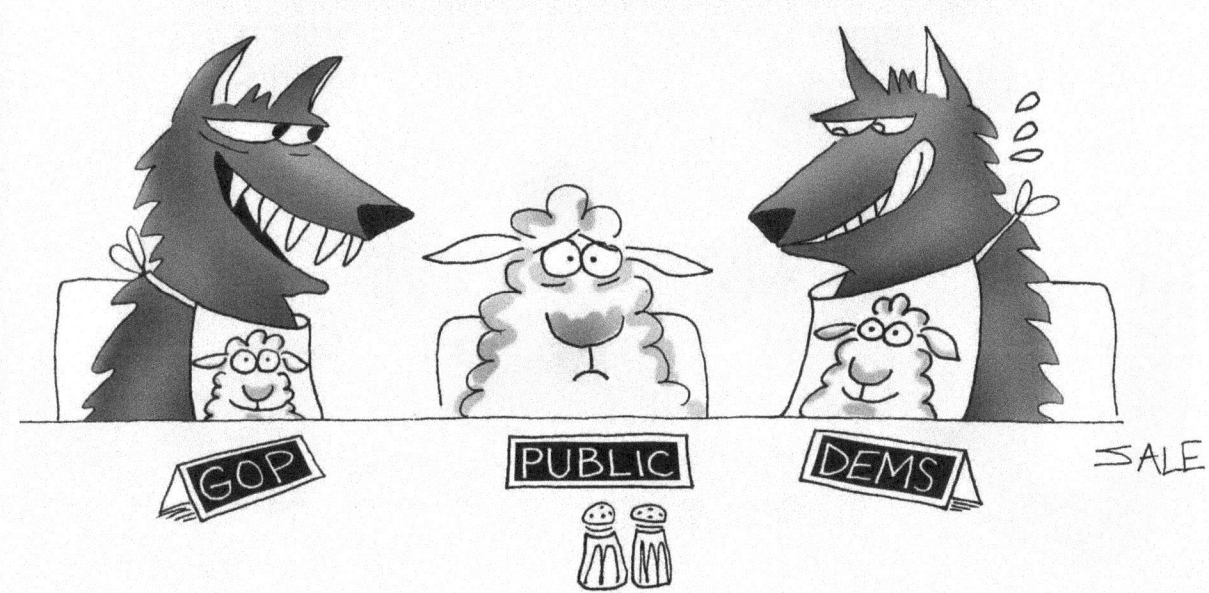

"How do you like your fifty percent prepared?"

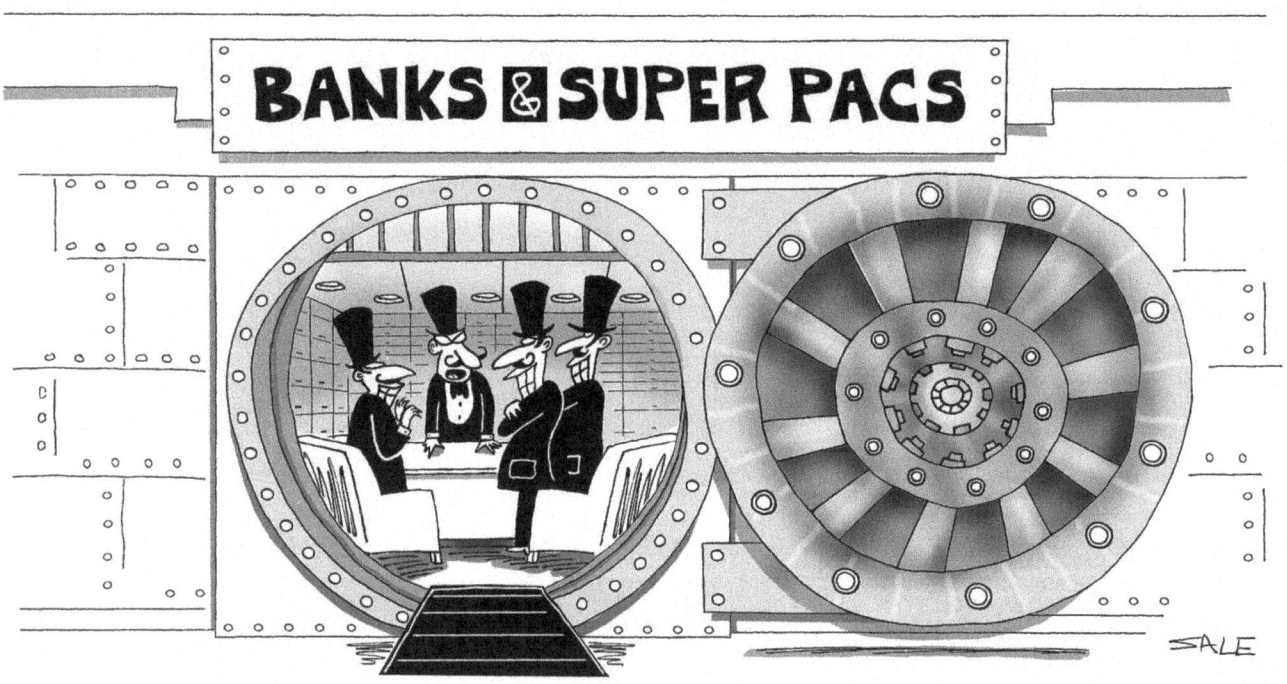

"Now that we've purchased both parties and secured the right to mortgage and pillage the future of the country — it's bonus time!"

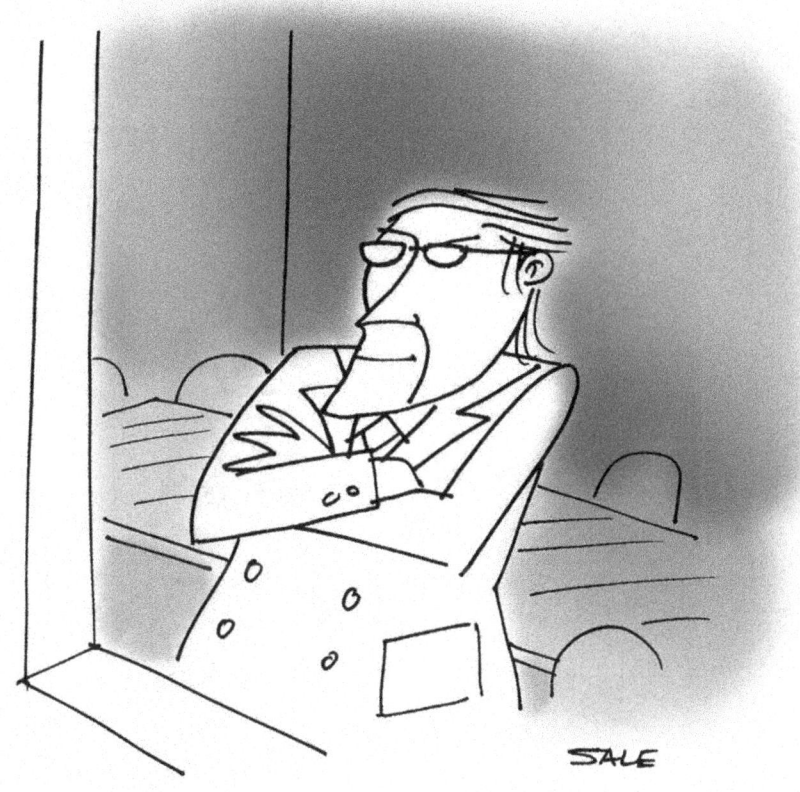

"Protest all you want," mused the corporate titan, *"As long as we own your courts and politicians - you meek shall inherit squat."*

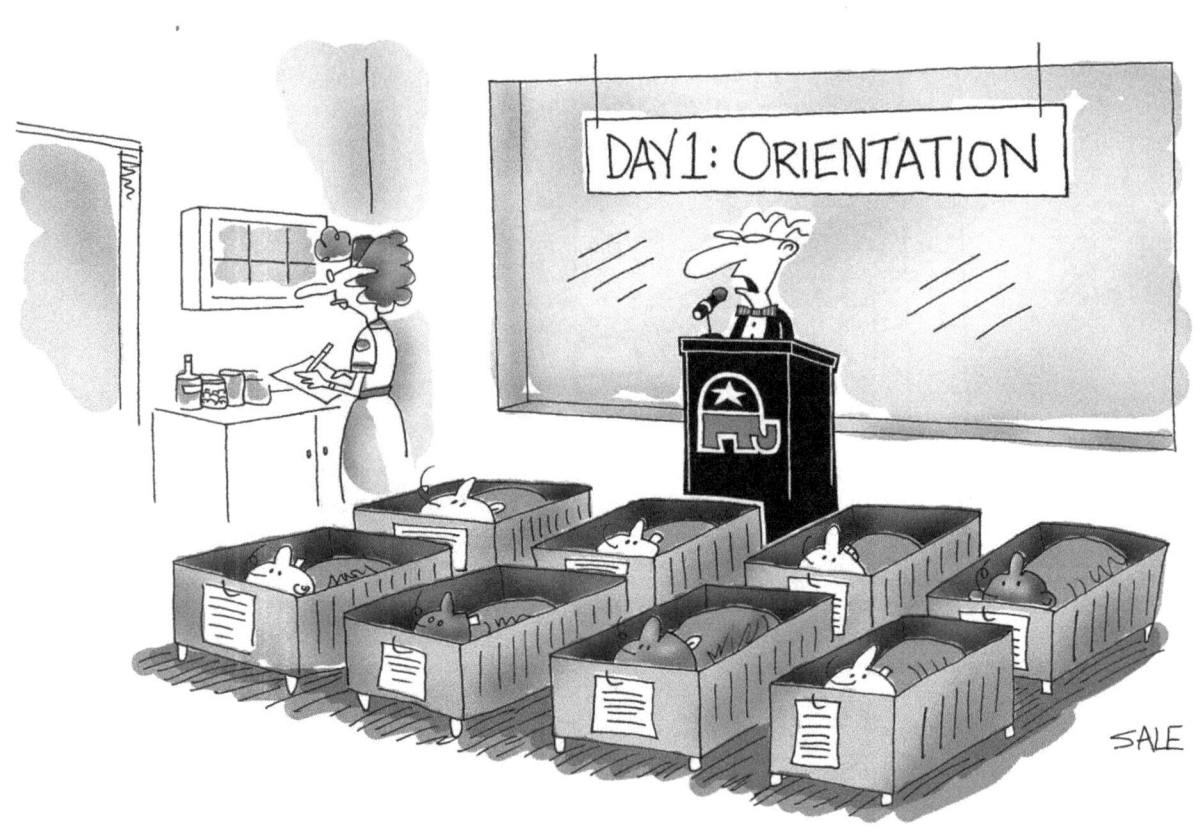

"*Listen up you babies. We fought hard for your right to be born — even killed for it, but from now on you little moochers are on your own, especially you brown ones.*"

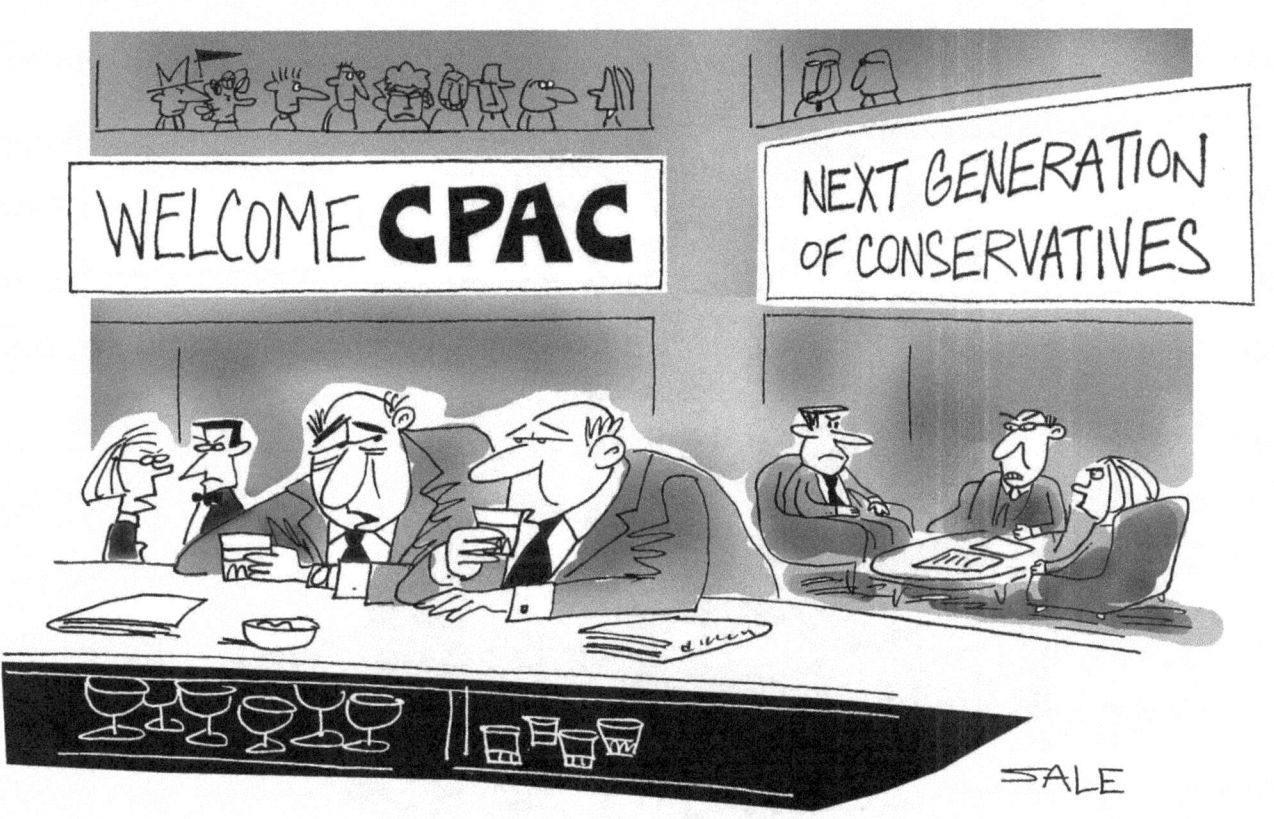

"I must be getting old. No matter how intolerant I get...I just can't keep up."

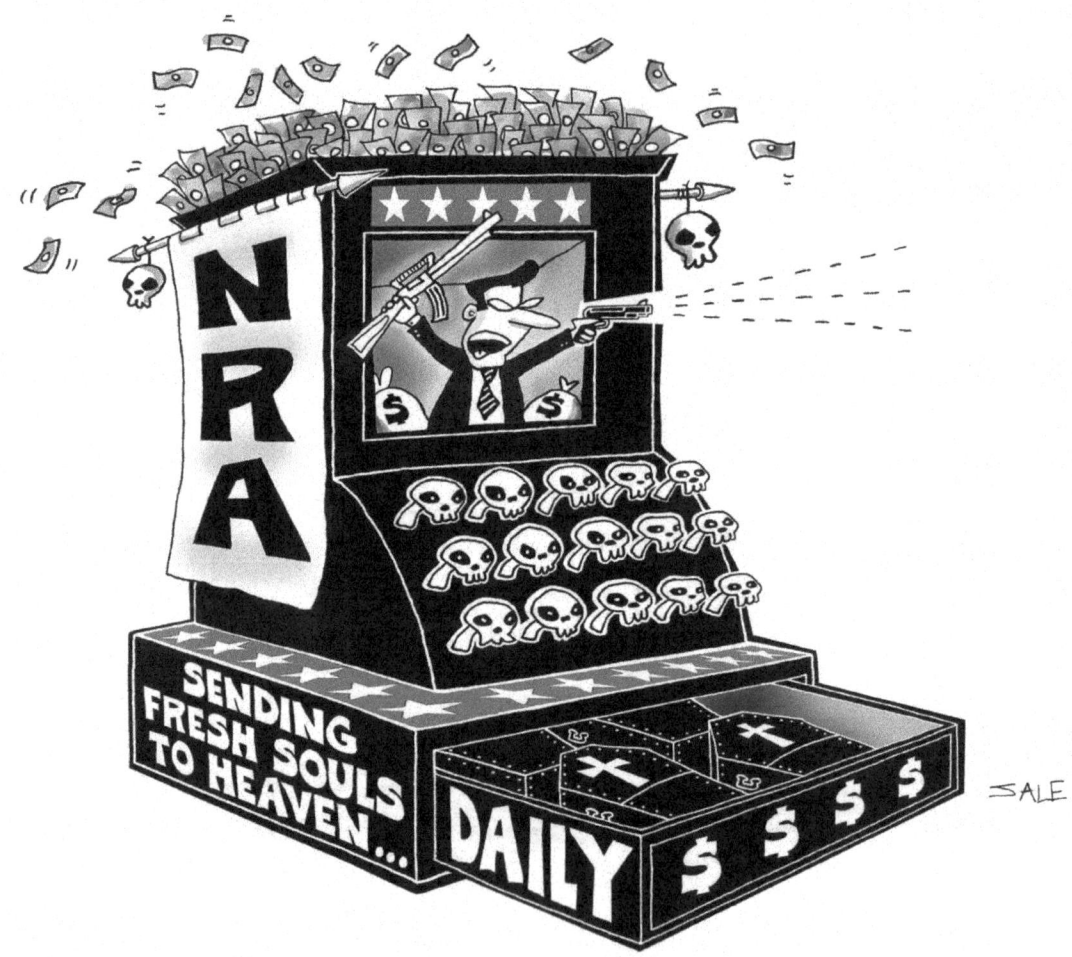

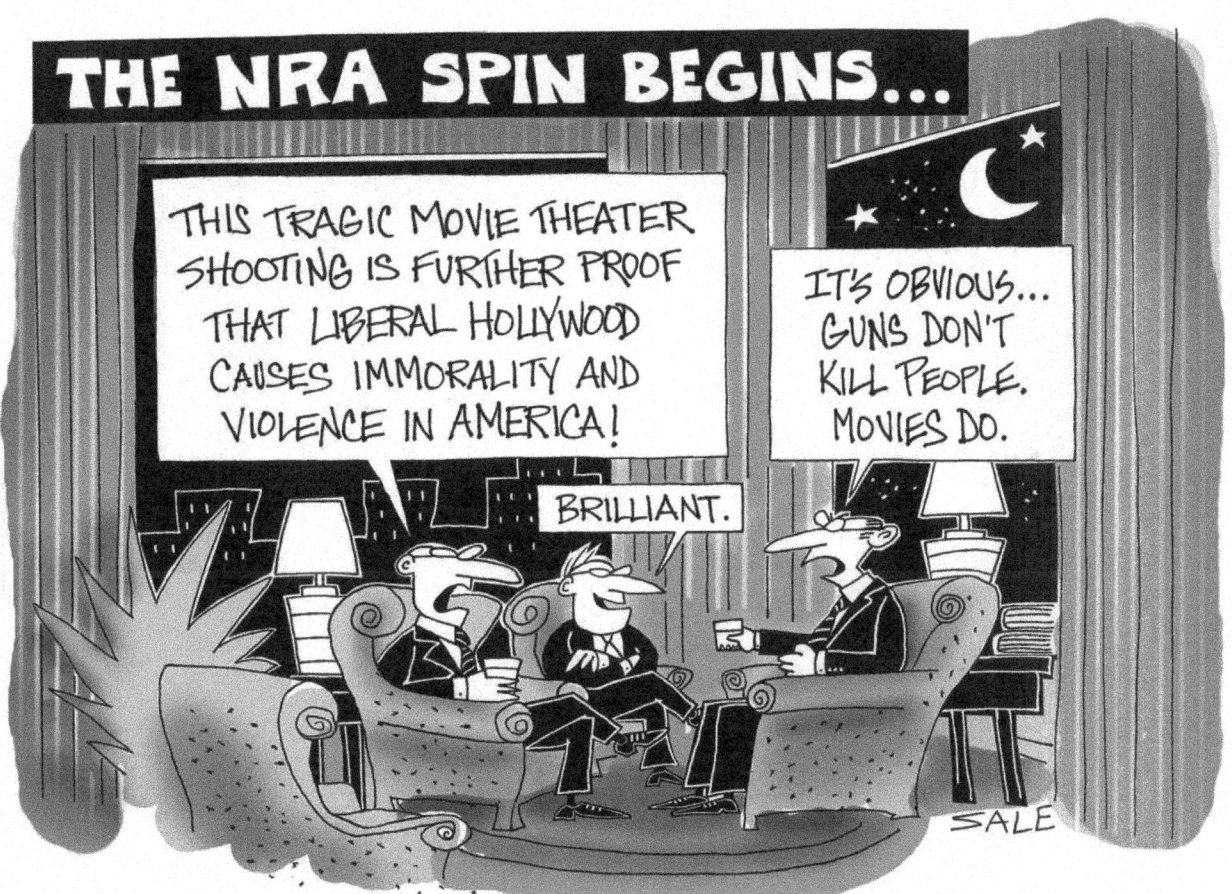

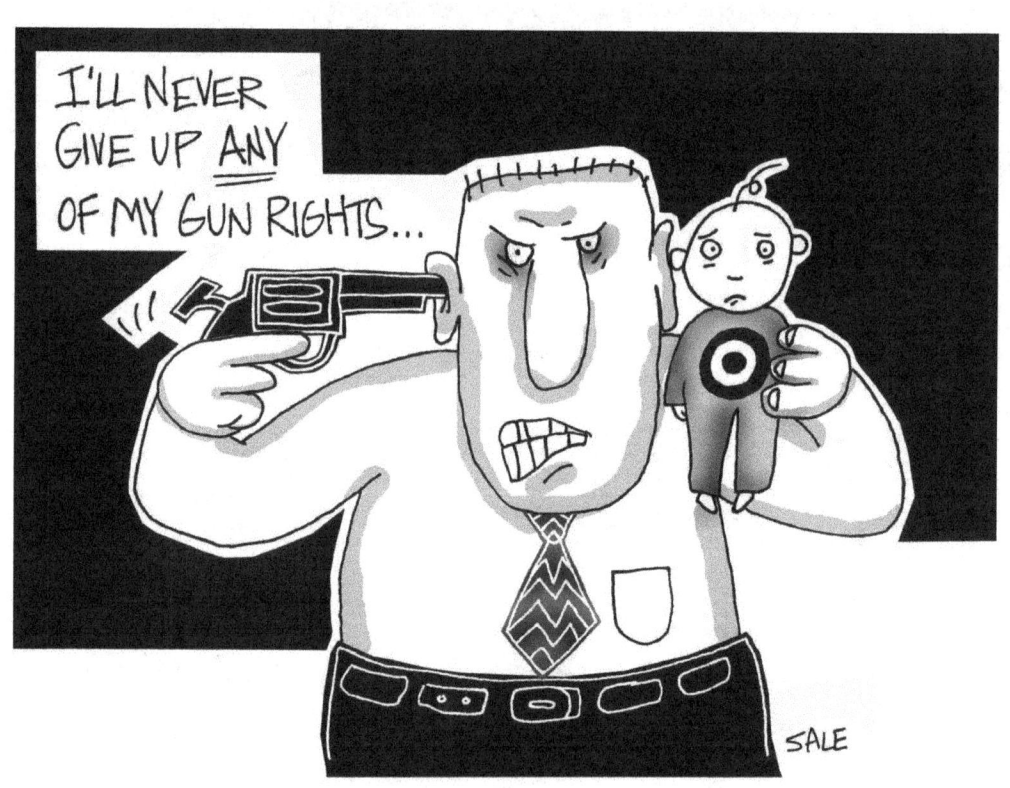

NO MATTER WHO MAY GET HURT.

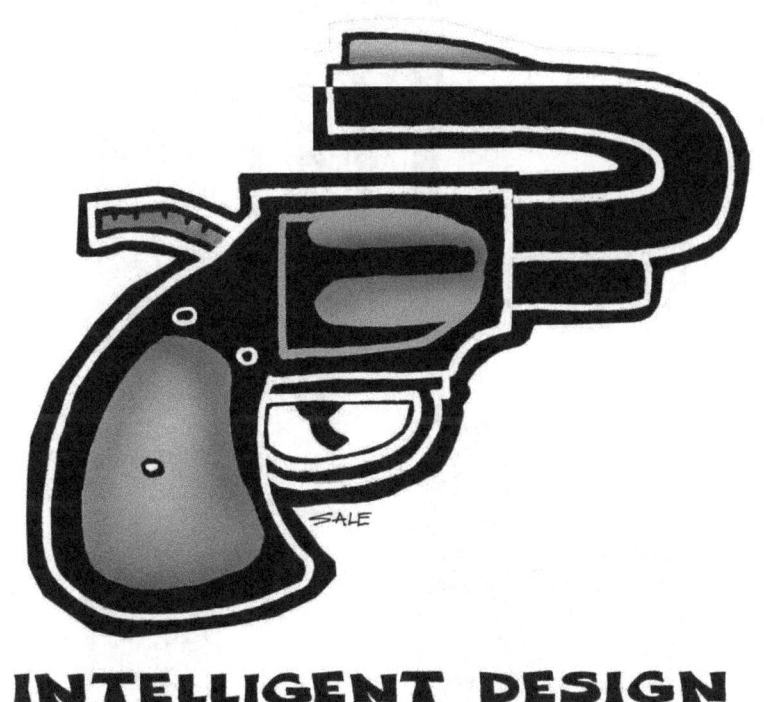

INTELLIGENT DESIGN

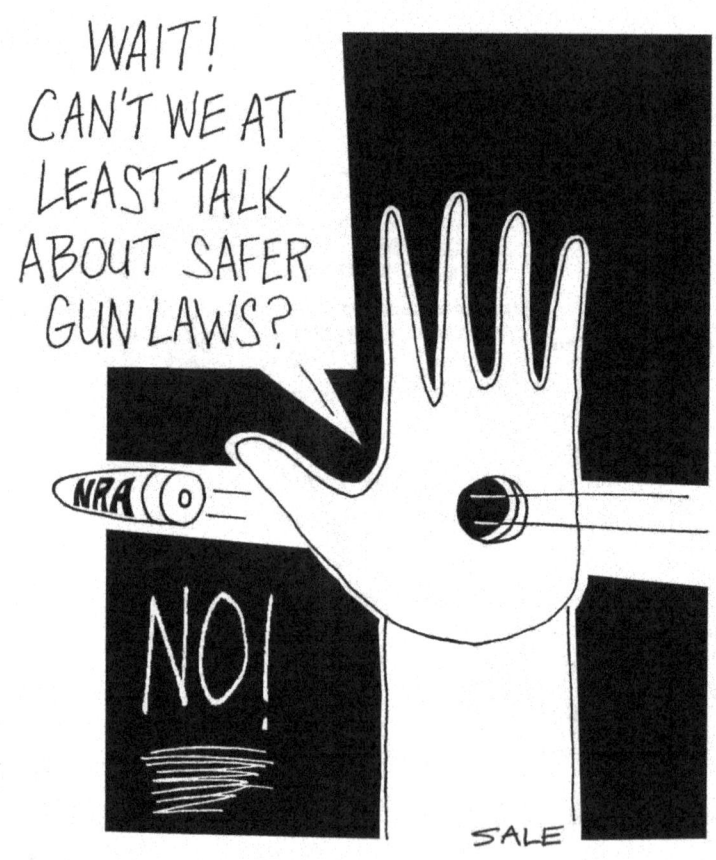

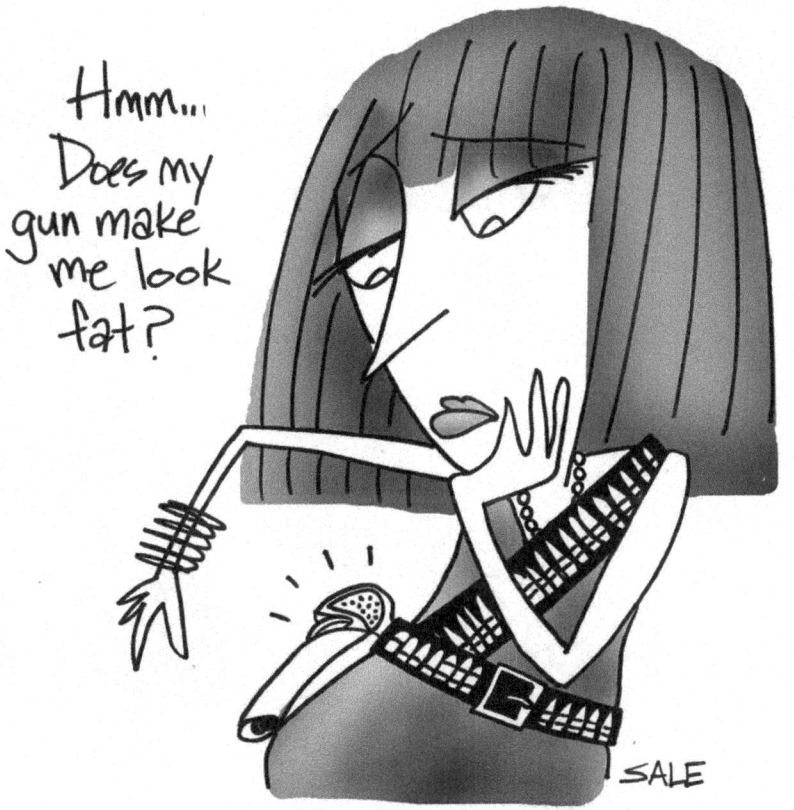

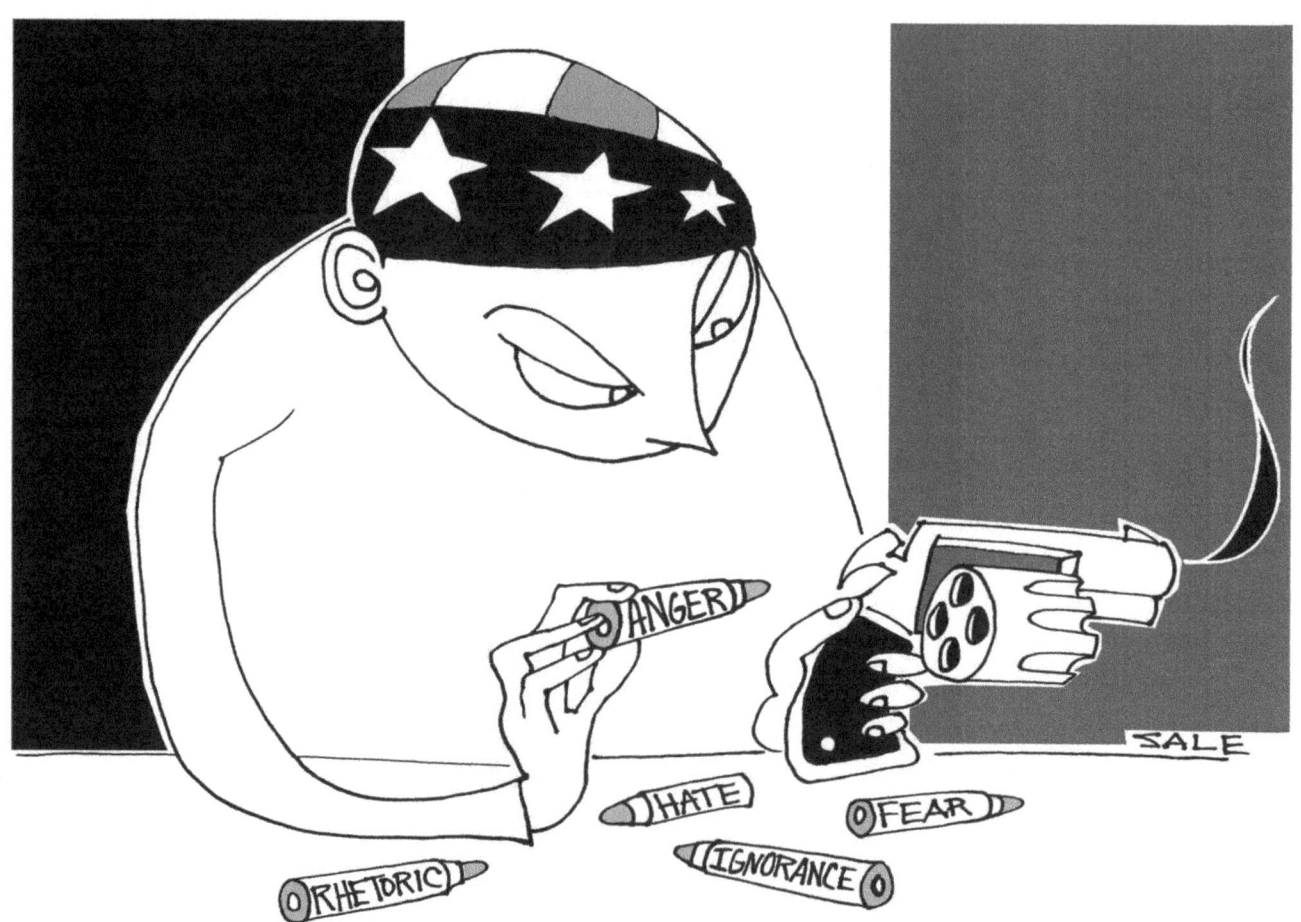

58

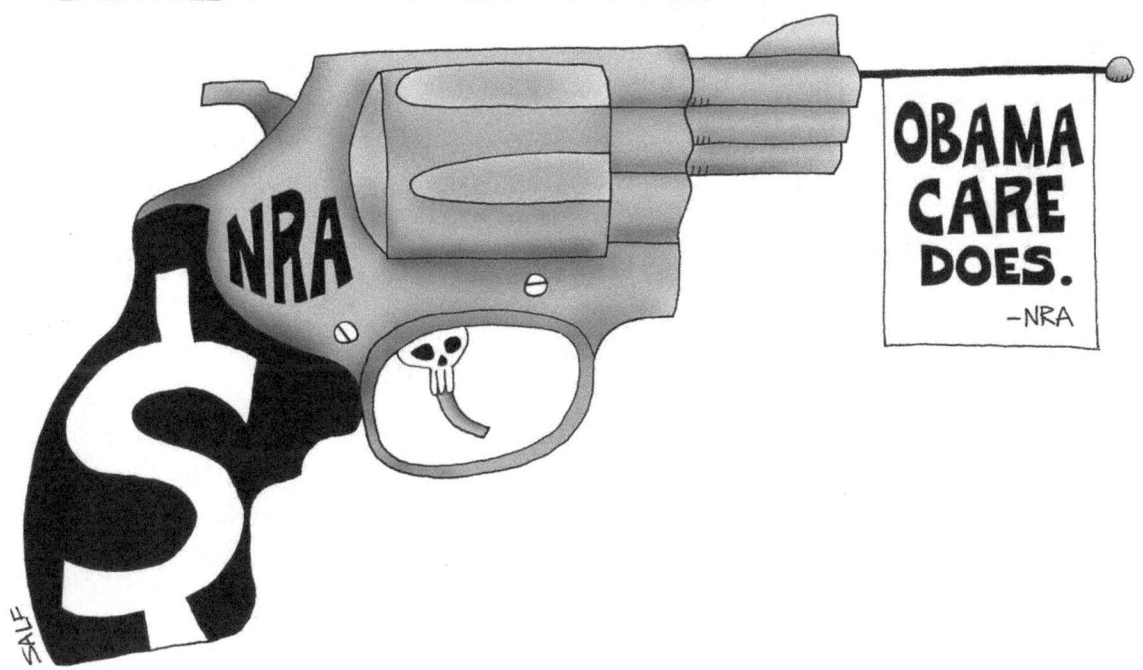

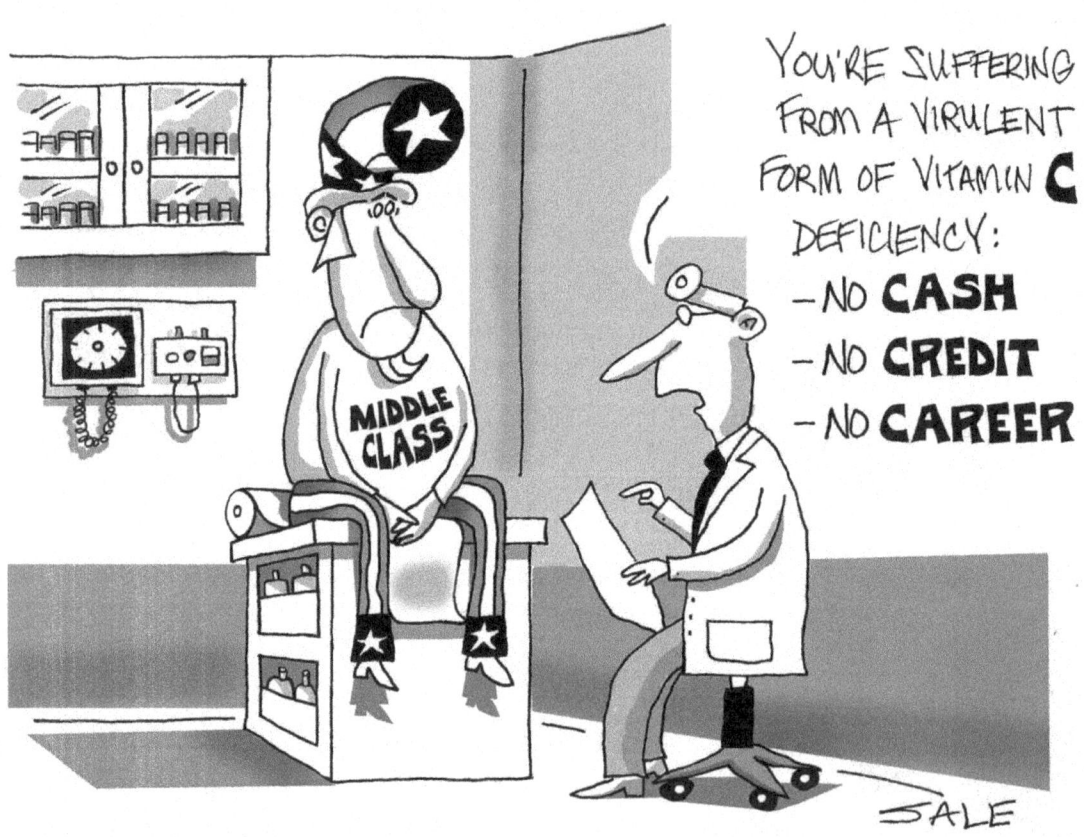

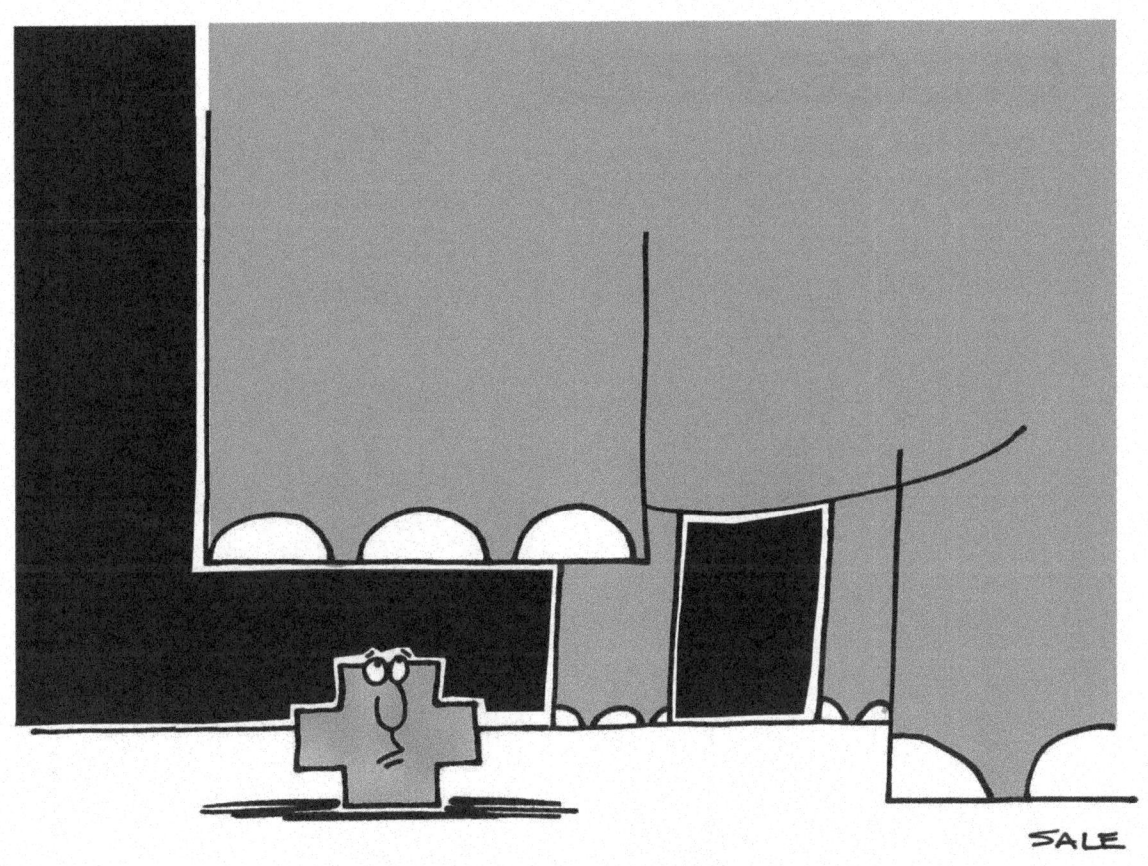

TAKING AIM AT OBAMACARE.

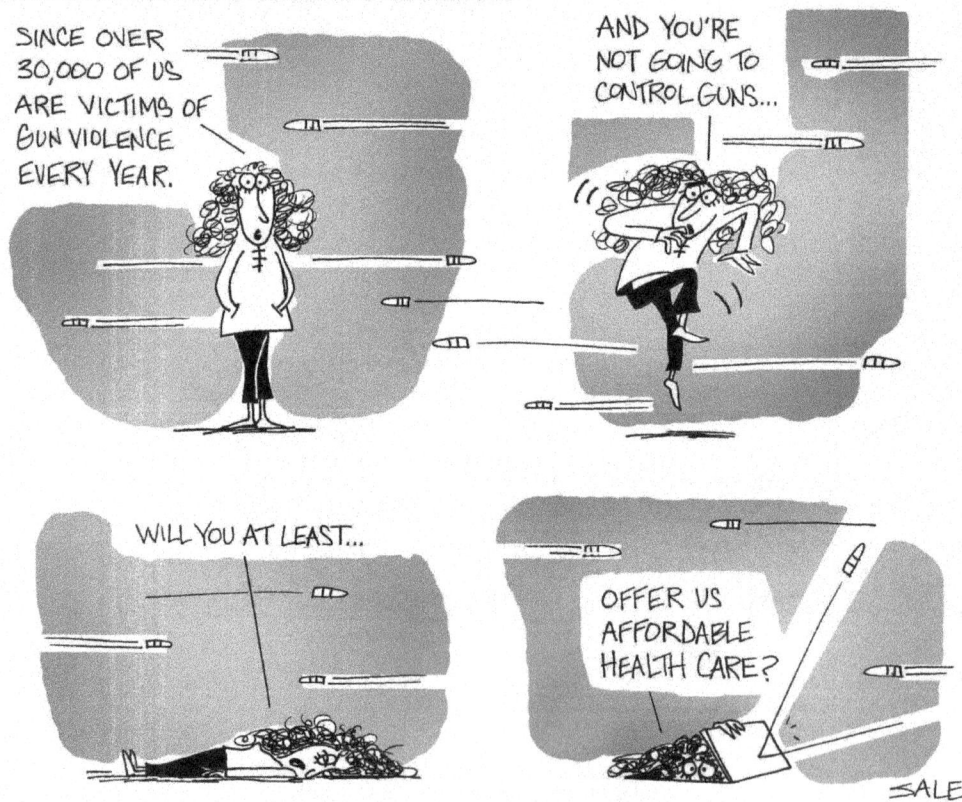

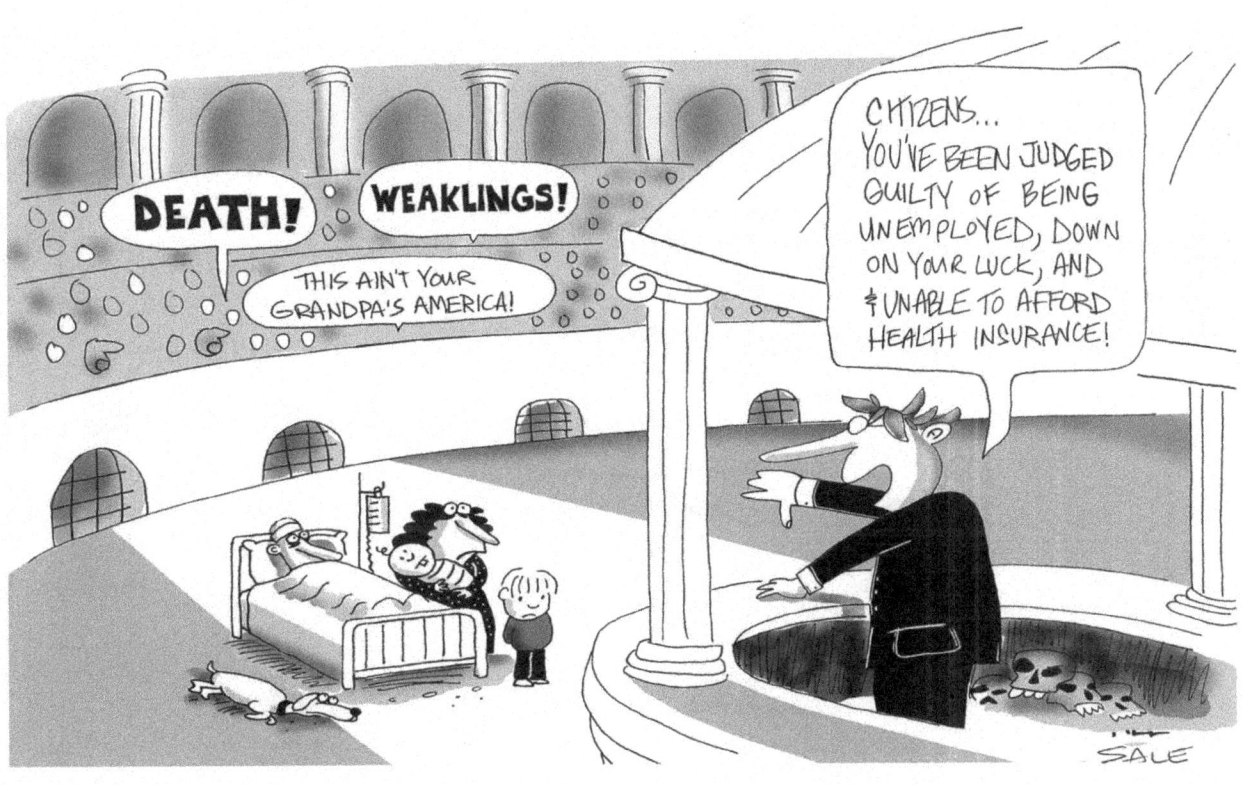

63

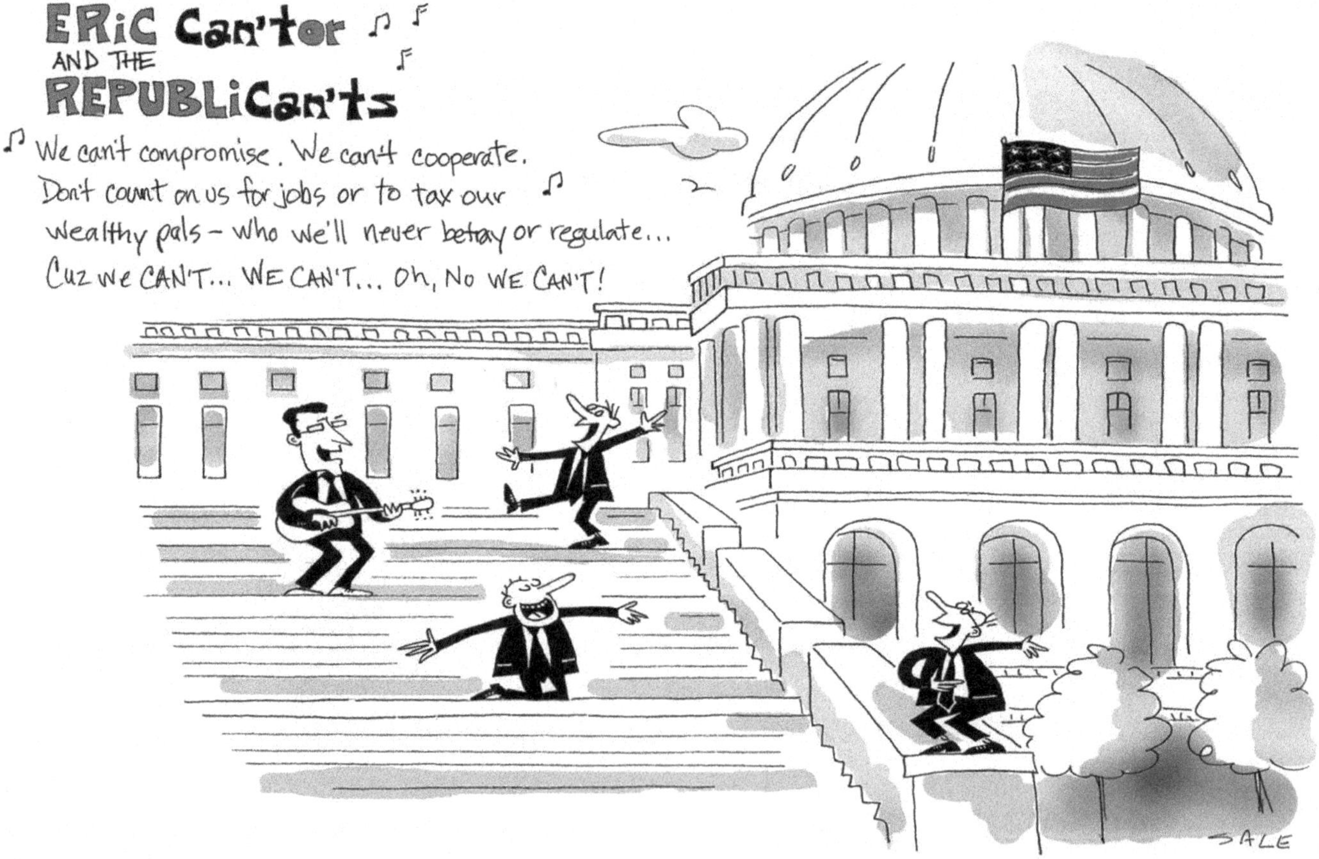

ERiC Can'tor ♪ ♪
AND THE
REPUBLiCan'ts

♪ We can't compromise. We can't cooperate.
Don't count on us for jobs or to tax our ♪
wealthy pals — who we'll never betray or regulate...
Cuz we CAN'T... WE CAN'T... Oh, No WE CAN'T!

SALE

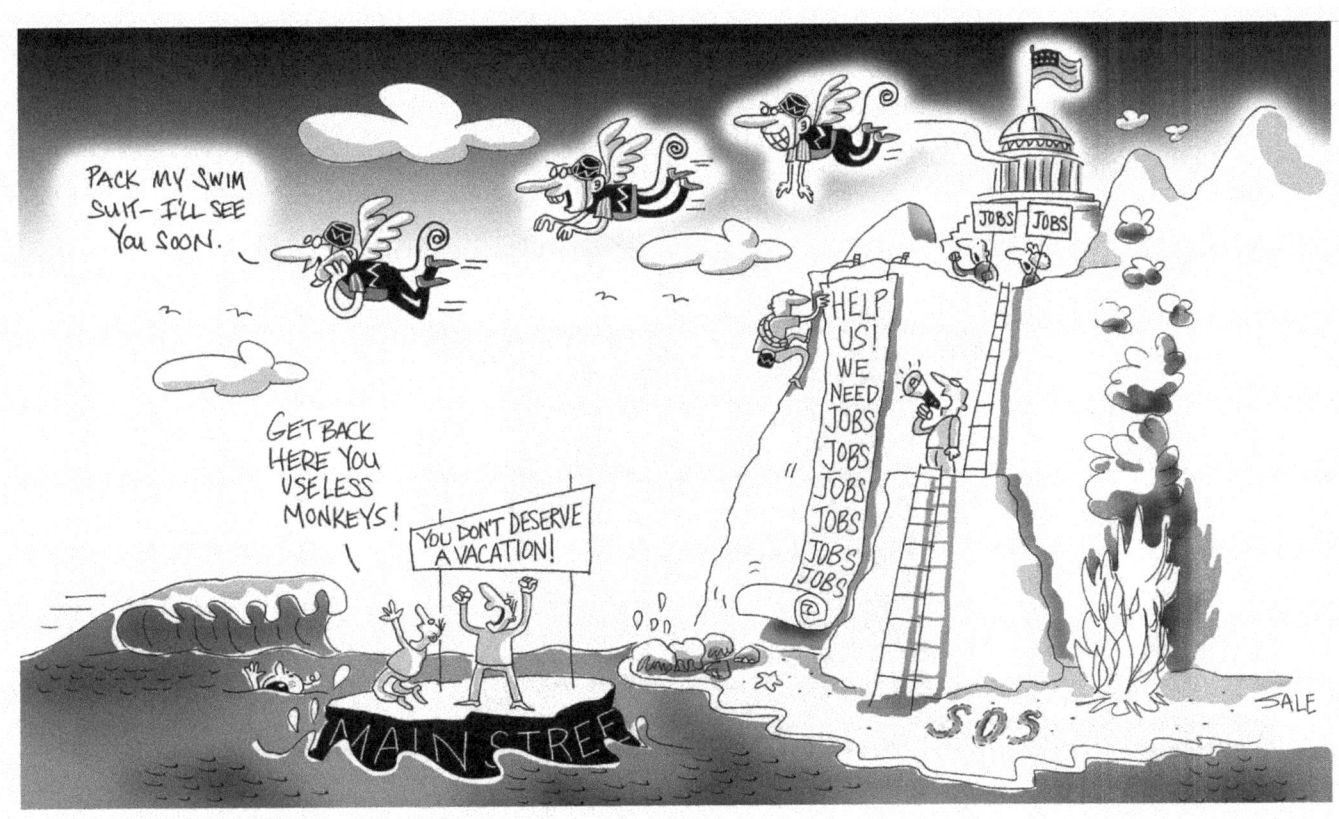

65

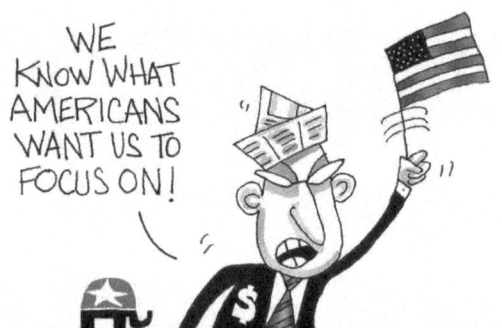

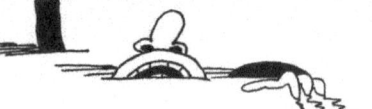

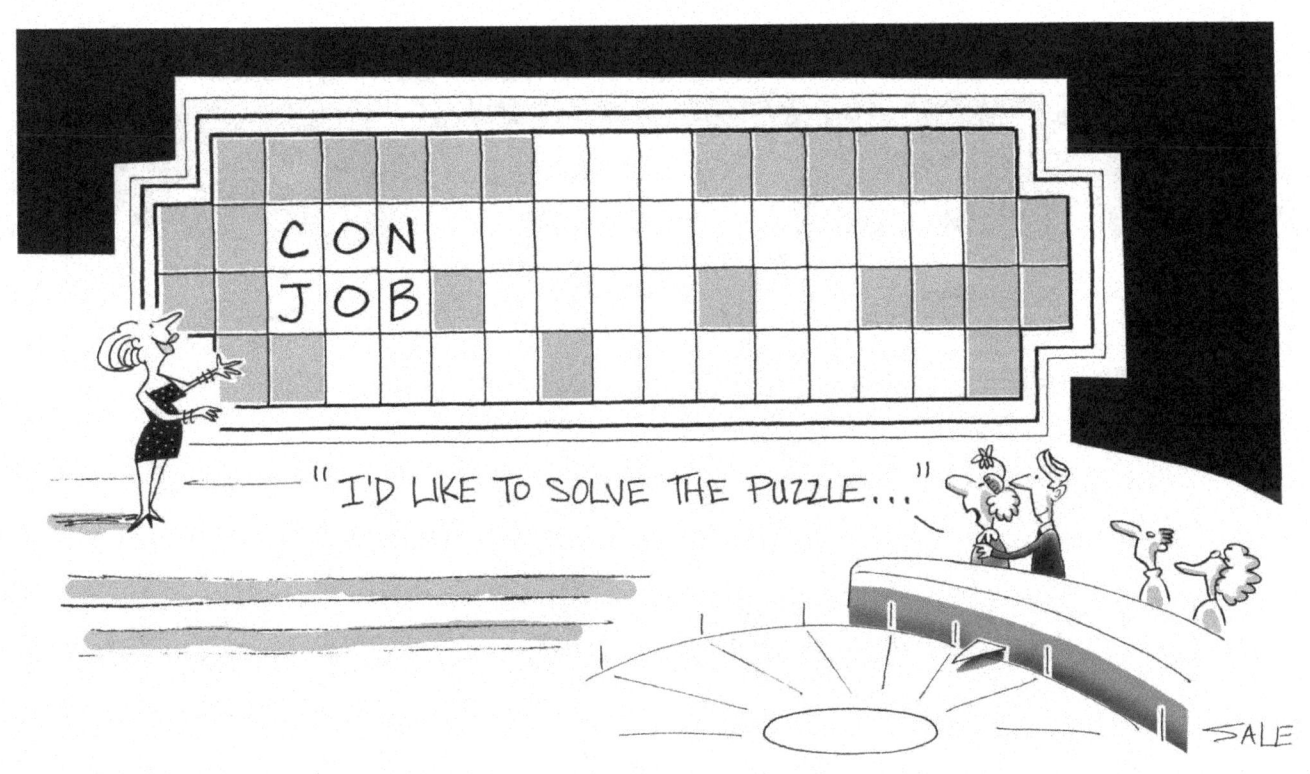

"THE CONSERVATIVES JOB PLAN TO SAVE AMERICA."

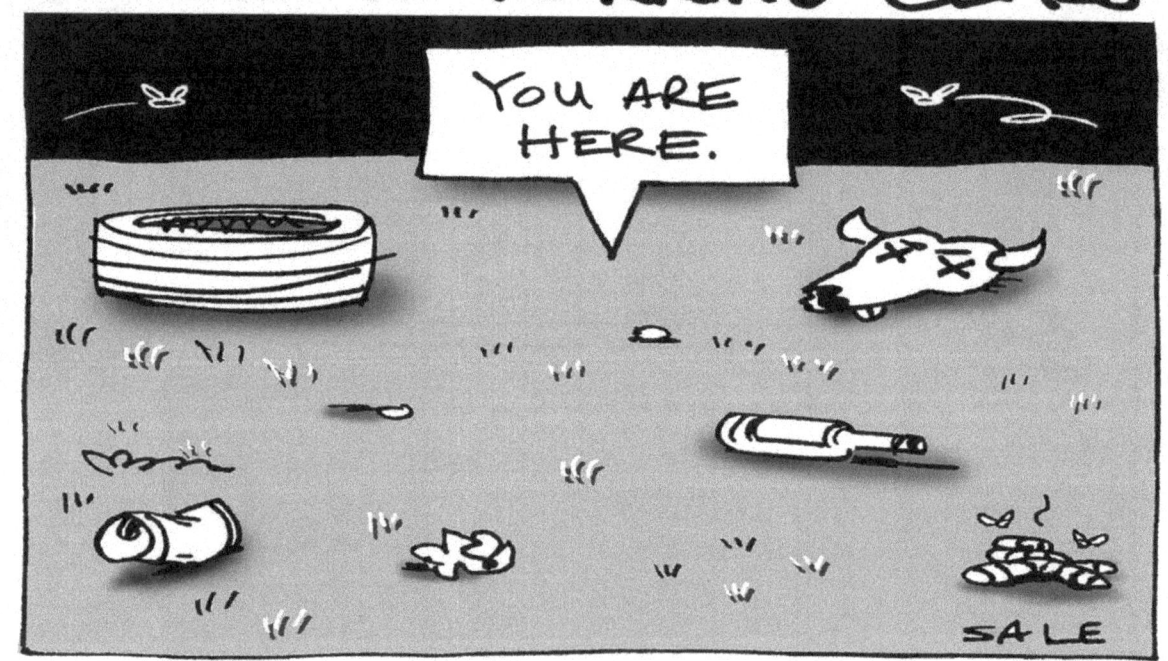

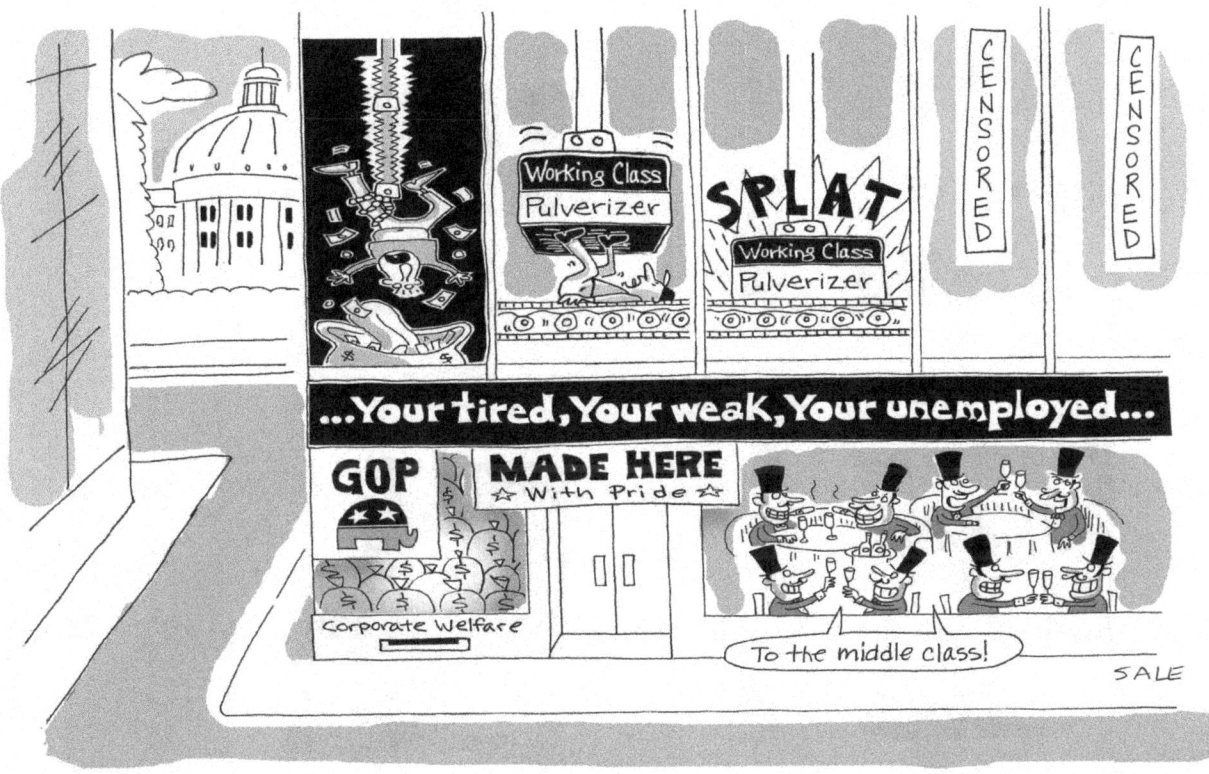

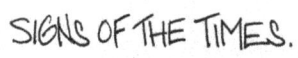

SIGNS OF THE TIMES.

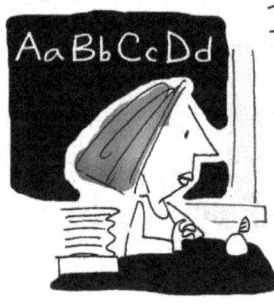

WHEN I GROW UP I WANT TO BE A PRIEST.

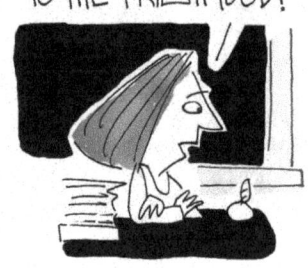

HAS GOD CALLED YOU TO TO THE PRIESTHOOD?

NO, MY FATHER HAS.

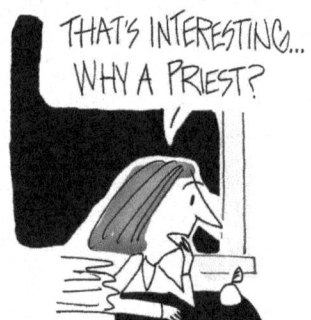

THAT'S INTERESTING... WHY A PRIEST?

JOB SECURITY.

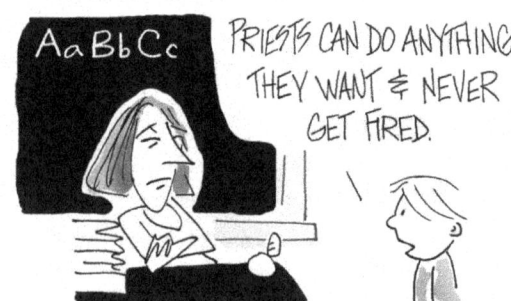

PRIESTS CAN DO ANYTHING THEY WANT & NEVER GET FIRED.

SALE

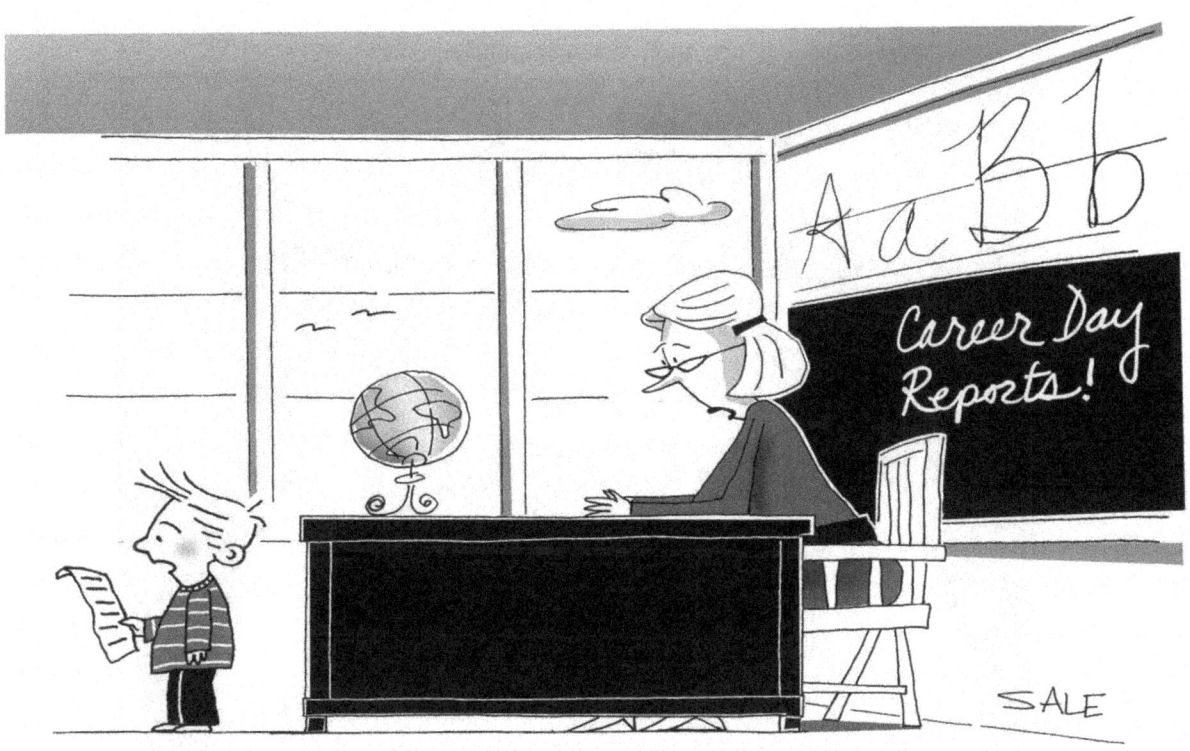

"After getting my feet wet in student government and local politics, I plan to do a brief stint in Congress as preparation for my ultimate career as an influence-peddling millionaire Washington-insider, author and speaker."

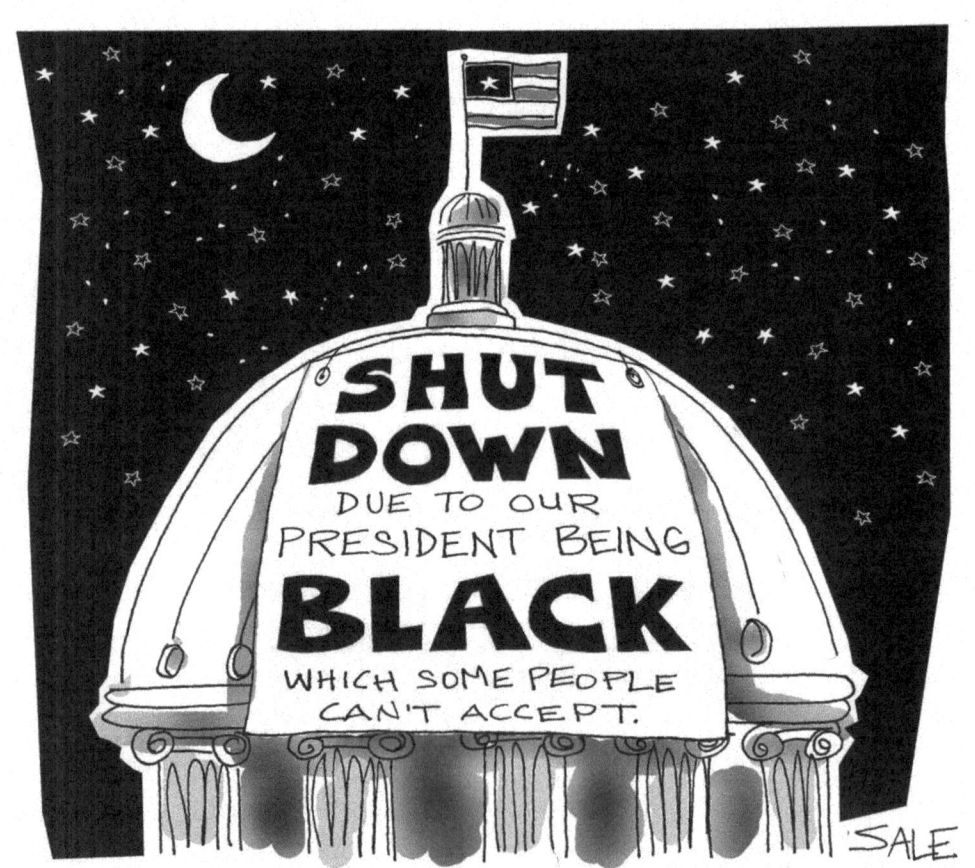

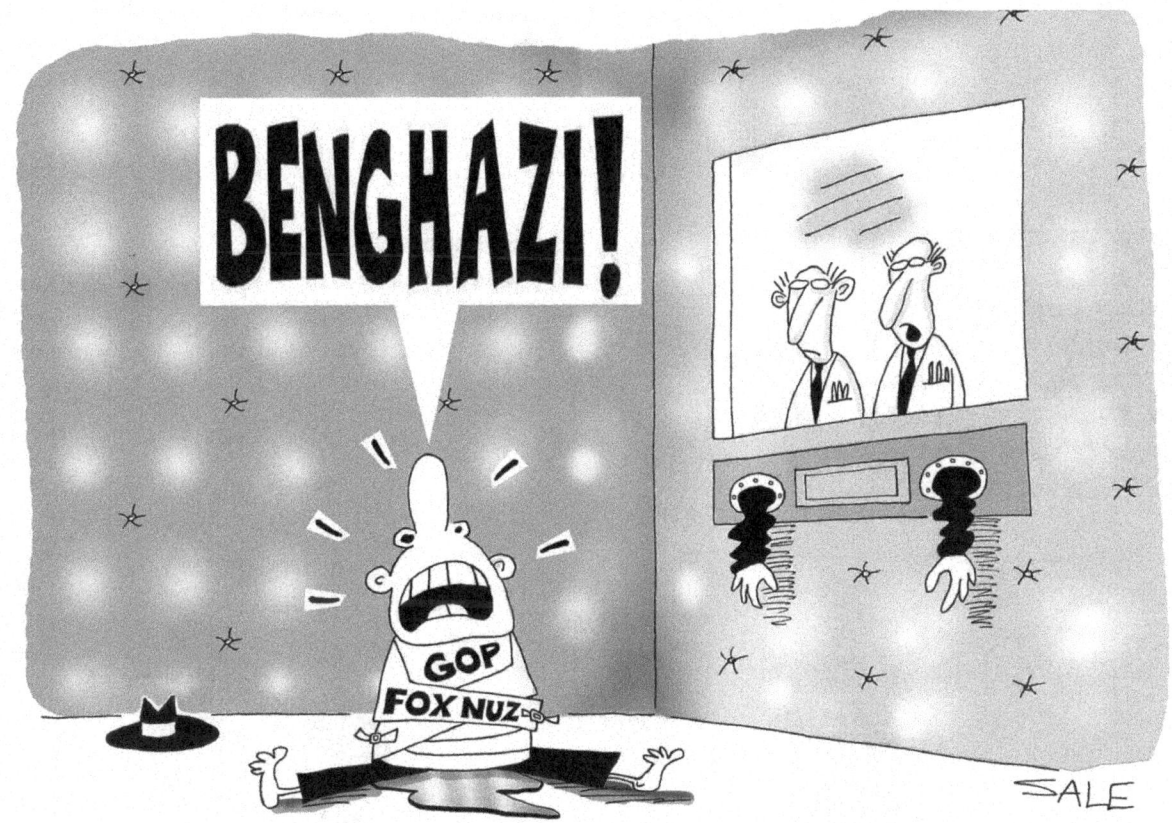

"Ignorant bombastic rants, accompanied by a shameless compulsion to mislead Americans for political gain...Yep, he's got Benghazi fever."

No Politician Left Behind - A Modest Proposal

I was thinking...
Since we elect and pay politicians salaries, why can't we set performance standards and hold them accountable with consequences for not meeting them?

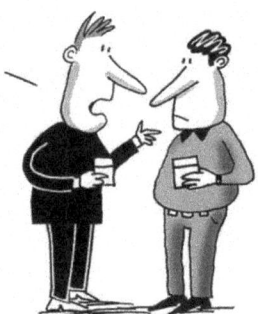

For example...
"You will be fired if you:
Don't show up for work, or for votes, or go on vacation before finishing your work, or storm out of meetings..."

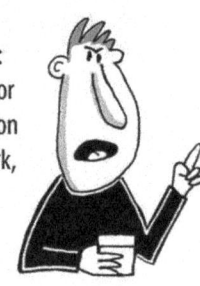

"Lie to, or mislead the public, take money from anyone, use government assets for personal use, publicly insult your boss.."

"Filibuster or obstruct the business of governing or prevent others from doing their jobs..."

SALE

How about threatening to shut down the government?

Instant dismissal – maybe worse.

Sounds like a good start and perfectly reasonable to me.

I know
I'd be fired
for a lot less.

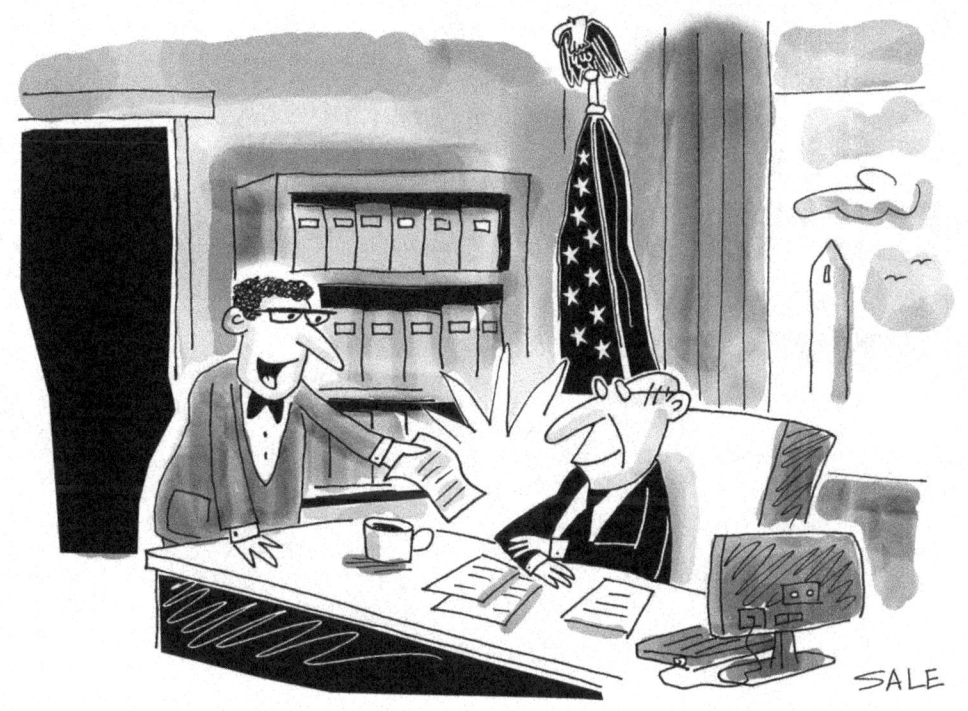

"This week's campaign donor list has arrived, Congressman, along with updated instructions on how to vote."

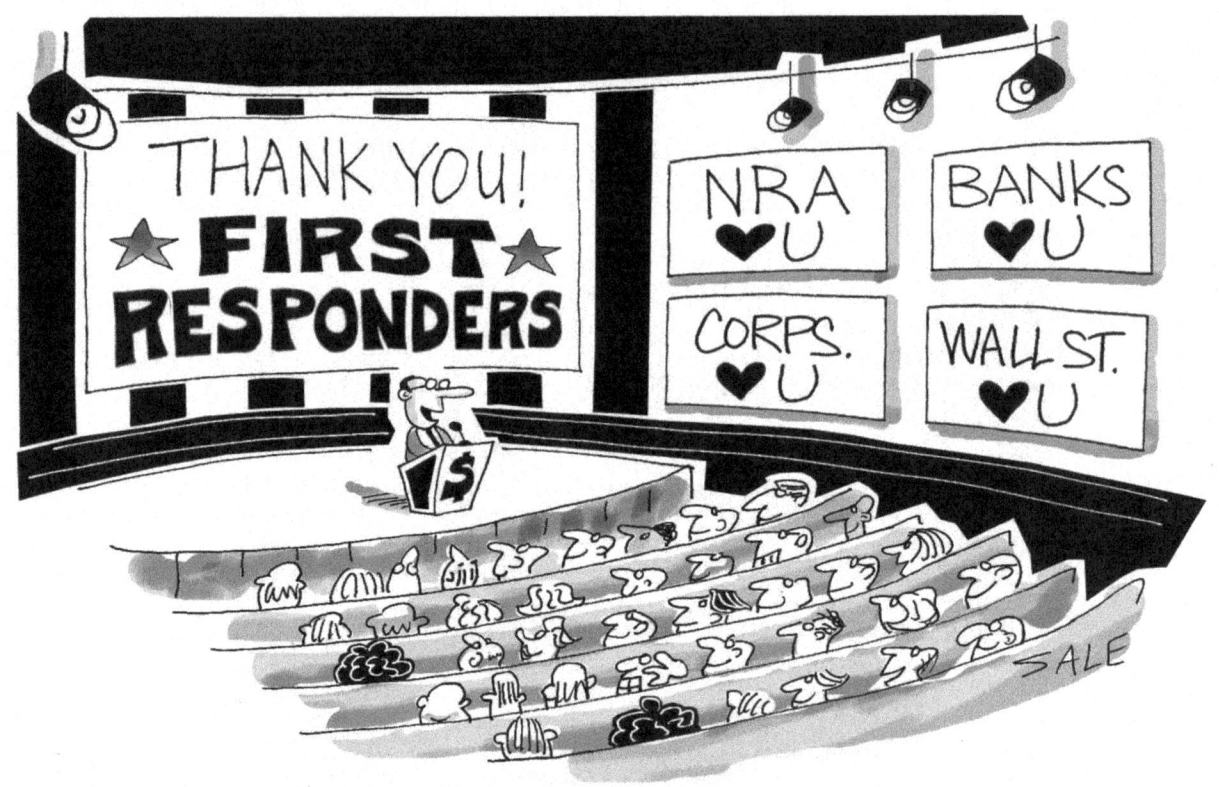

"Members of Congress and dear friends, whenever we're attacked, you are always the first through the door to protect us...and we are eternally grateful. So have a great time tonight, enjoy the open bar and don't forget your swag bags!"

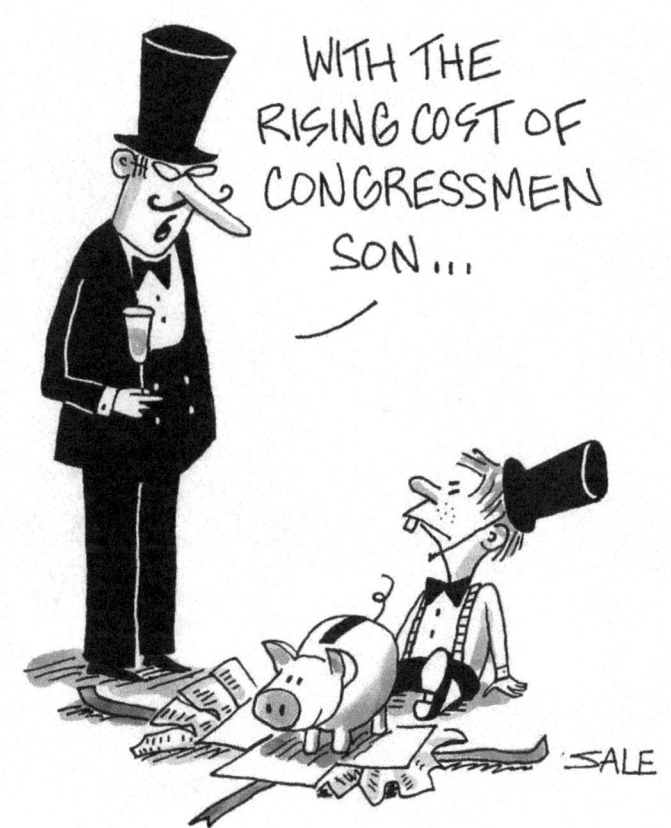

"It's never too soon to start saving."

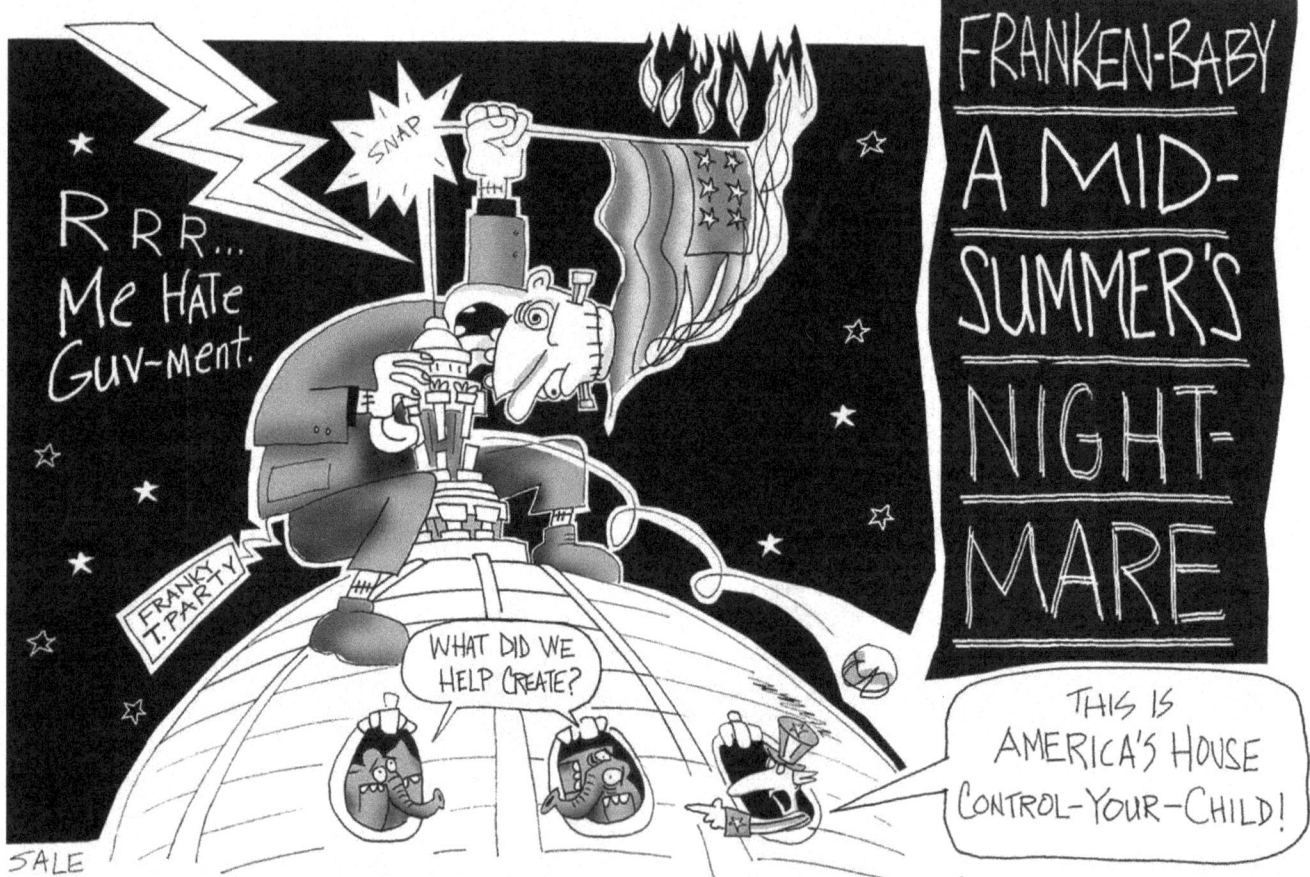

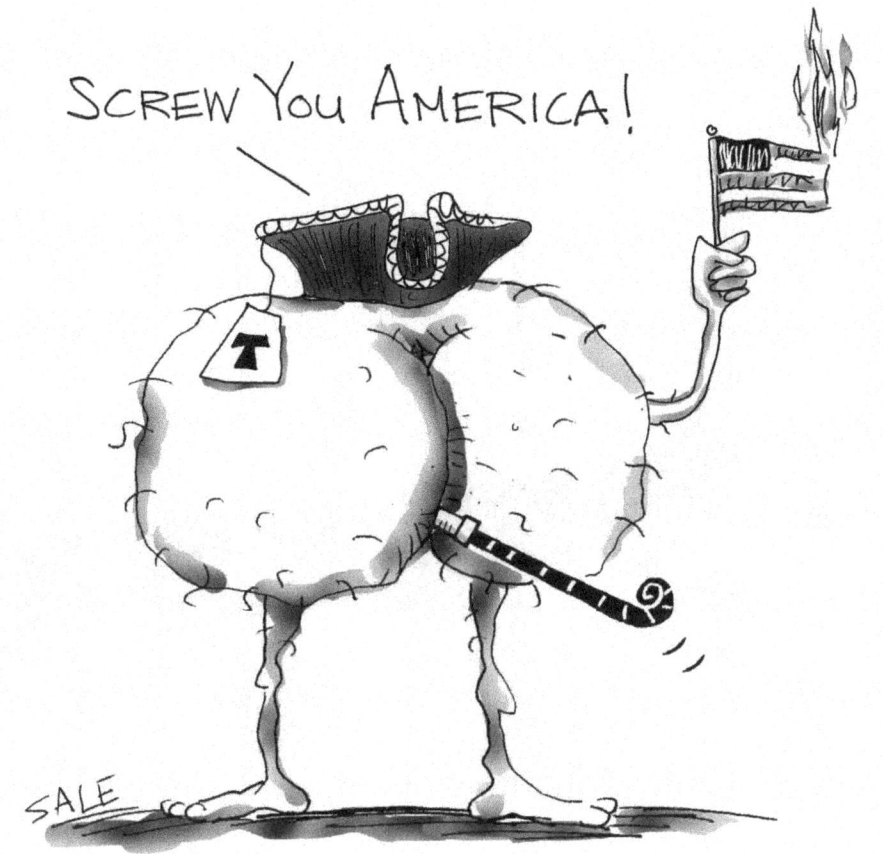

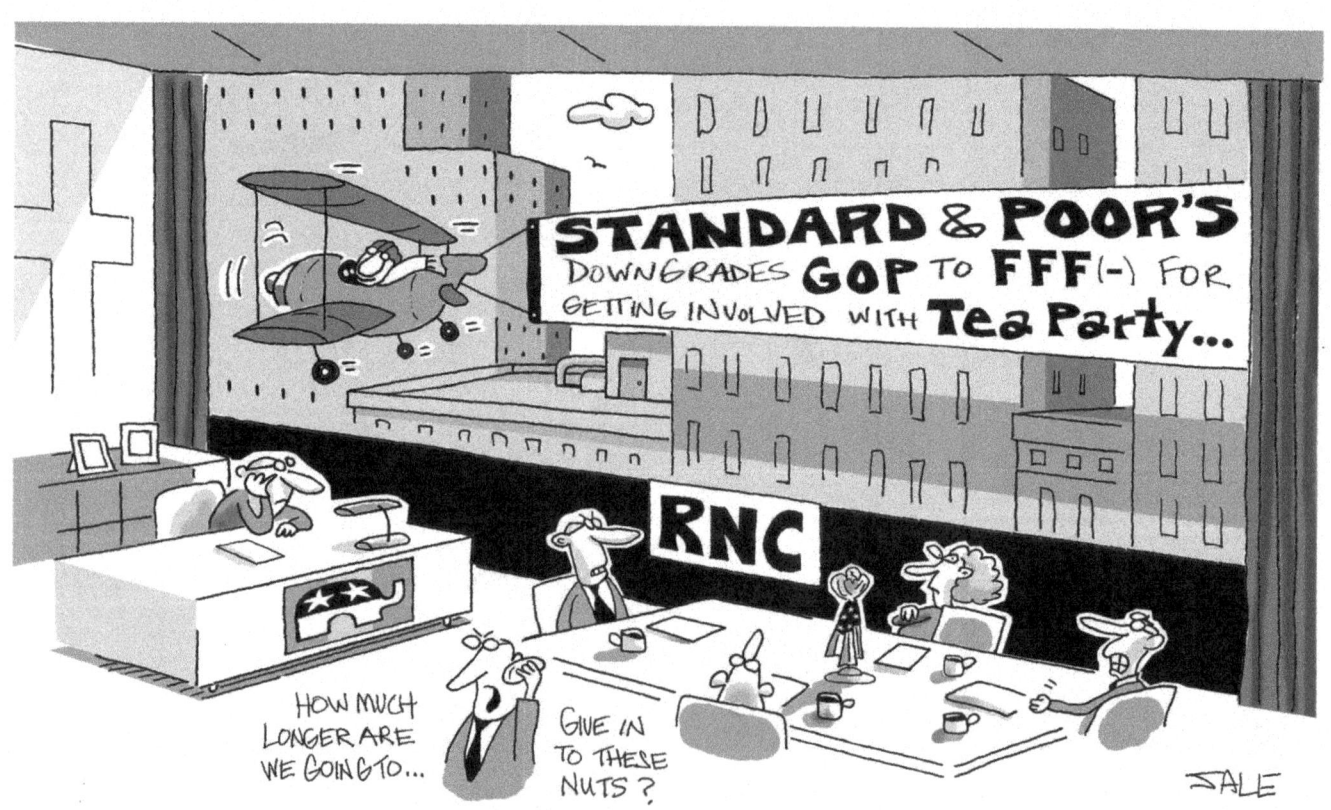

80

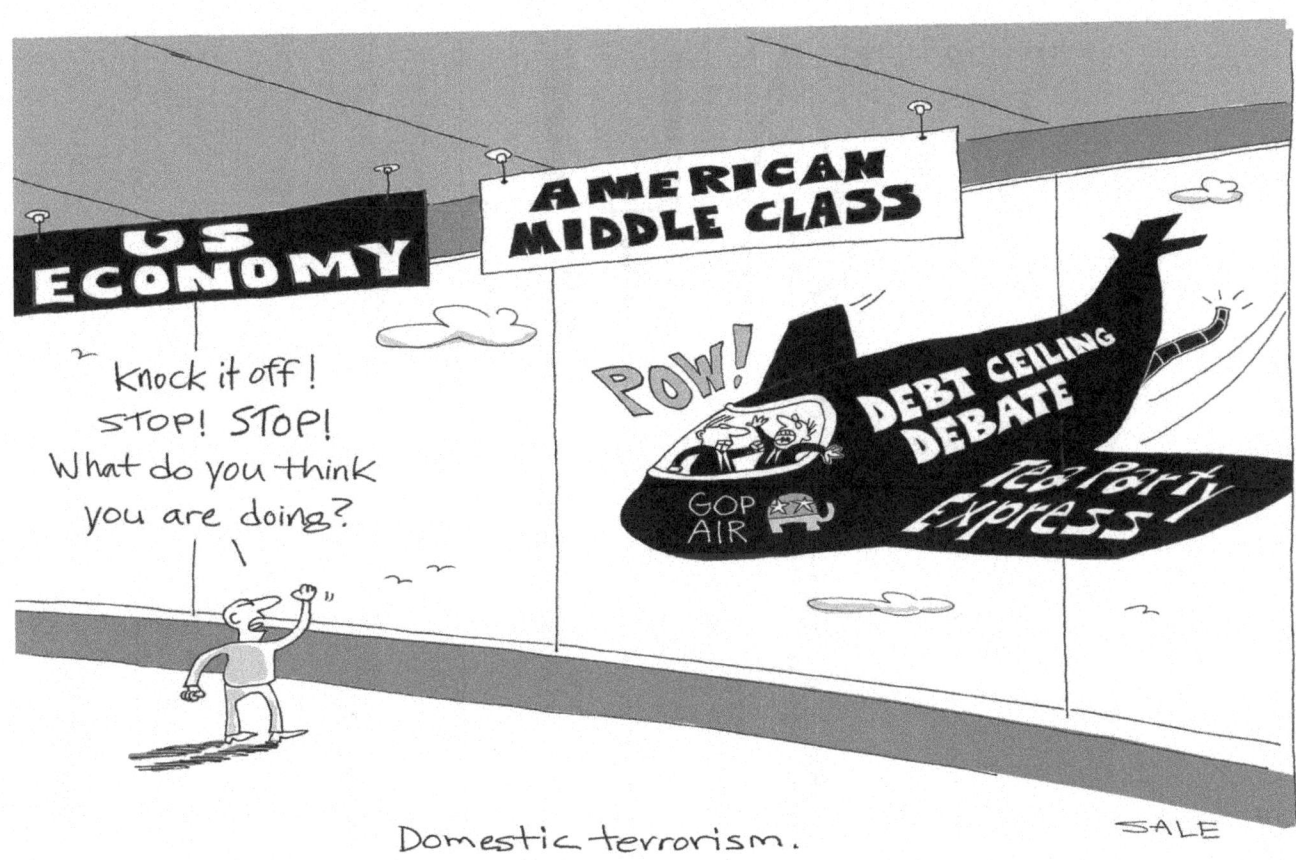

Domestic terrorism.

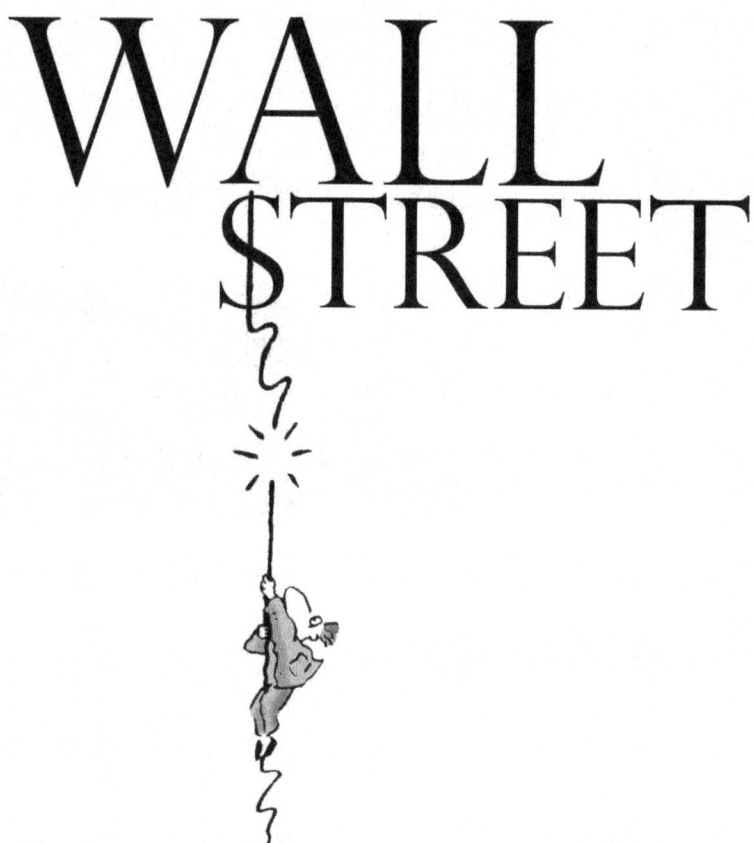

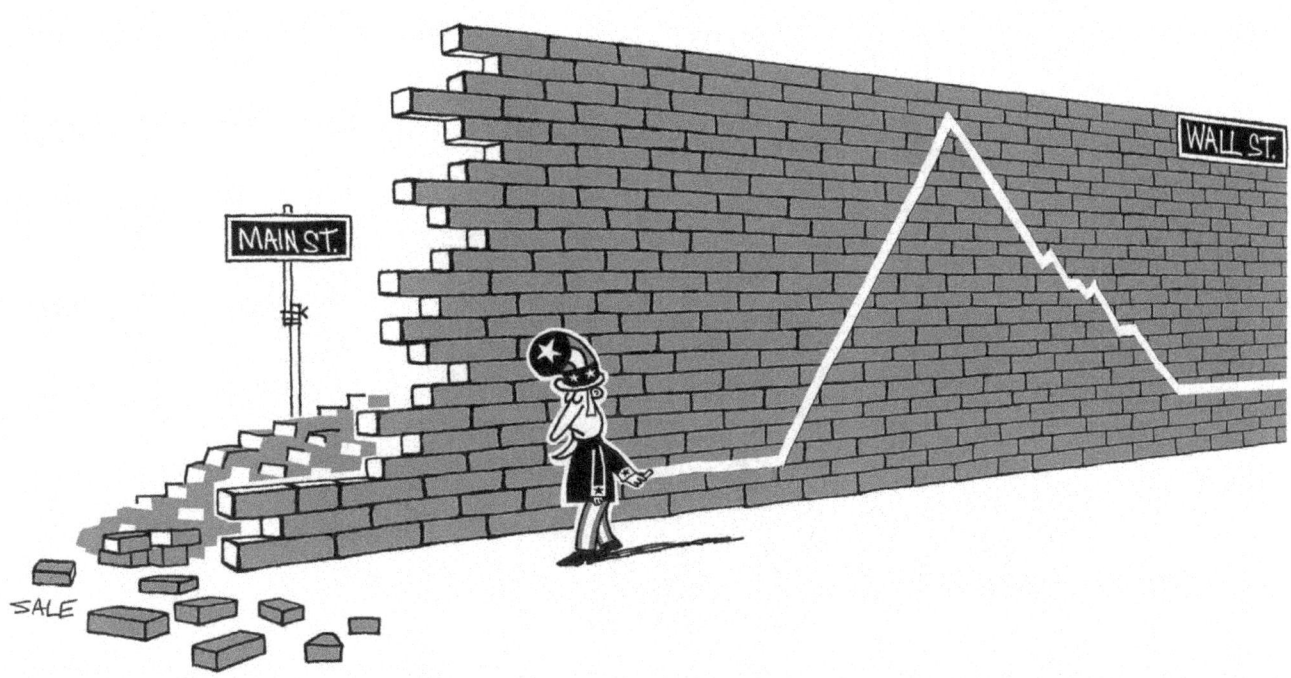

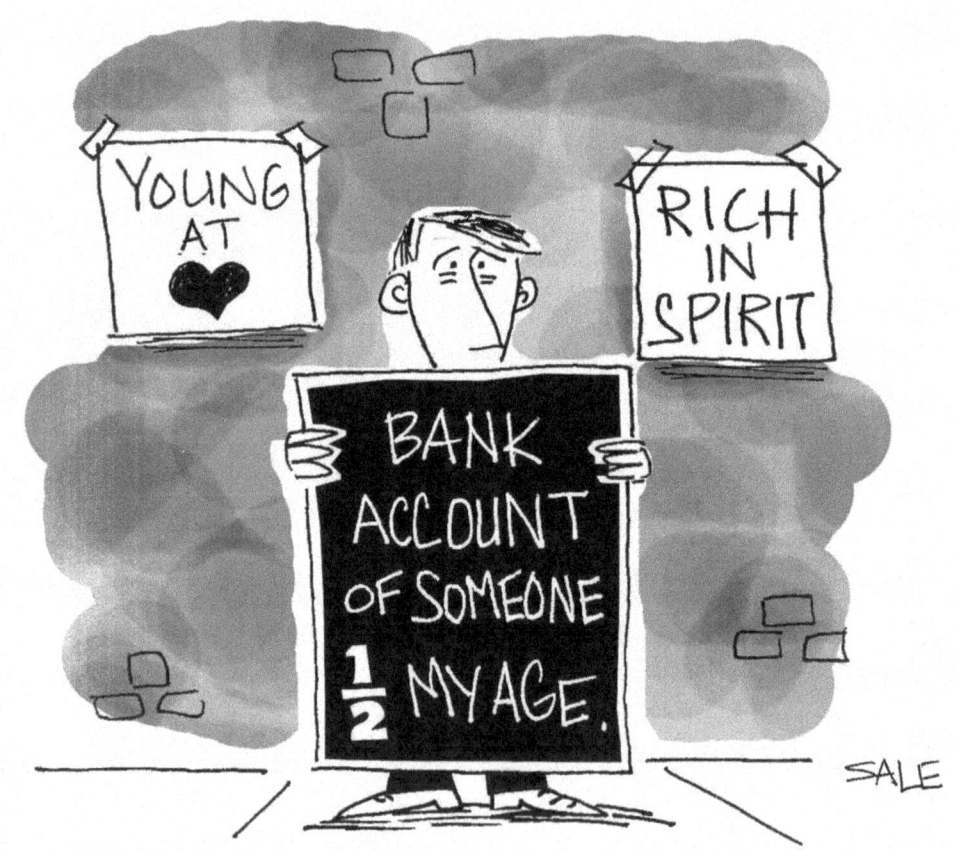

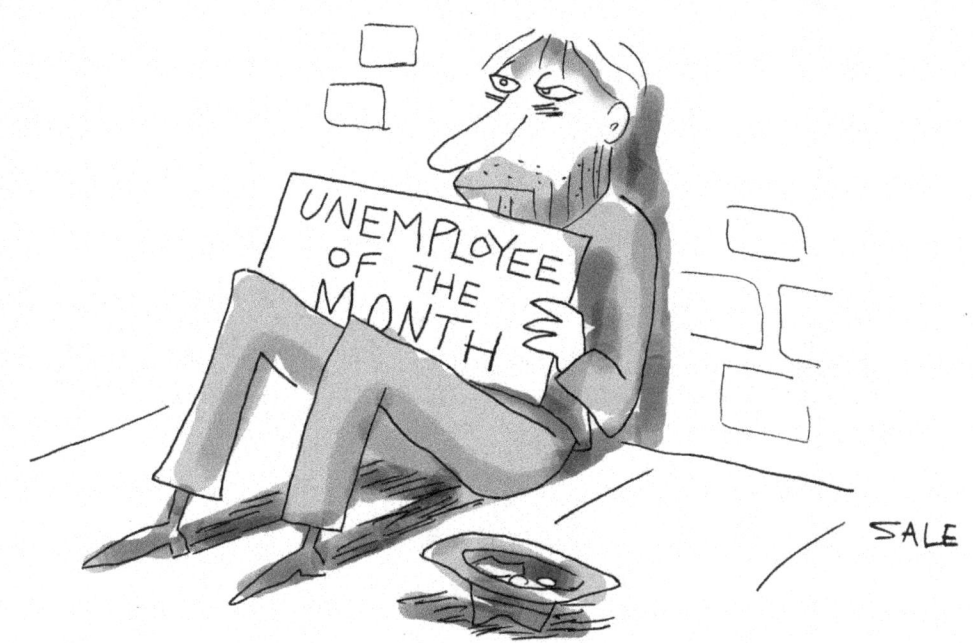

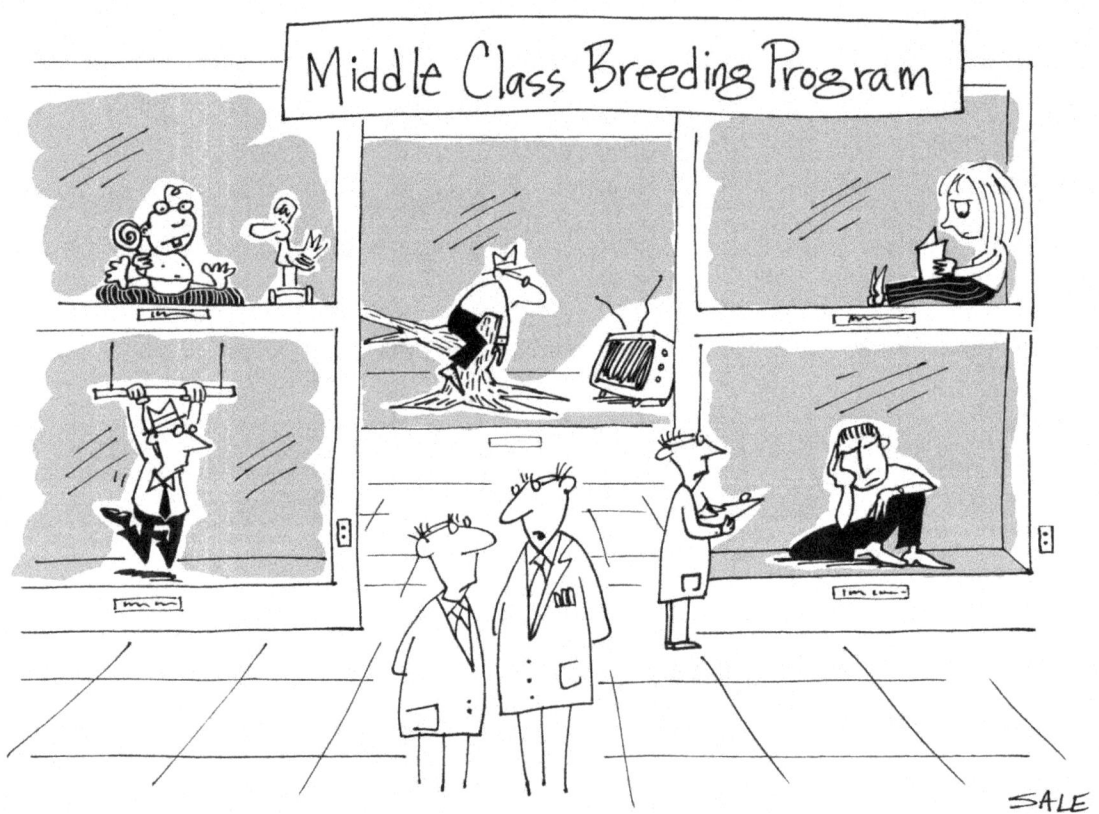

"We're hoping to re-introduce them into society someday."

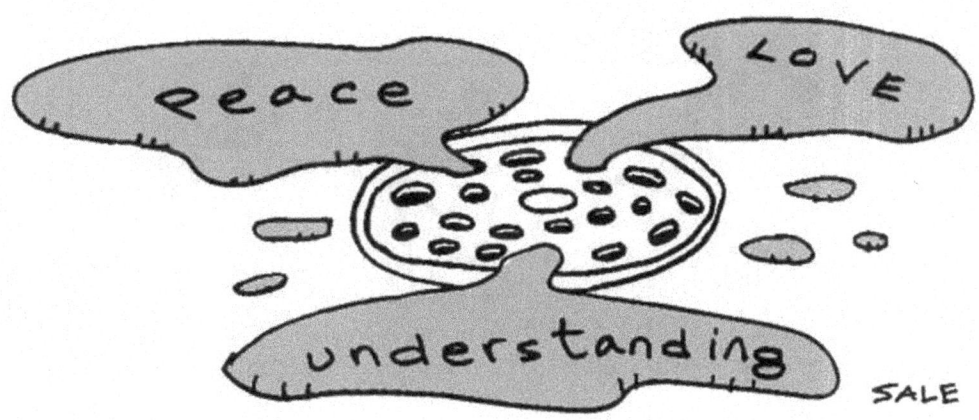

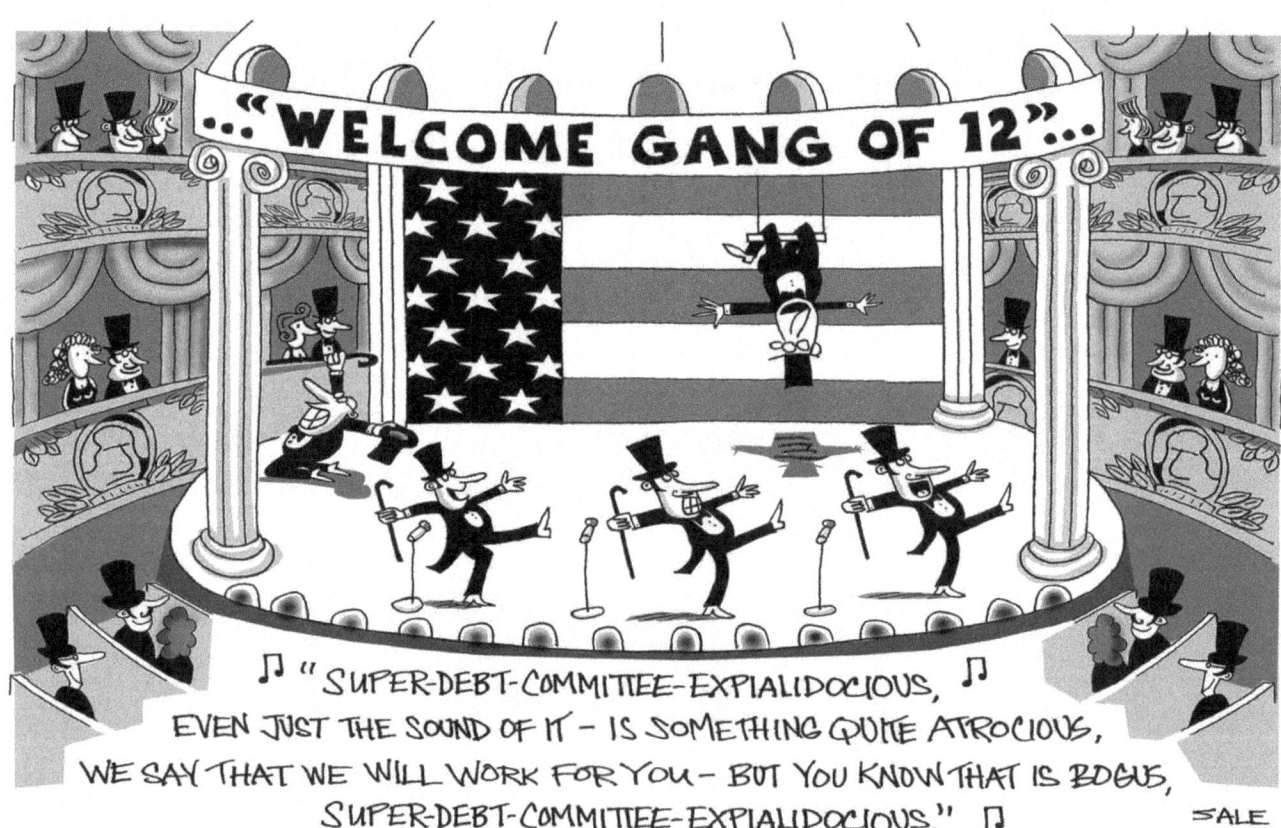

88

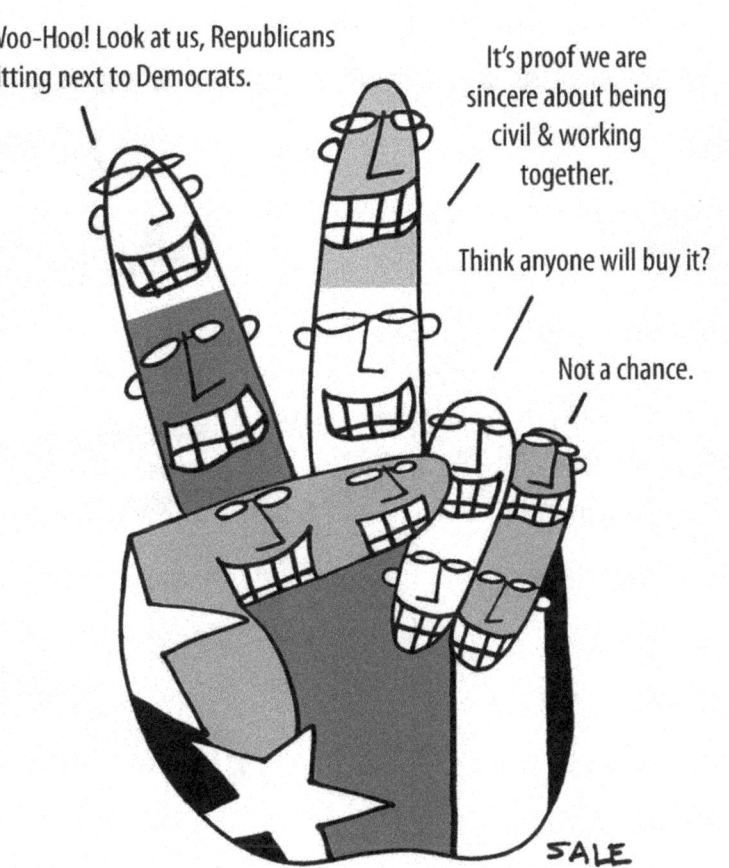

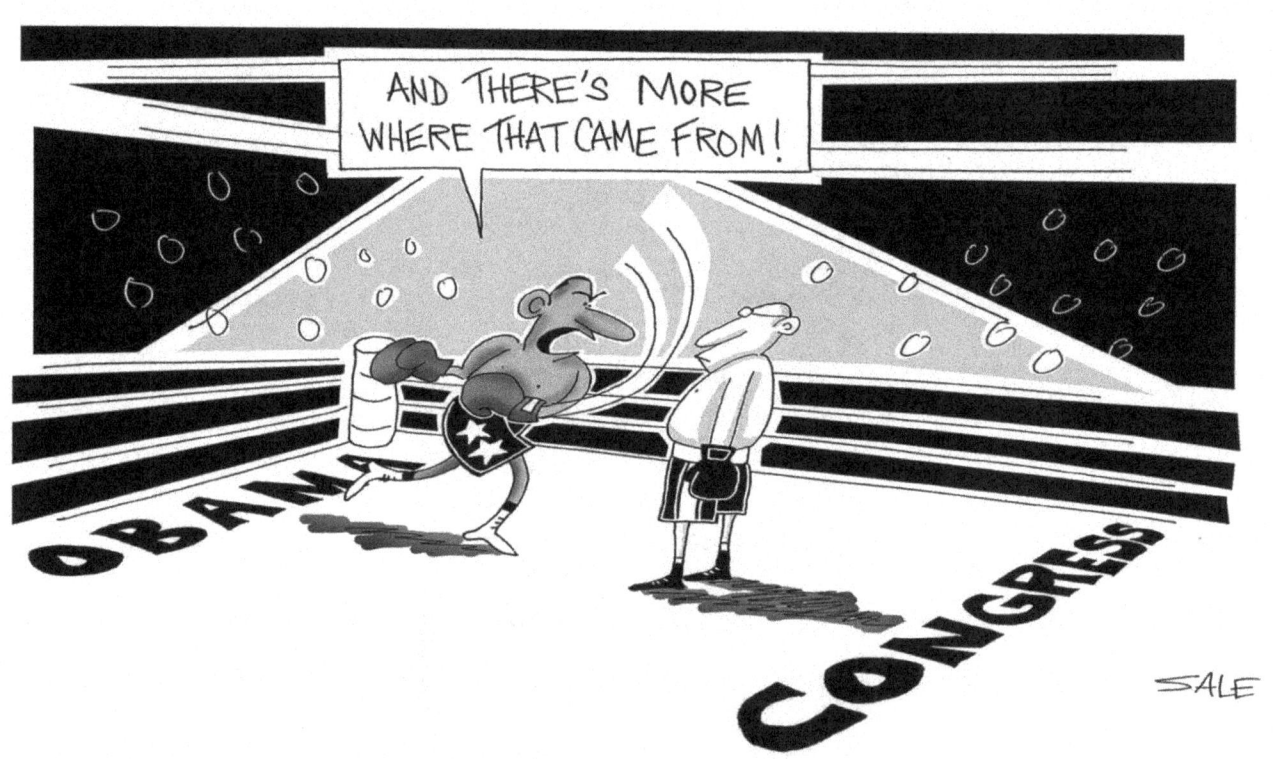

Hawaiian without a punch.

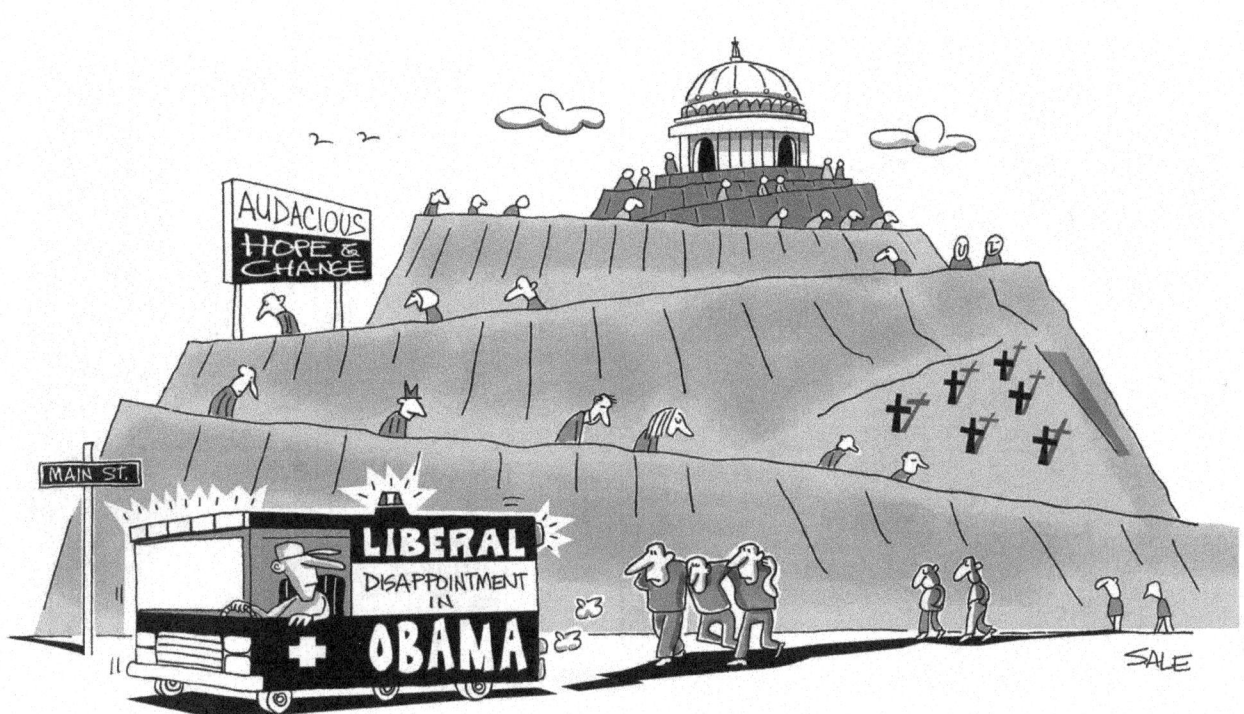

91

The Master Negotiator:

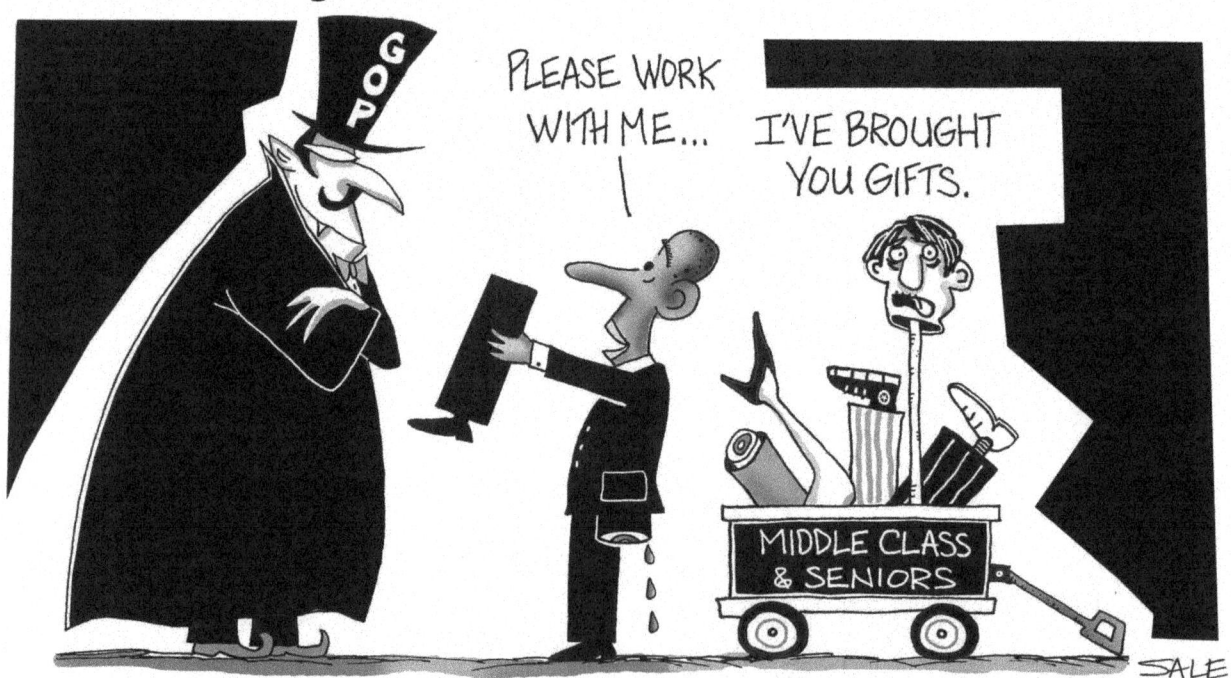

"Plus, I'll let you taser Nancy Pelosi and Elizabeth Warren."

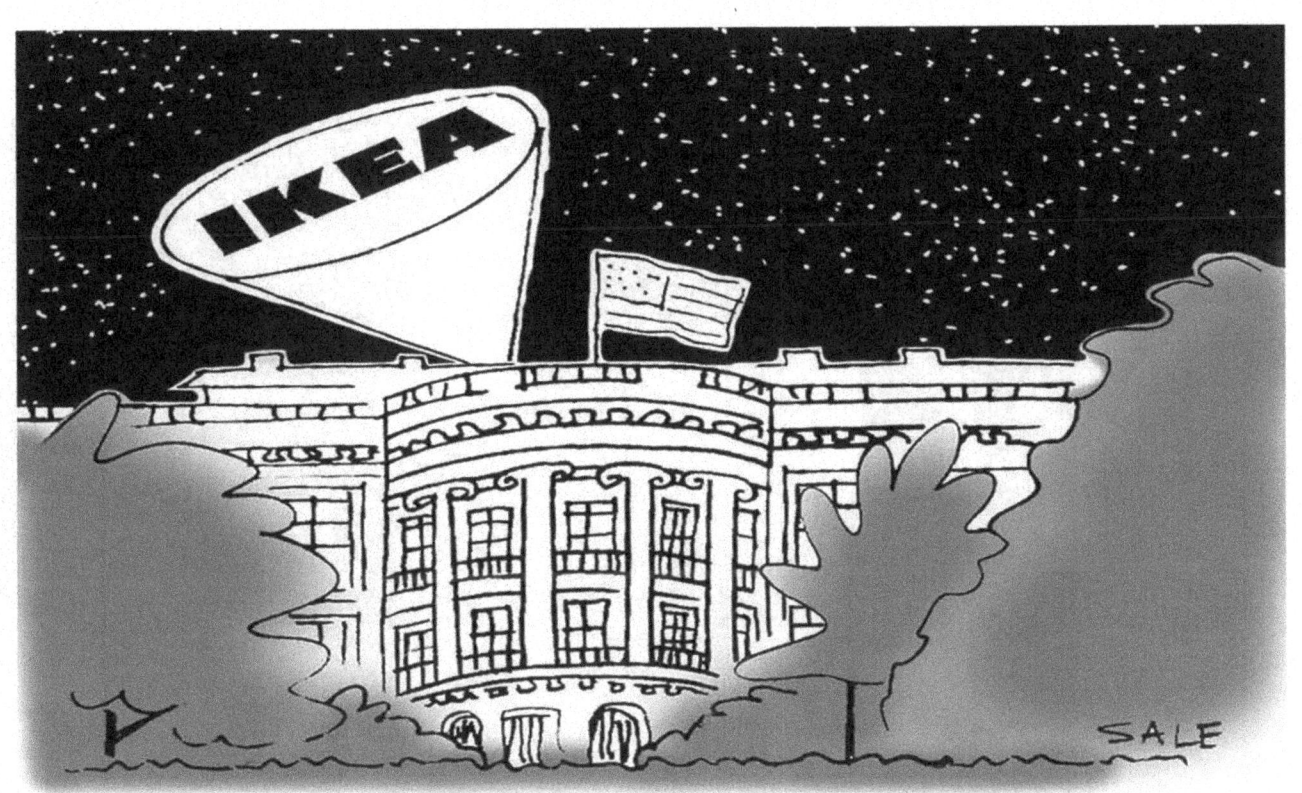

"When tax breaks and bailouts failed to rebuild the economy, a call went out to the experts at putting together complicated things with lots of parts and few instructions.

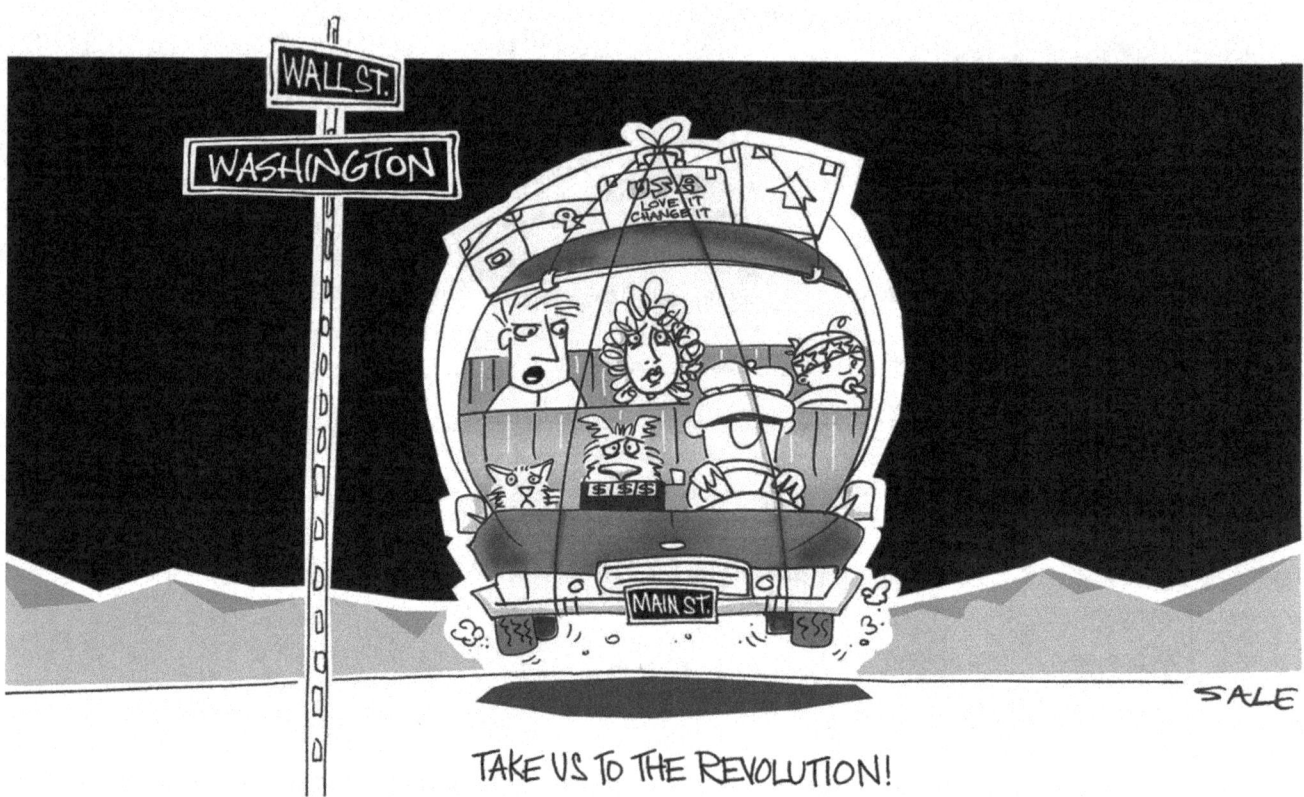

TAKE US TO THE REVOLUTION!

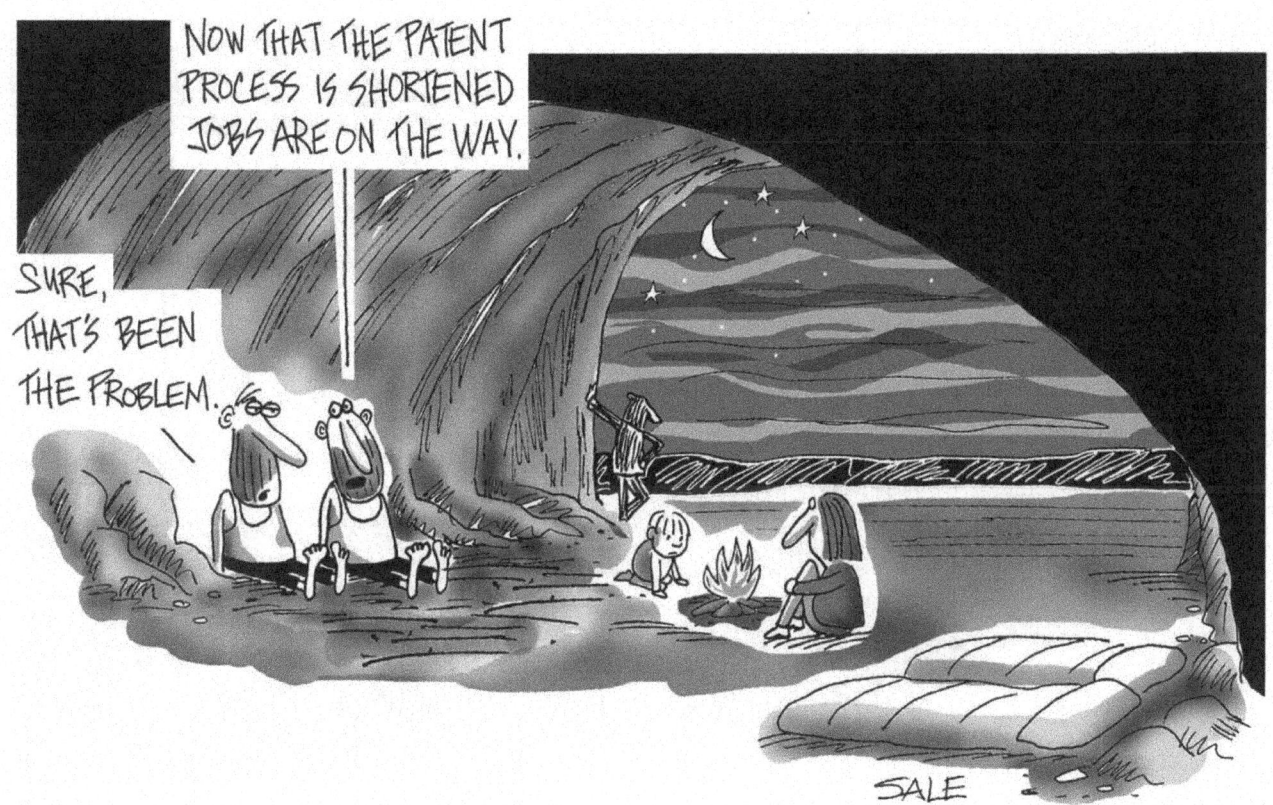

95

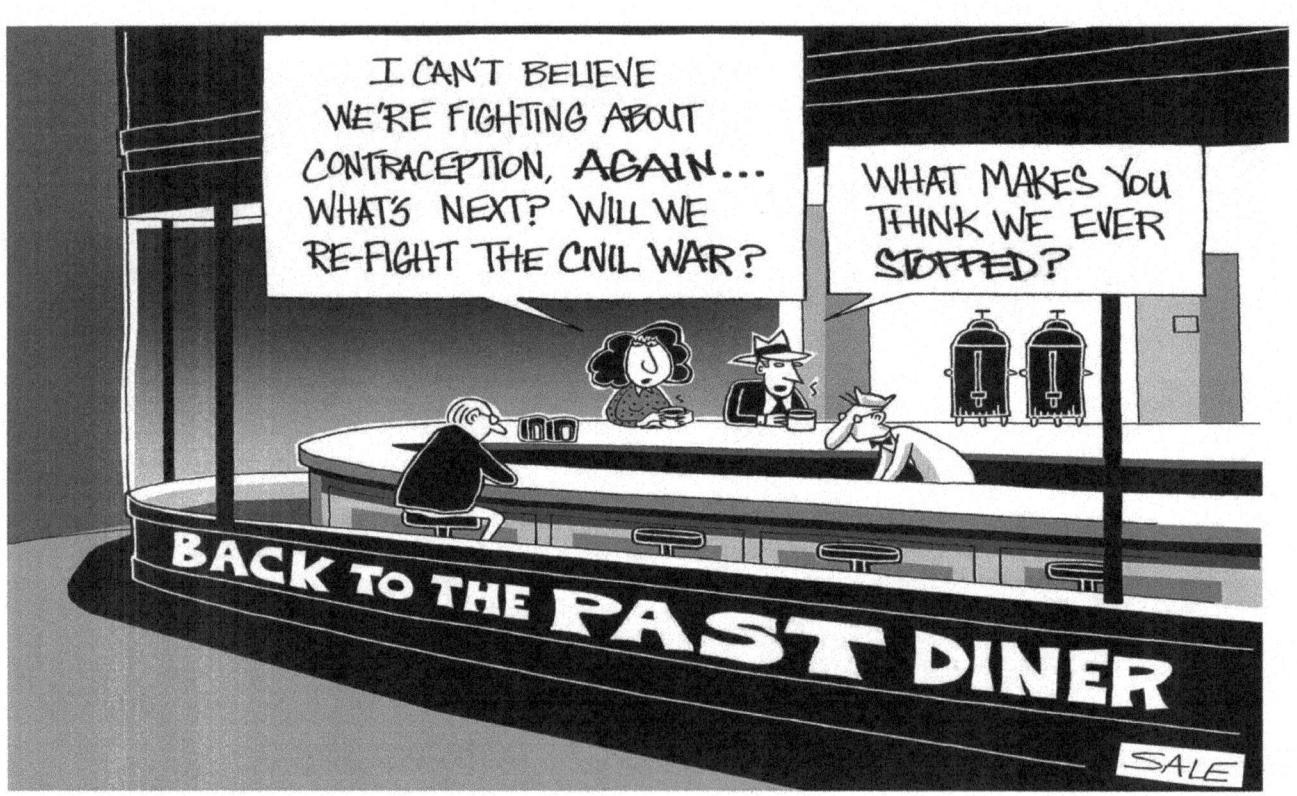

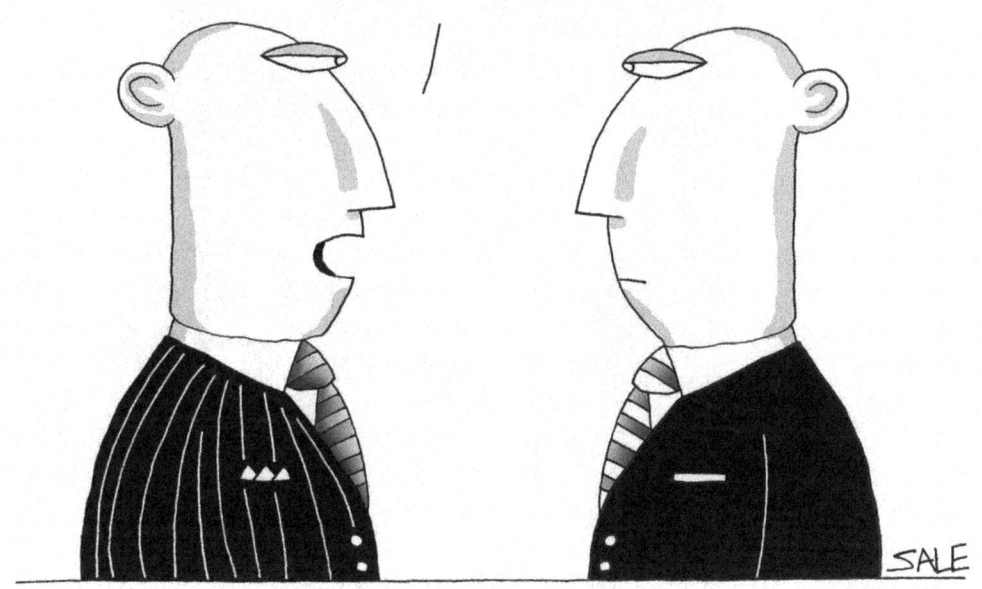

"It made me sick."

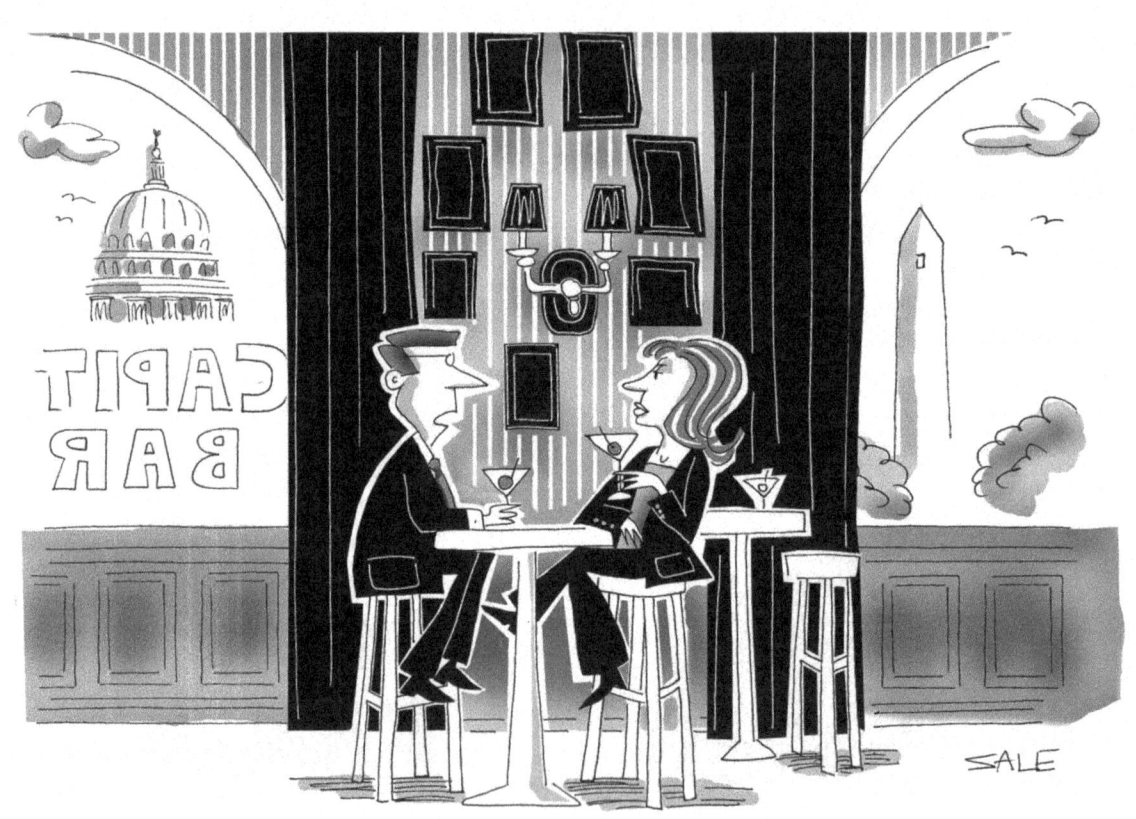

"Personal convictions aside, what's your ideology?"

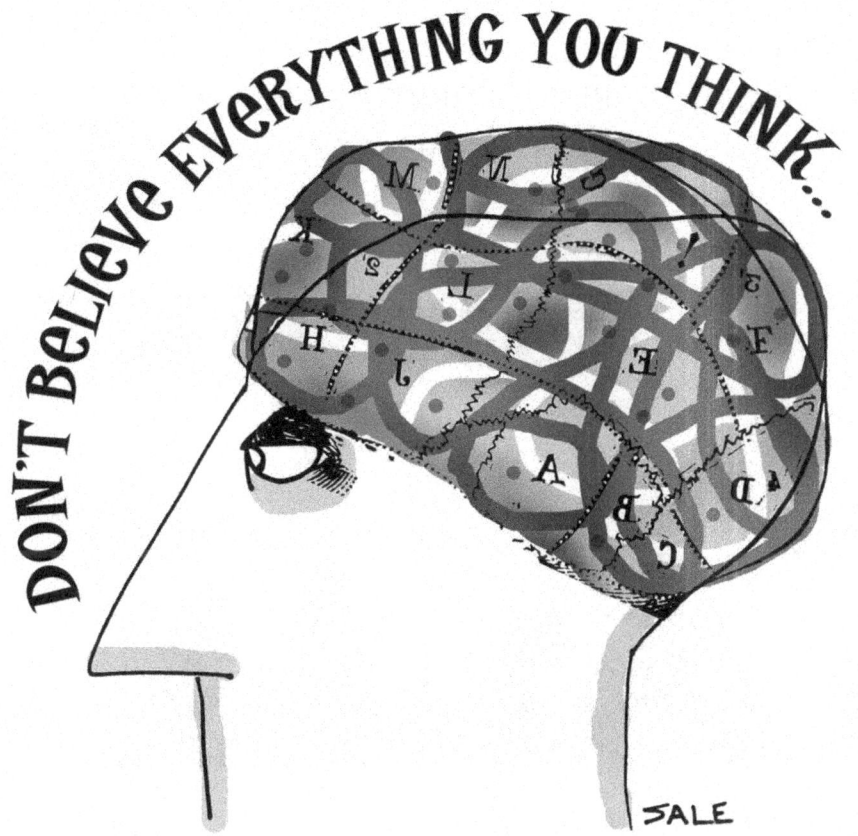

99

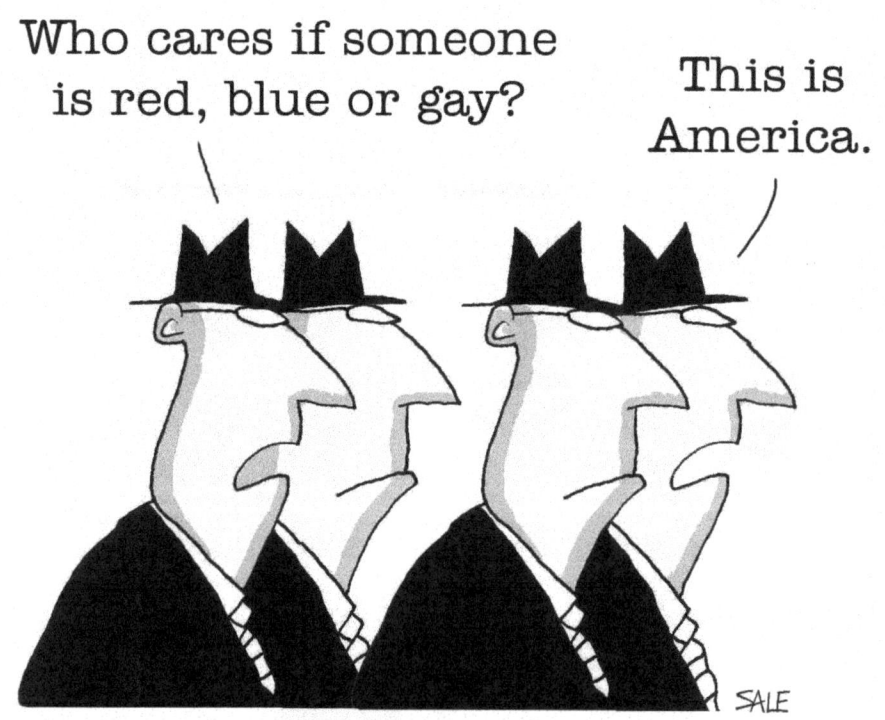

"We judge people by how much they have, who they know, what they look like, how they pray and if they can sing."

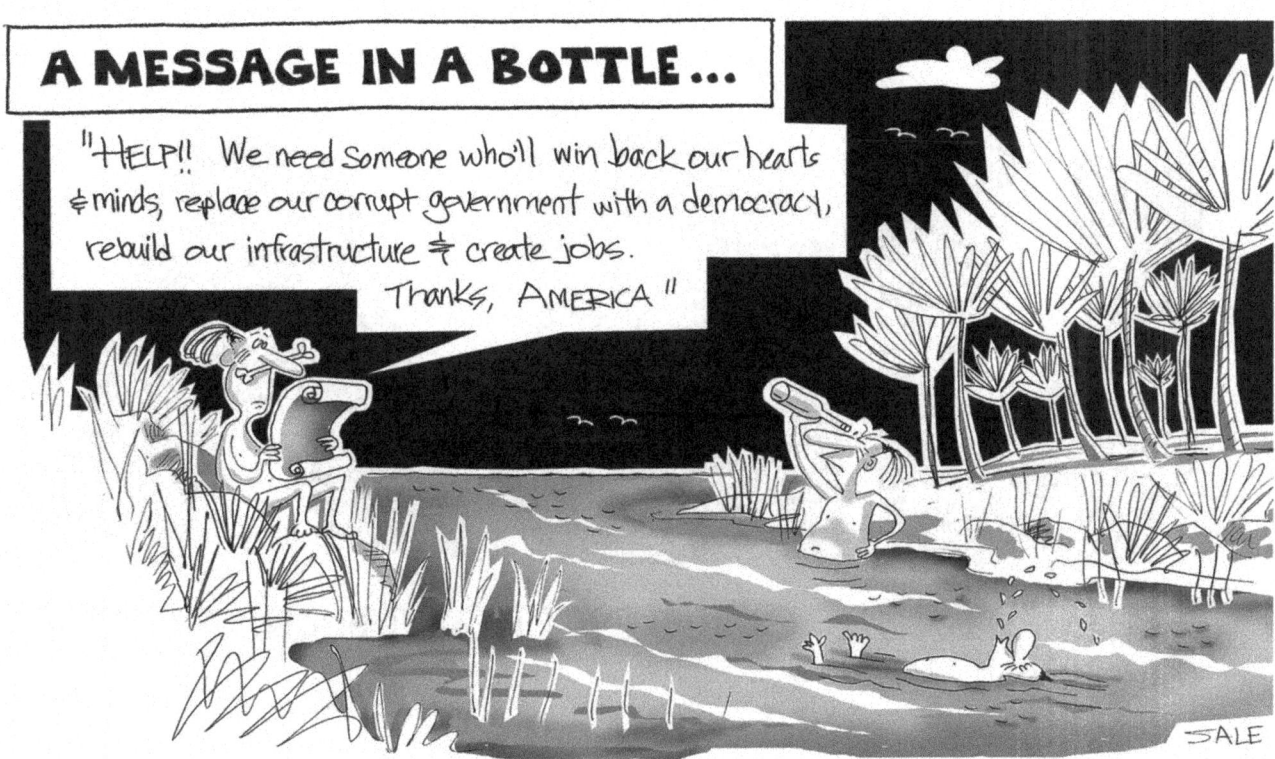

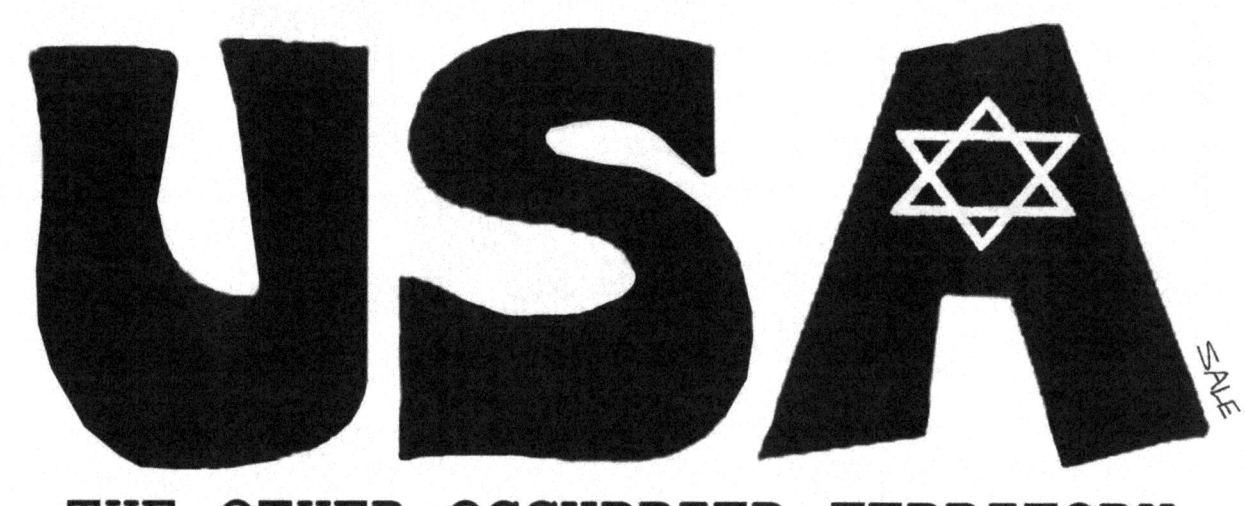

THE OTHER OCCUPPIED TERRITORY.

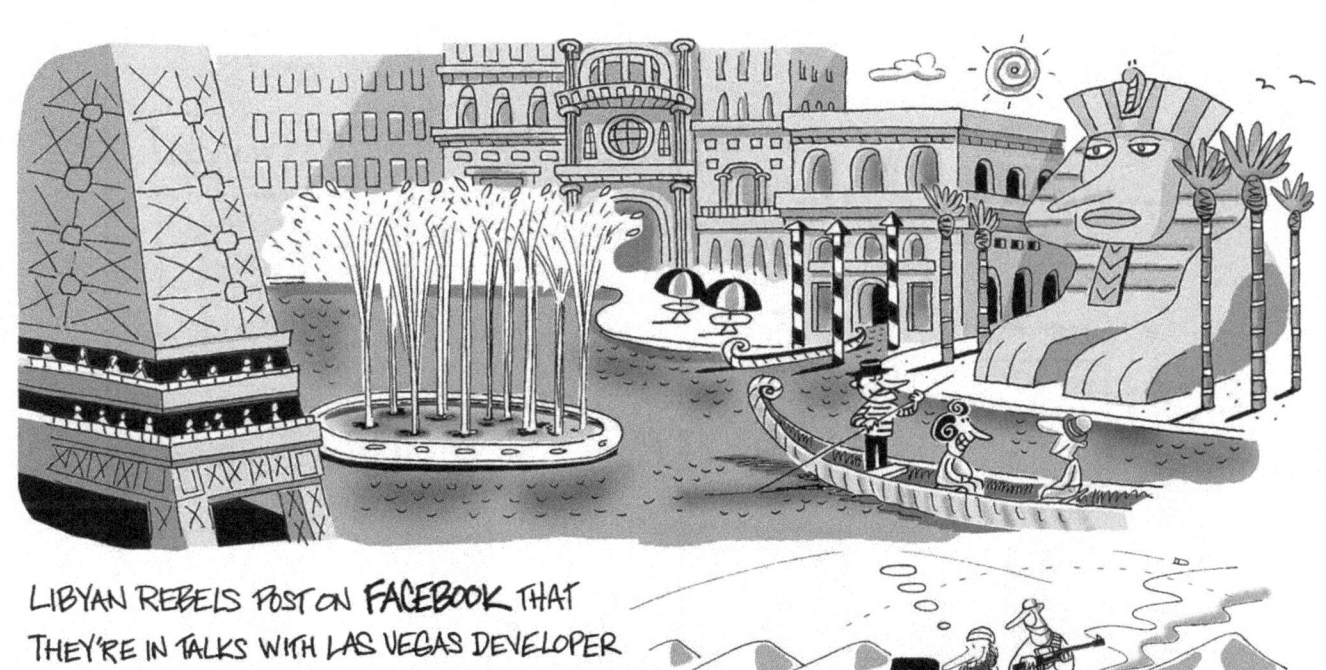

LIBYAN REBELS POST ON **FACEBOOK** THAT
THEY'RE IN TALKS WITH LAS VEGAS DEVELOPER
STEVE WYNN TO REBUILD LIBYA, "THE WAY YOU
MAKE ANCIENT CULTURES IN THE DESERT IS MOST AWESOME."

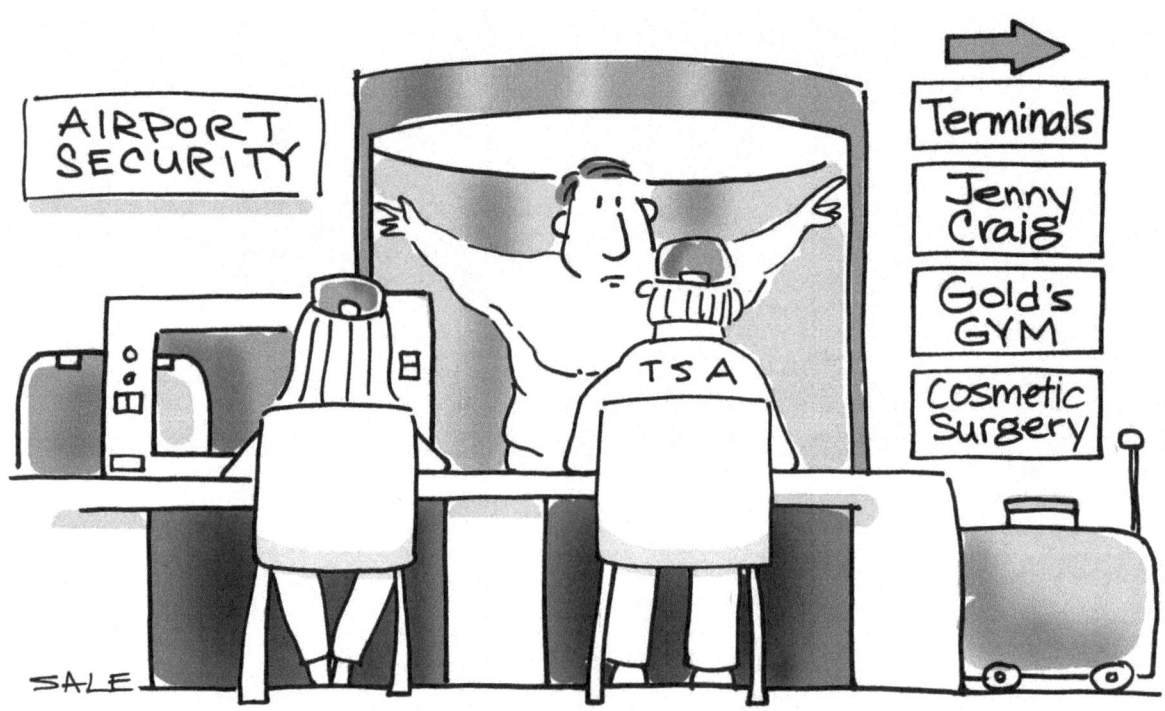

Groping for Security or Will Terrorism Lower My Cholesterol?

Could there be unexpected benefits to the Keystone Cops humiliating grope fest that has become America's feckless airport security system? Could the Underwear and Shoe bombers do for American health and fittness what Jared did for *Subway* and the submarine sandwich?

Will the potential humiliation of being viewed naked by strangers inspire us to get healthy and fit again? Will we be too embarrassed to fly until we regain our girlish figure, lose thirty pounds and finally remove that third nipple? When you no longer resemble twenty pounds of sausage in a five pound sack, you're empowered with a sense of pride and accomplishment, but there may be even more collateral benefits.

For instance, a leaner, lighter traveler will save the airlines fuel costs, which will help them remain solvent in these tough economic times, saving American jobs. Travelers will save on extra luggage fees since our new smaller clothing will fit more easily into a single bag. Being healthier will lower health costs and insurance premiums, which will help solve the national healthcare crisis. And finally, a fit, pumped up America will be even better able to pummel terrorists. Maybe a little groping does a body good.

So...Assume the position for your country! Now where did I put that thigh master?

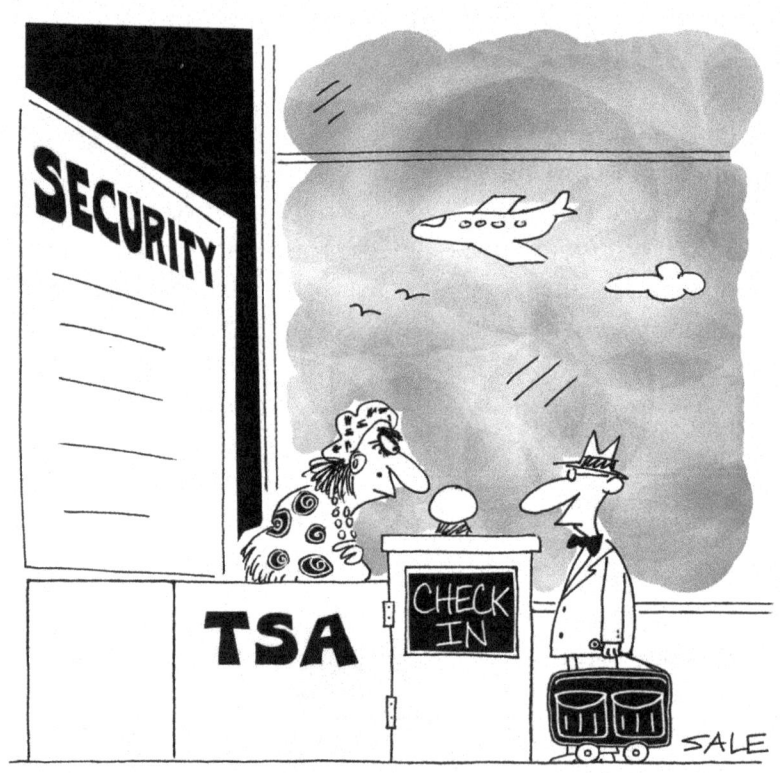

Airports try new and less intrusive screening procedures.

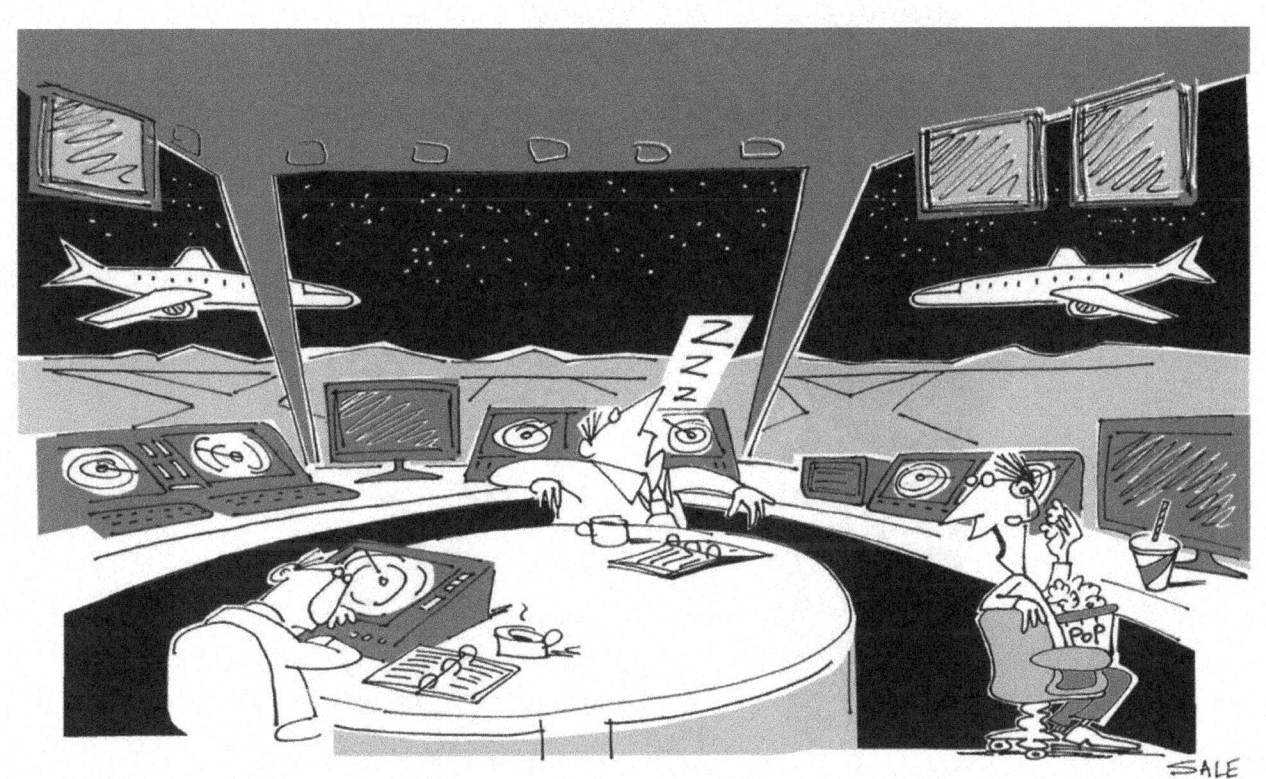

"Wake up, guys! Airplane is on Netflix!"

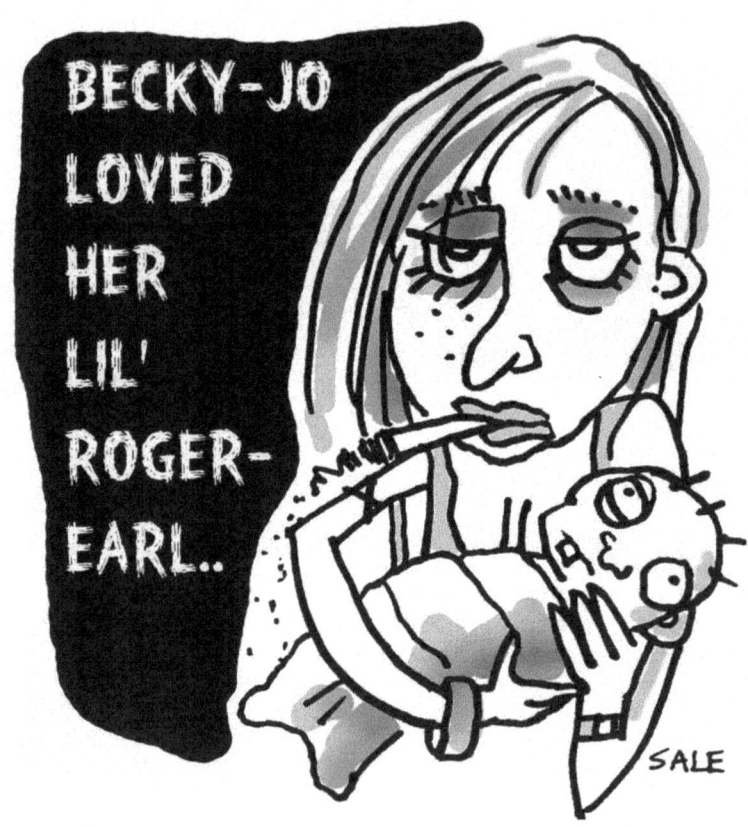

*But there were days she questioned her congressman's
insistence that she become a single mother.*

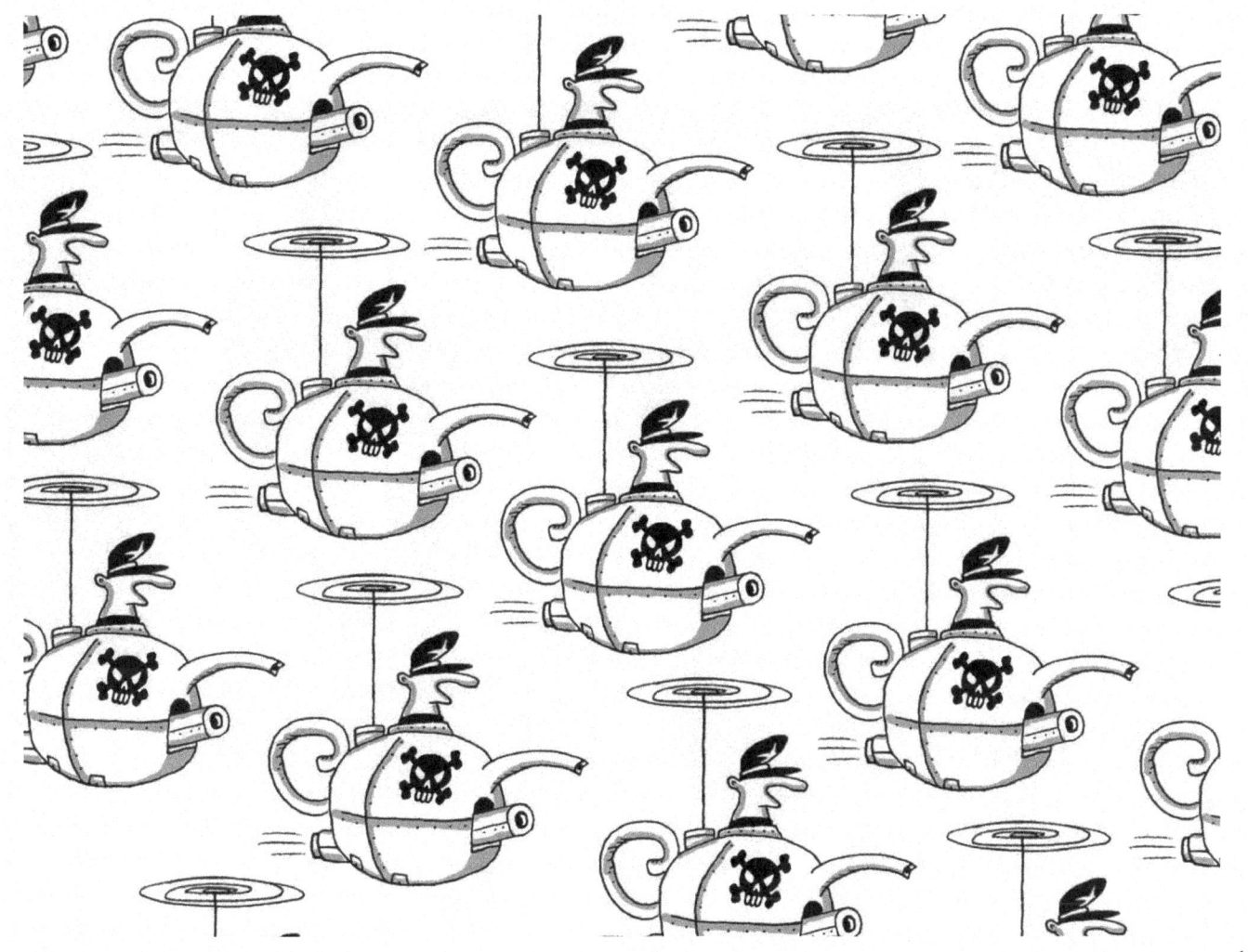

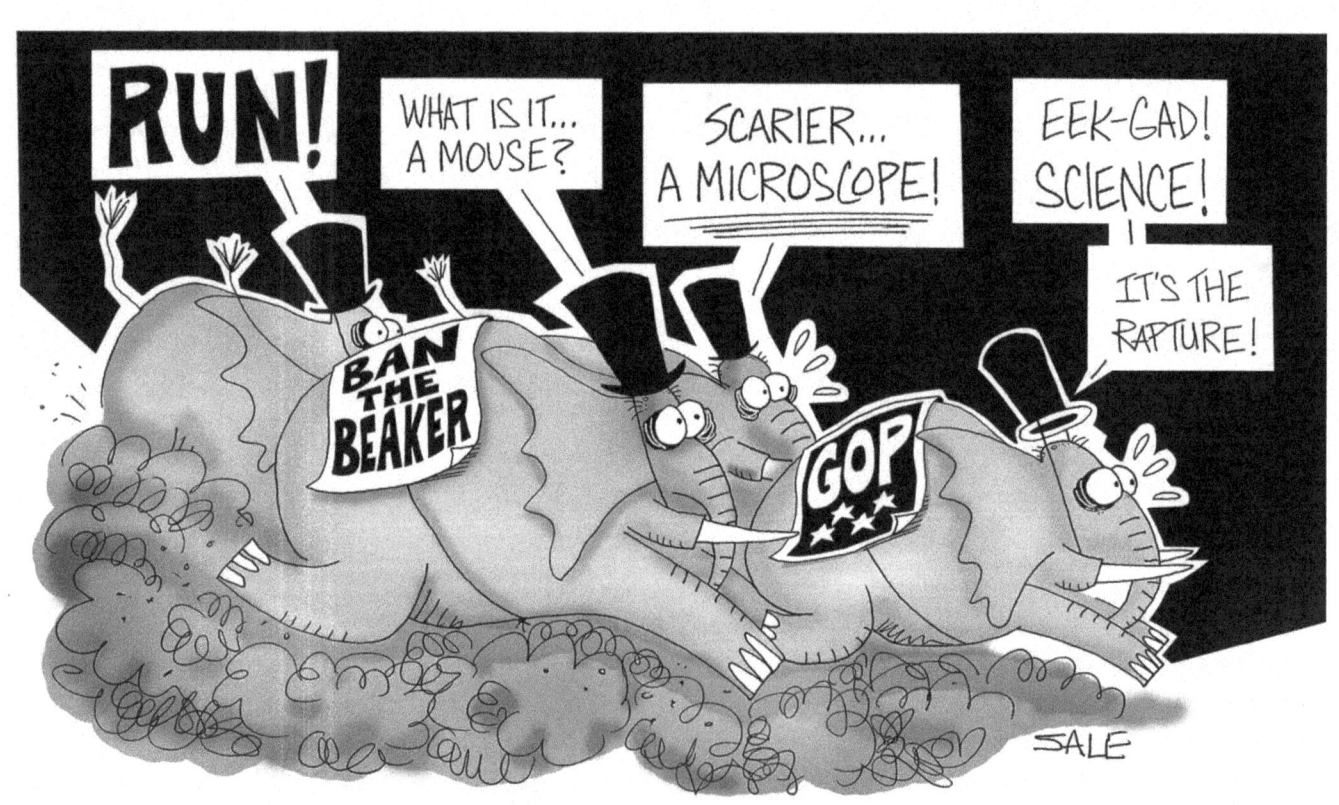

White House Committee on Science & Technology

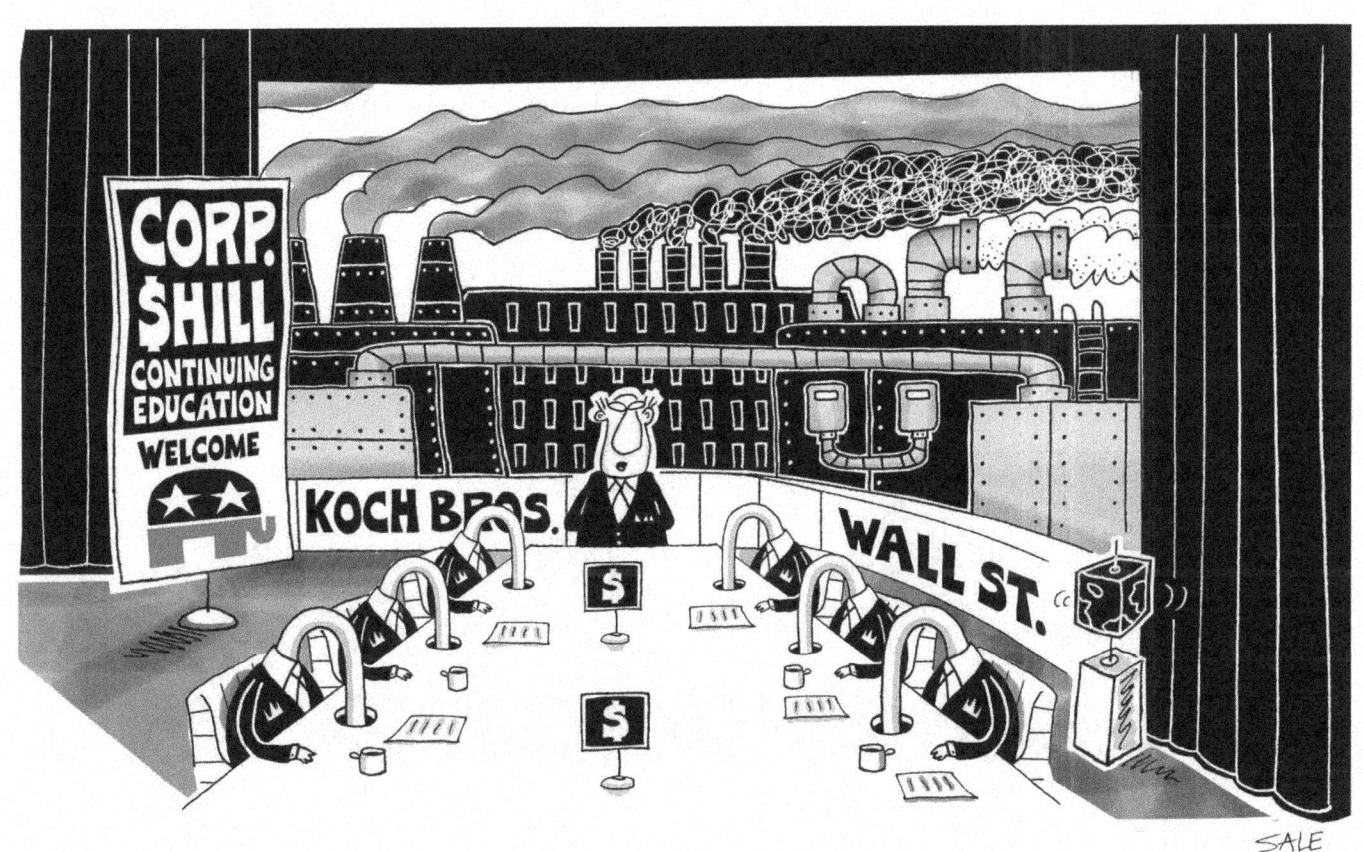

"Today's topic is climate change. Assume your position."

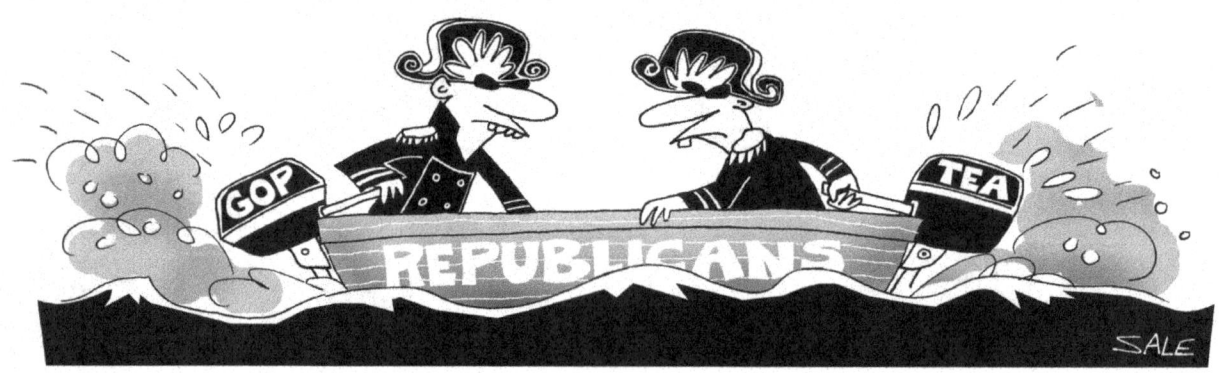

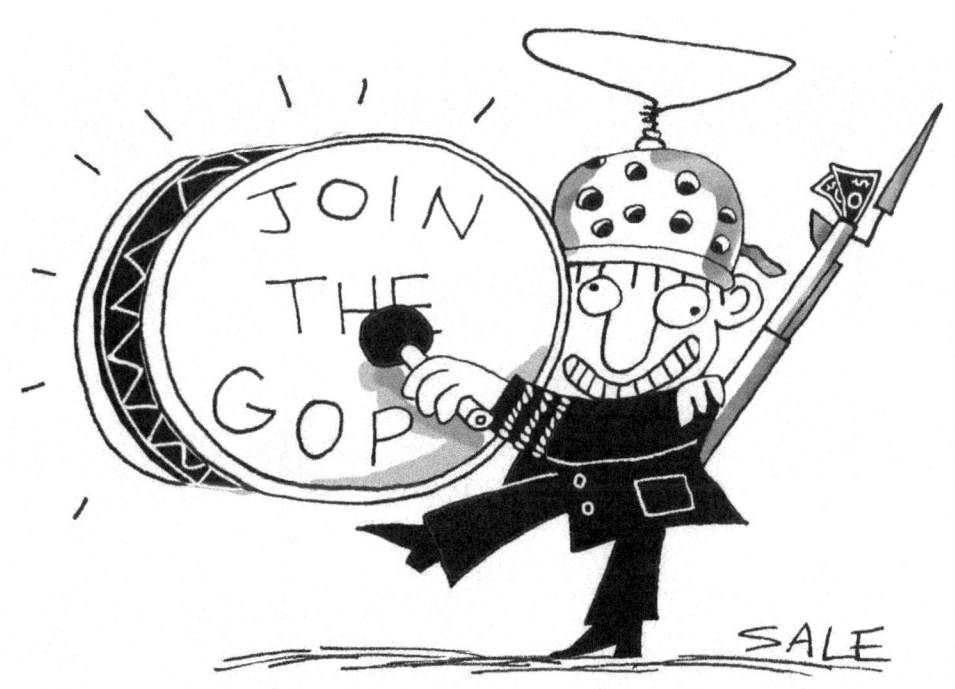

"*Make friends with people who have
the same mental disorders as you.*"

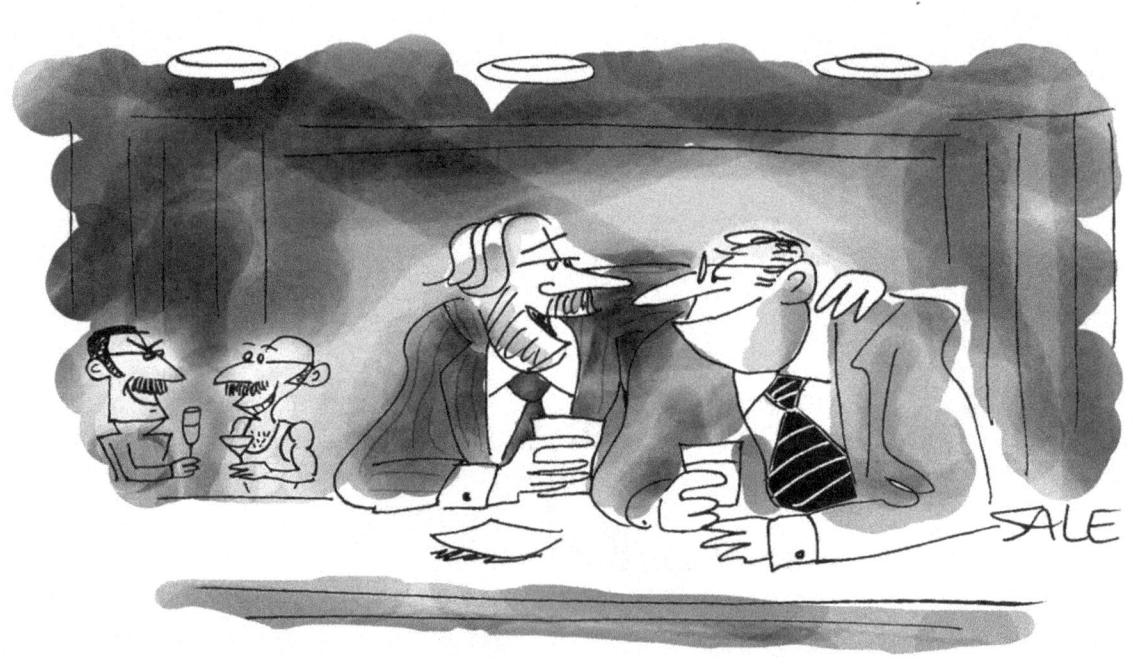

"If straight people are so creeped out by gay people,
why do they keep making us?"

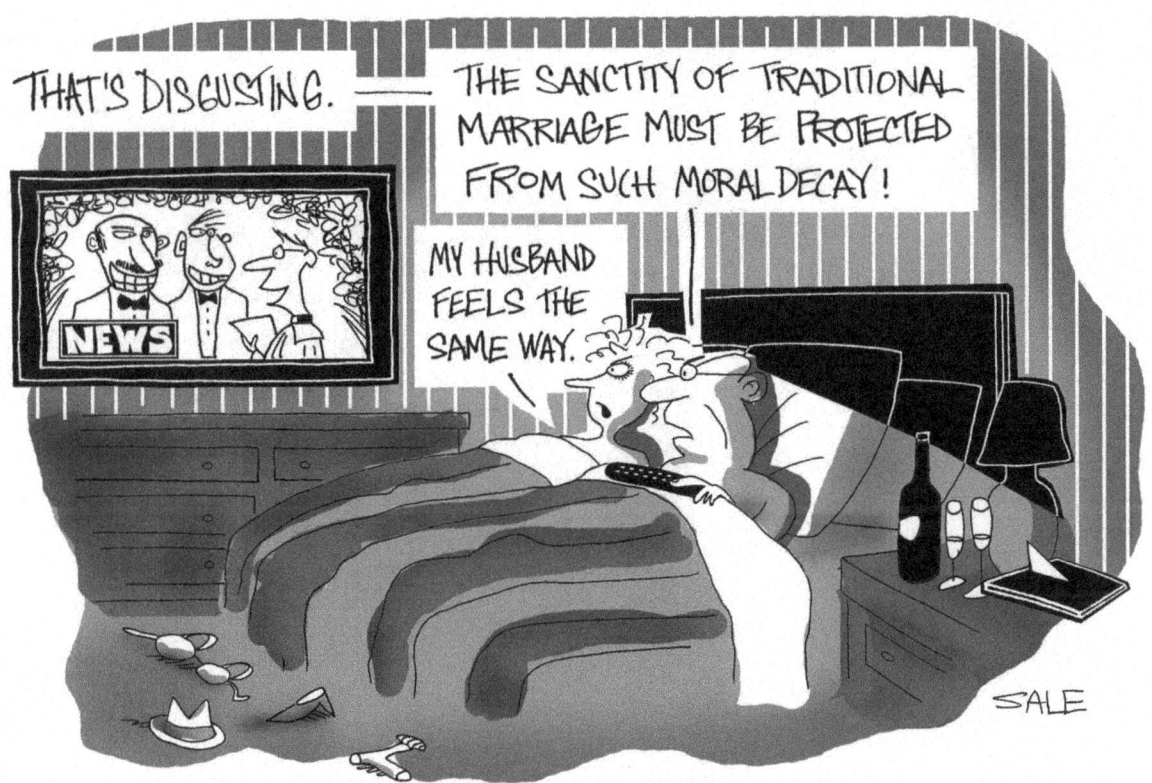

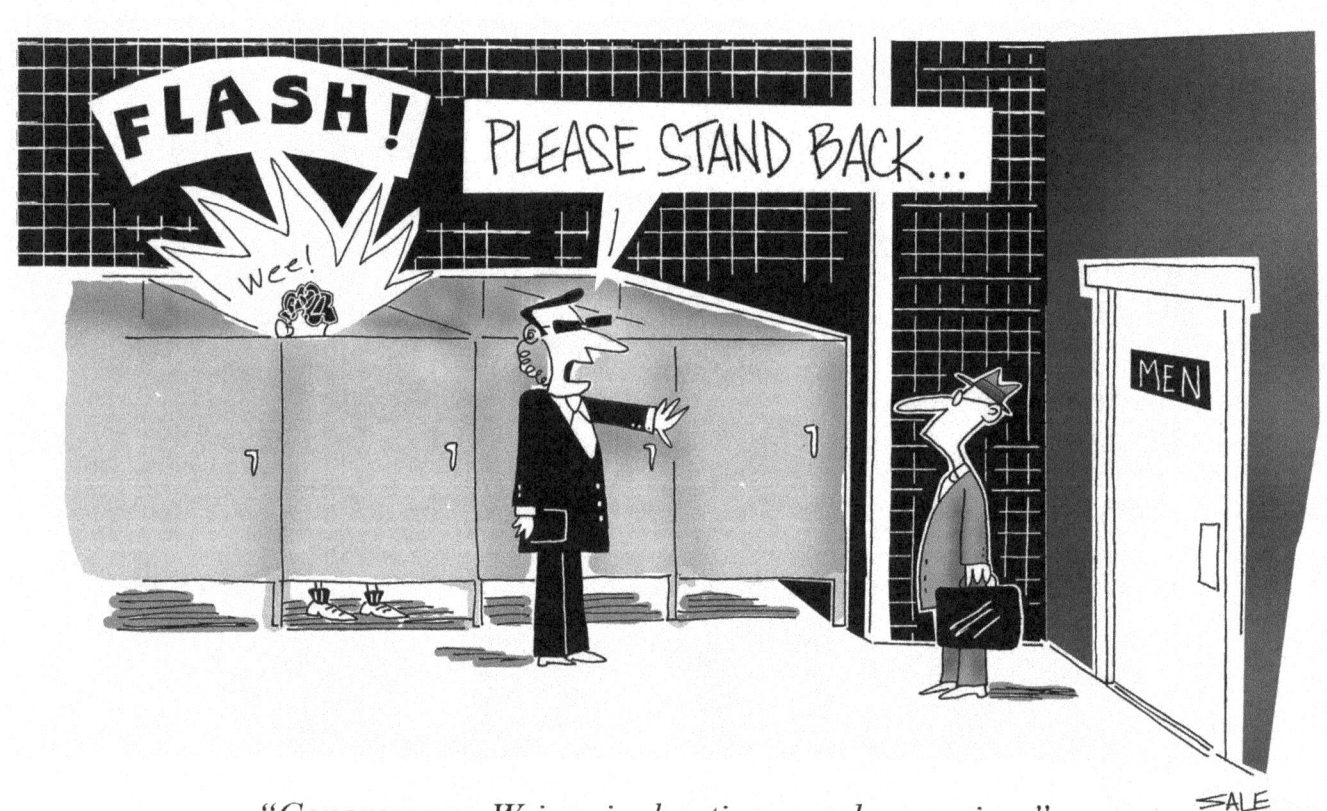

"*Congressman Weiner is shooting an ad campaign.*"

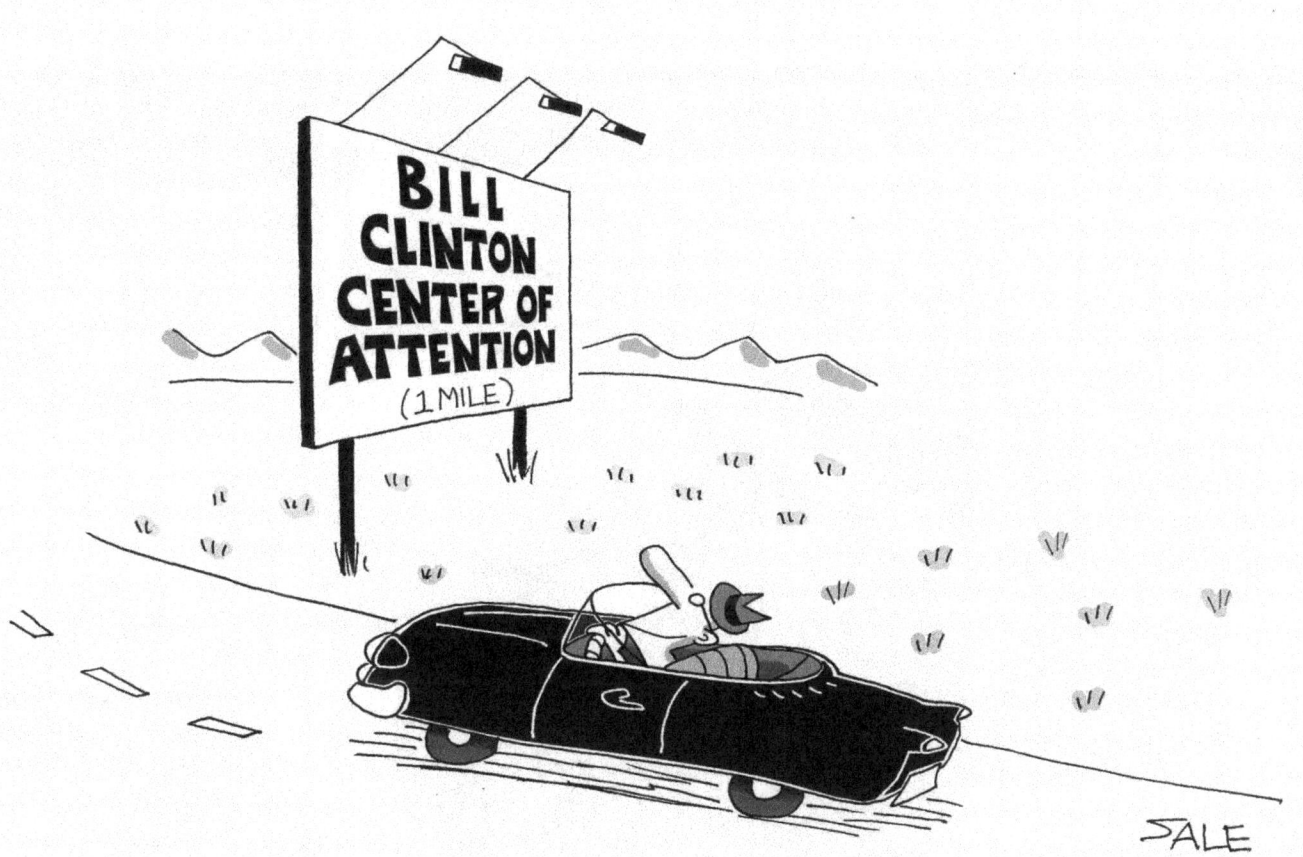

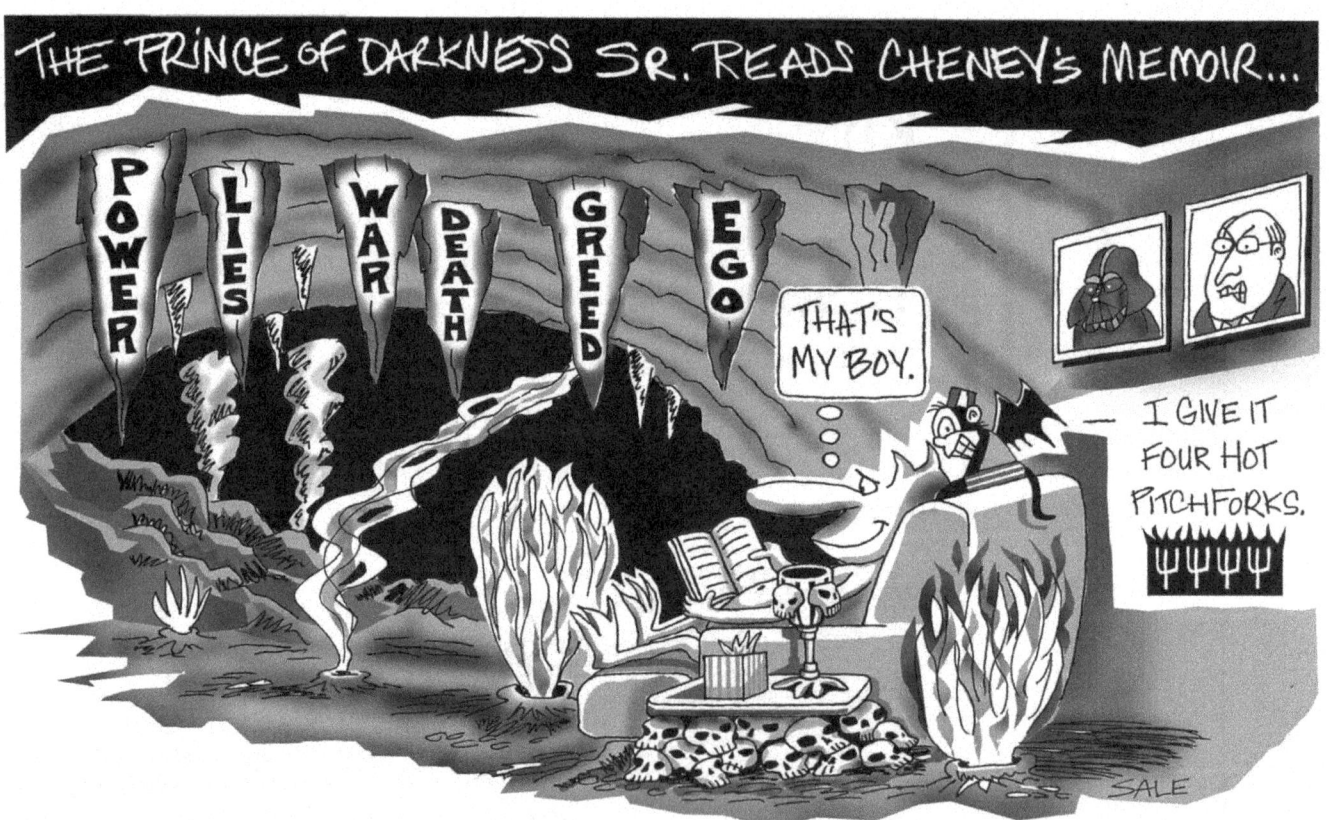

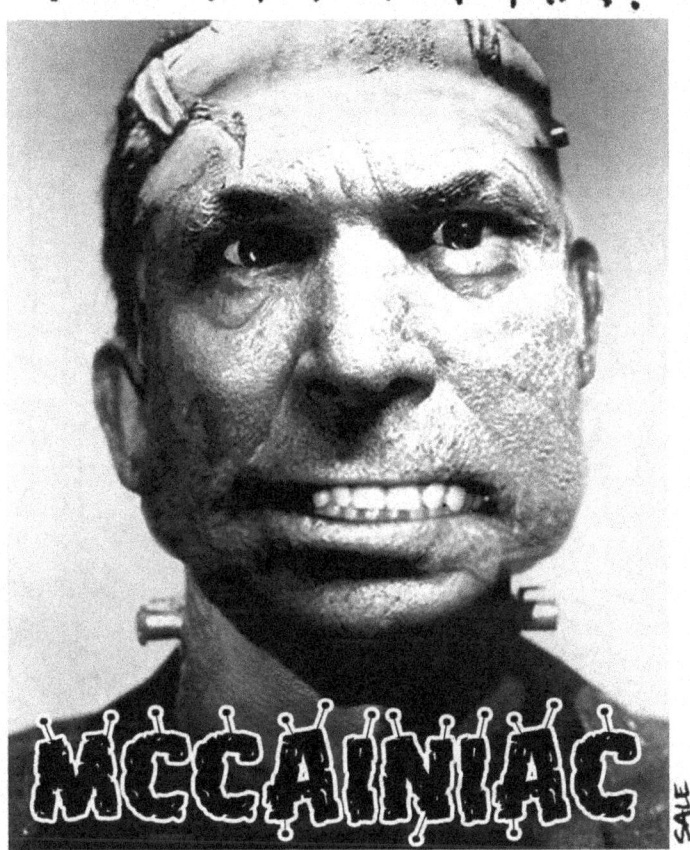

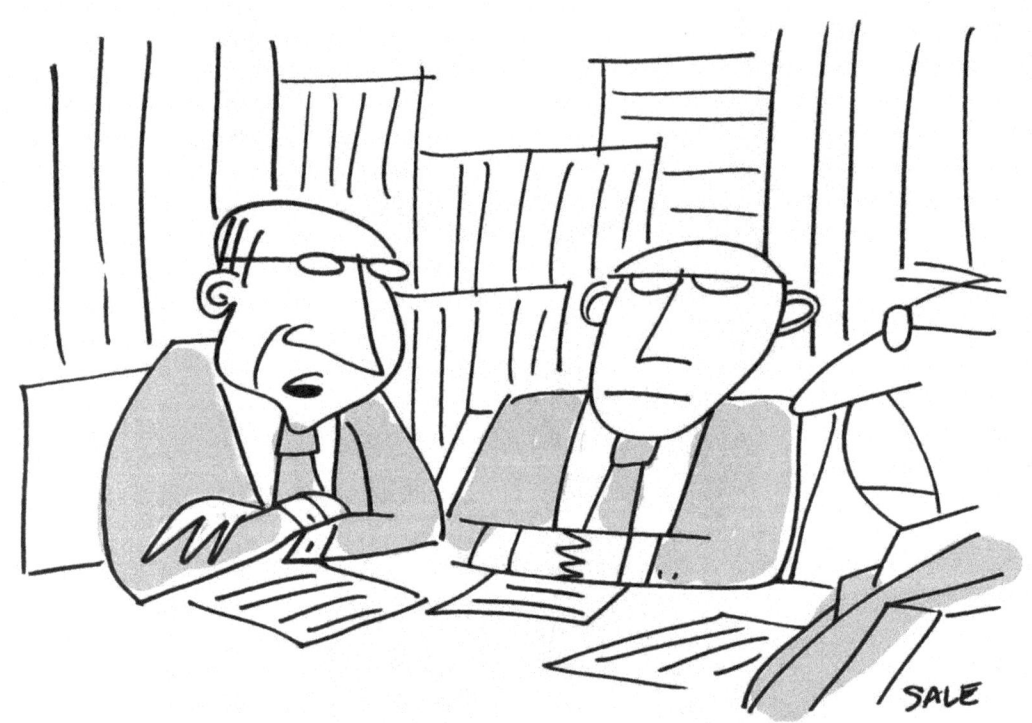

"Gentlemen, we all agree that honesty is a policy,
but is it our policy?"

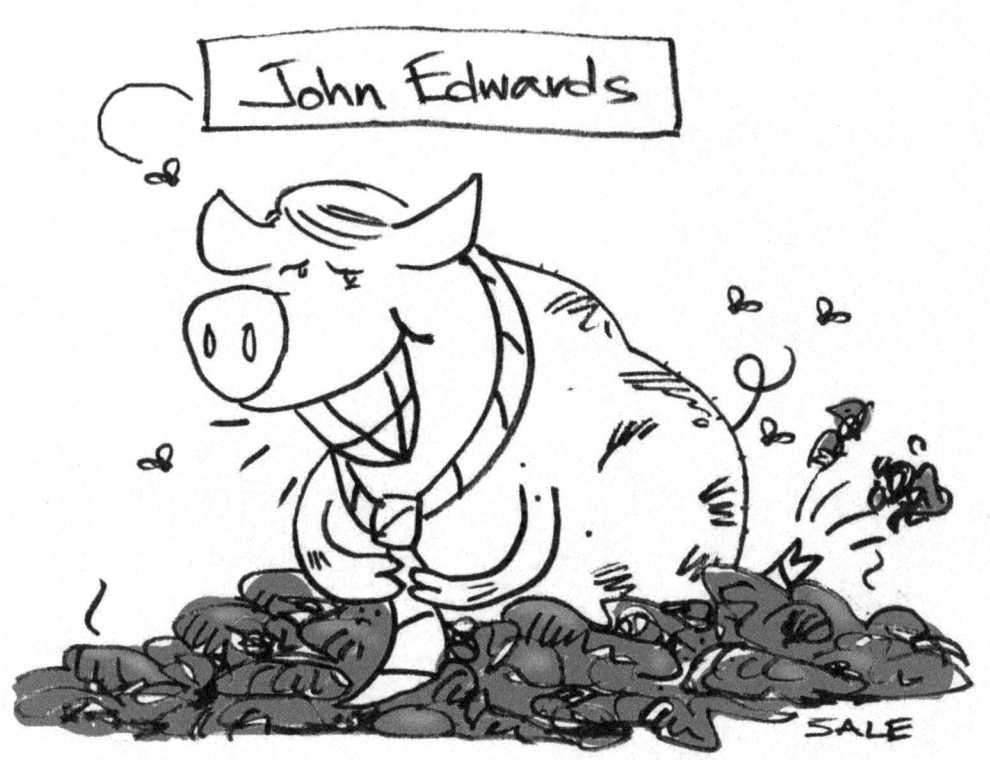

"Should this little piggy go to prison?"

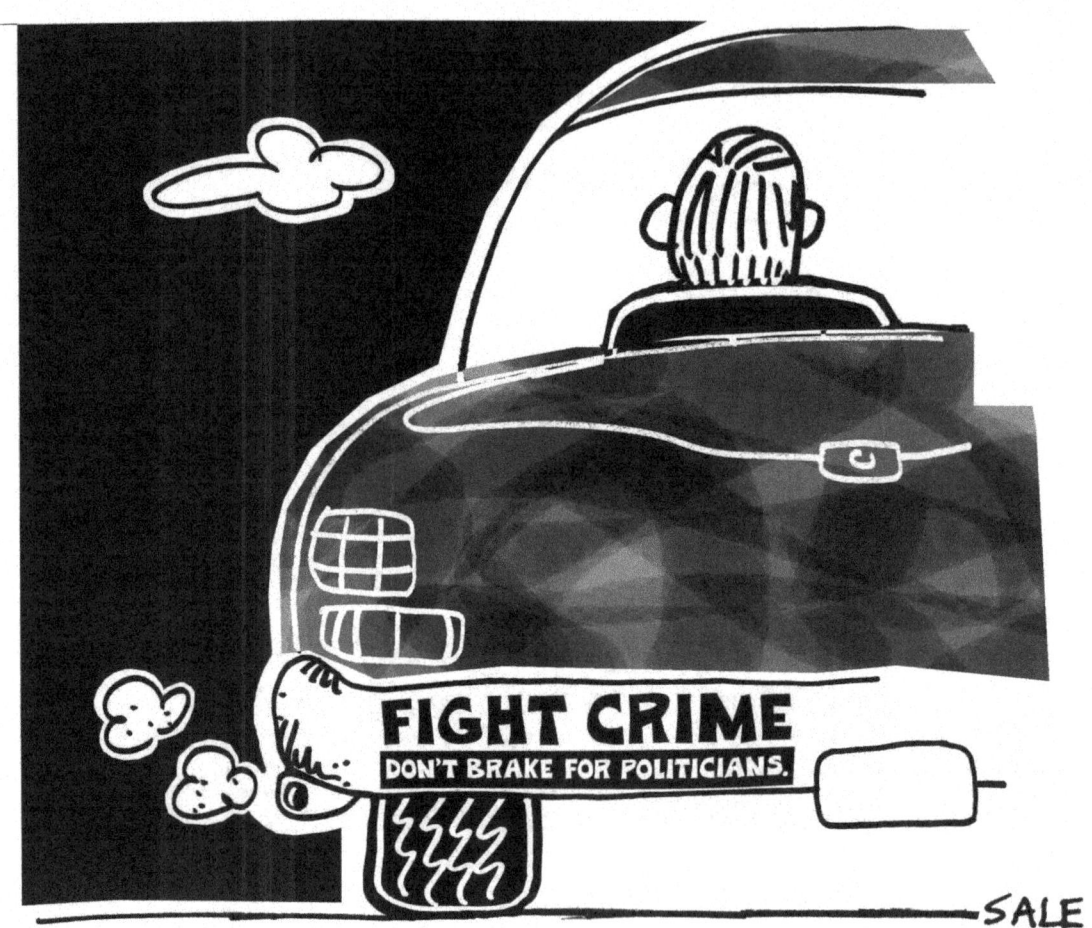

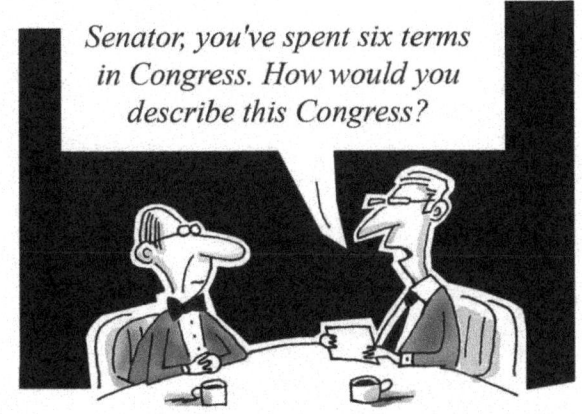

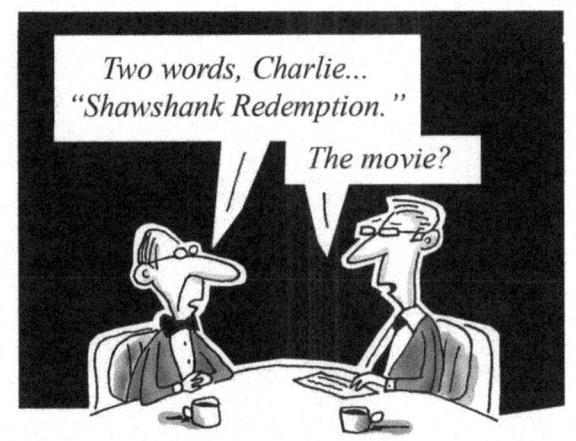

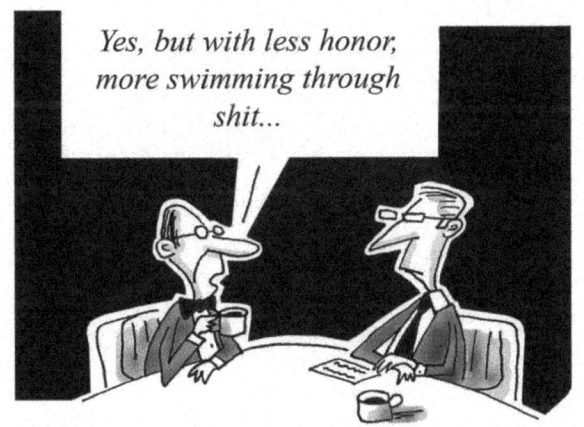

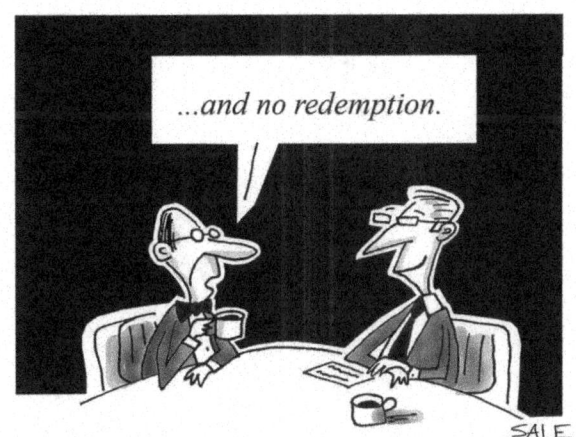

Pat Robertson makes God sick.

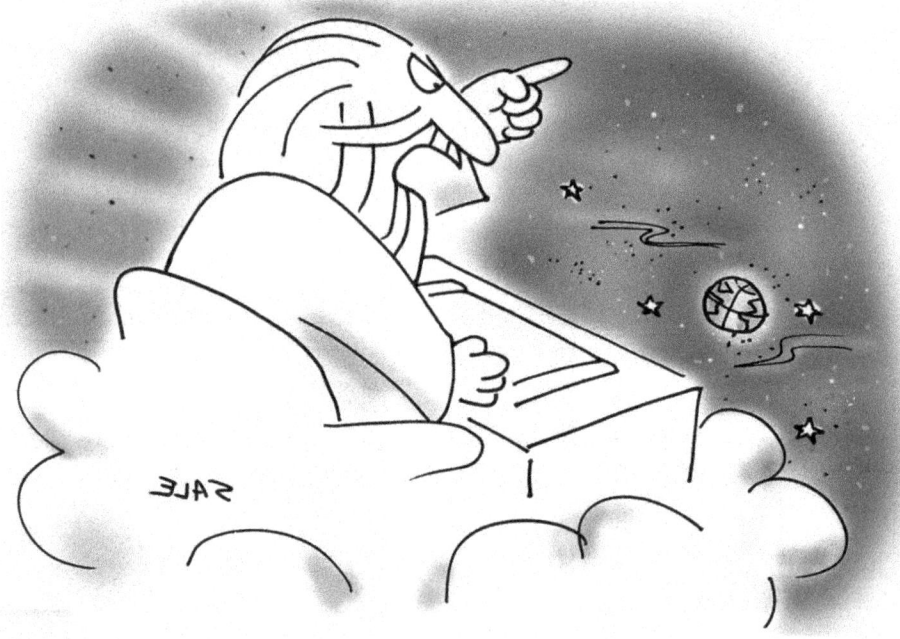

"Shut the hell up you lunatic!"

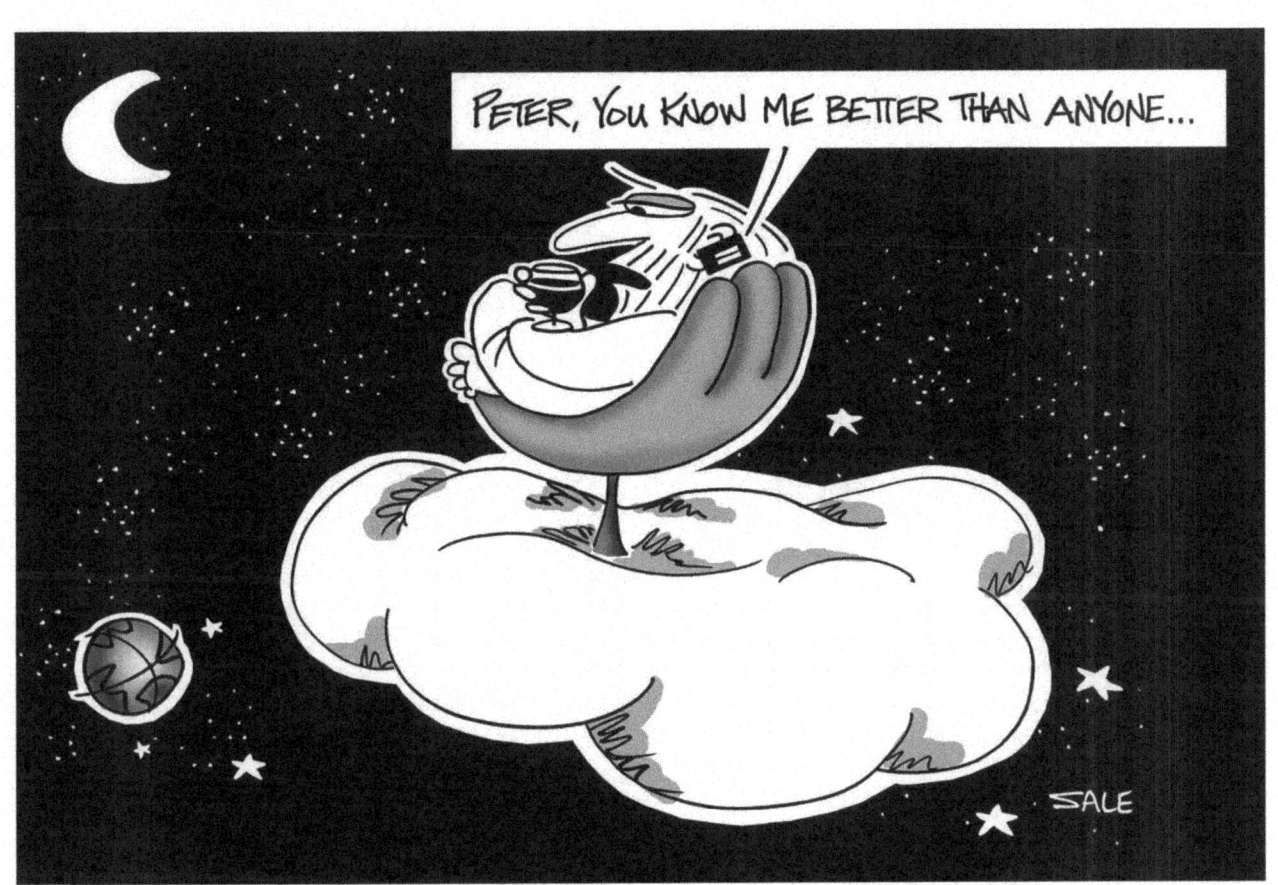

"Why do I attract so many crackpots?"

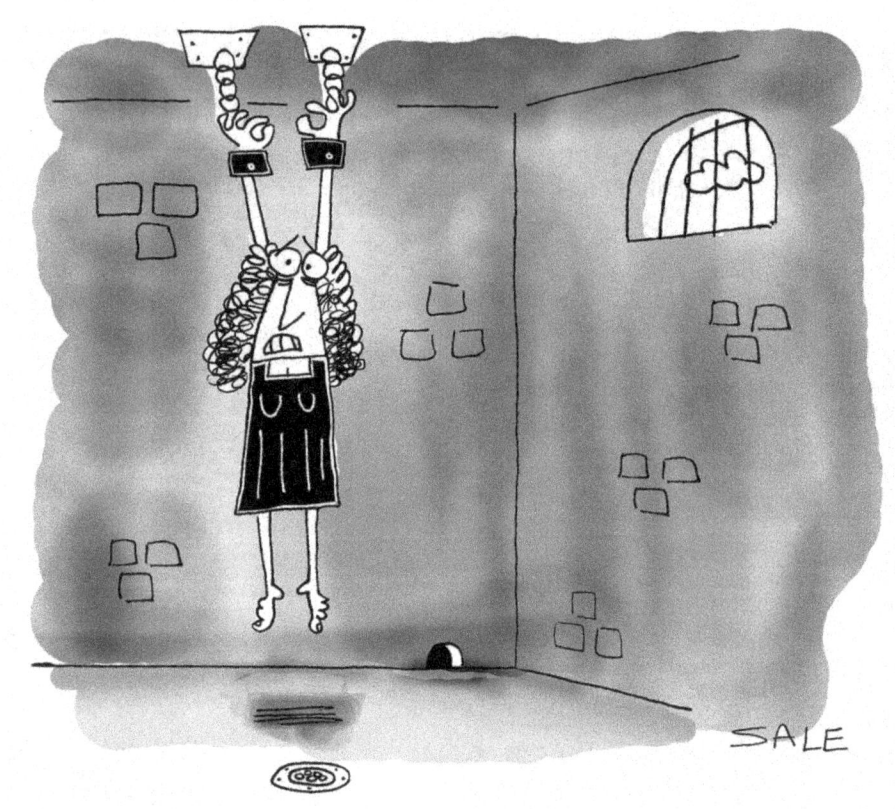

*Andrea learned the hard way that the kernels of unpopped
popcorn she re-popped belonged to Monsanto.*

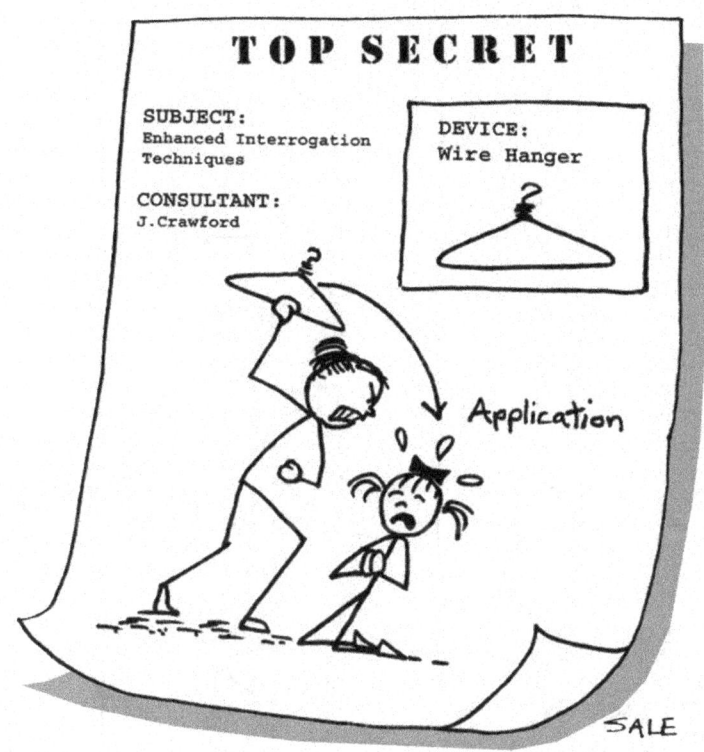

CIA memos reveal that Joan Crawford was a pioneer in the development of enhanced interrogation techniques.

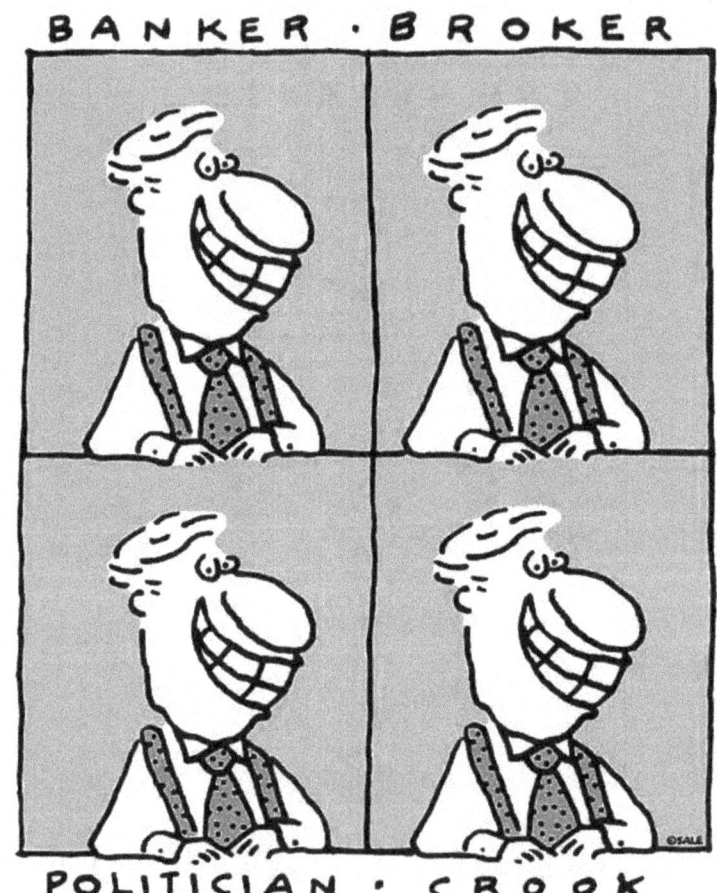

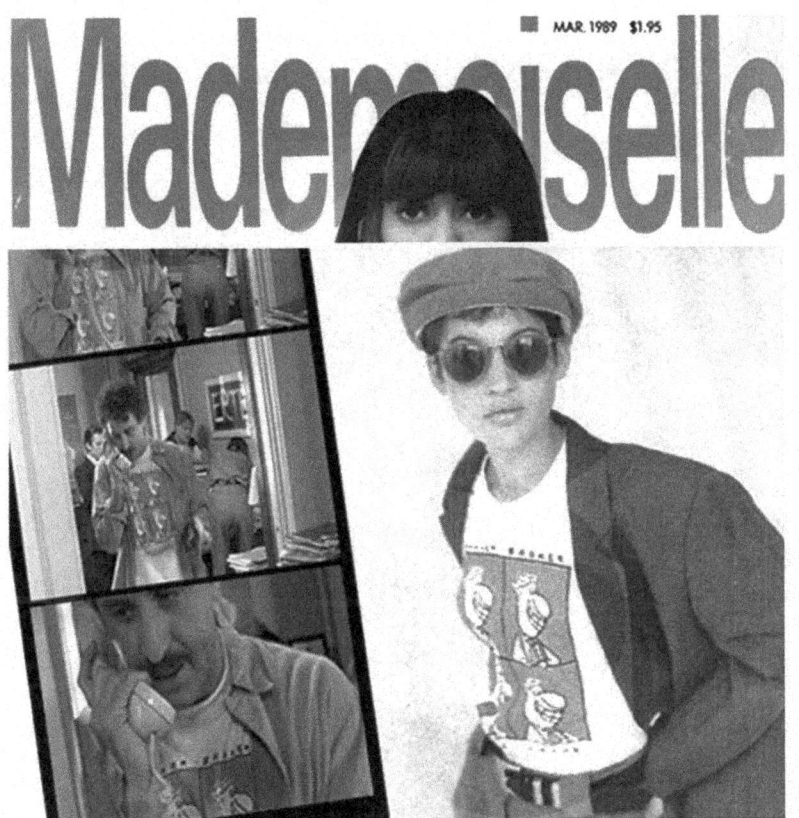

Mademoiselle

REVERSAL OF FORTUNE. Ron Silver wore my shirt when playing attorney Alan Dershowitz in the movie, *Reversal of Fortune,* starring Glenn Close and Jeremy Irons.

Banker, Broker, Lawyer, Crook was a reaction to the Wall Street banking scandals in the 1980's by Ivan Boesky, Michael Milken, Charles Keating and others. Sadly, it's worse and more prevalent today. Politicians have replaced lawyers as the sleaziest, lying, villianous, scumbags around. So, I made a **Banker, Broker, Politician, Crook** shirt.

> **THE JOKE'S ON YOU.**
> Every girl needs a quirky conversation piece in her closet! Try this great shirt with a message, "Banker, Broker, Lawyer, Crook." Raise its level of sophistication with a blazer and khakis combo.
>
> – Madamoiselle

THE JOKE WAS ON ME. I was watching the movie when my shirt suddenly appeared on screen. I began shouting, "That's my shirt!" People looked at me like I wasnuts. No one told me it was used in the film.

129

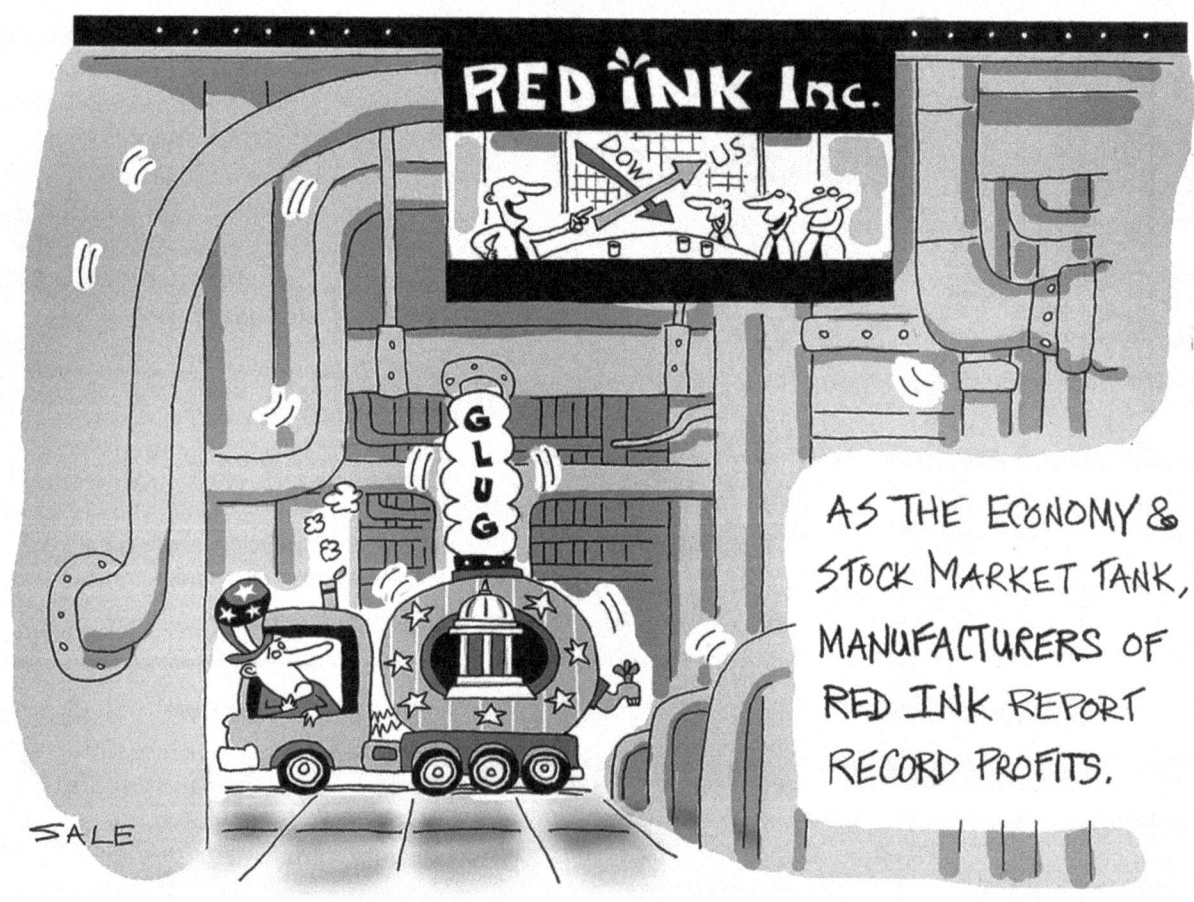

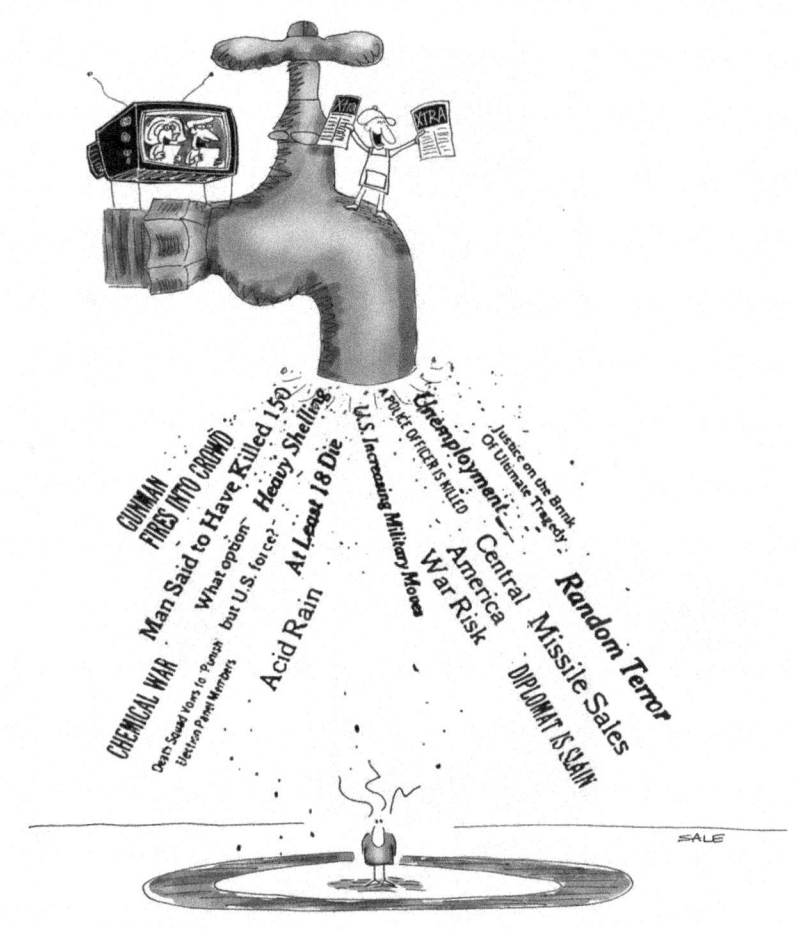

ONLY BAD NEWS.

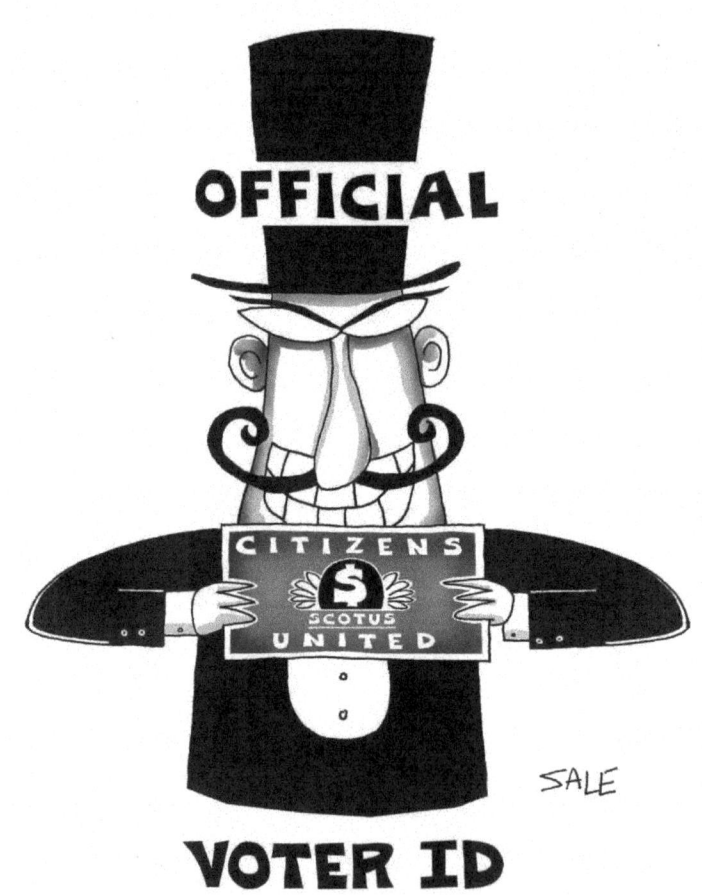

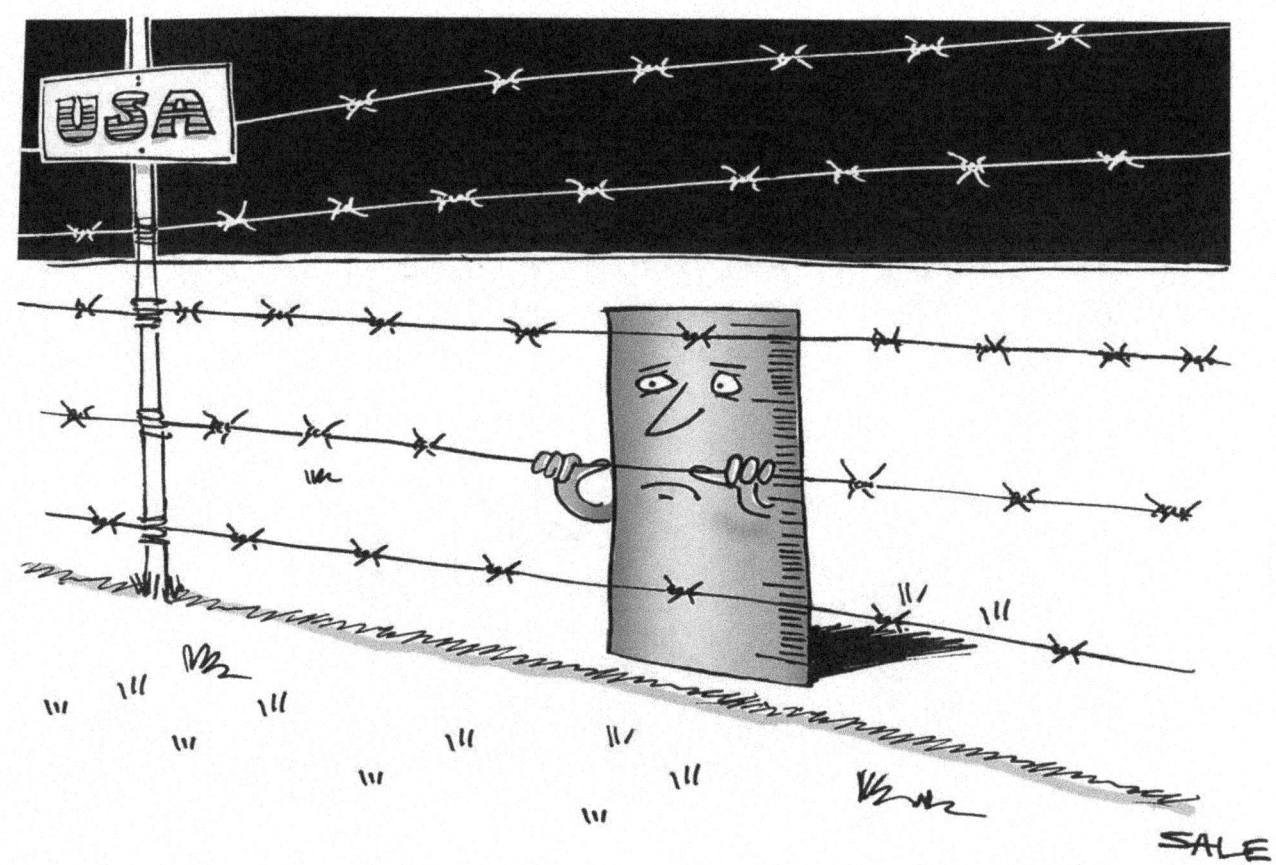

America kept out the metric system but can't keep out the Mexicans.

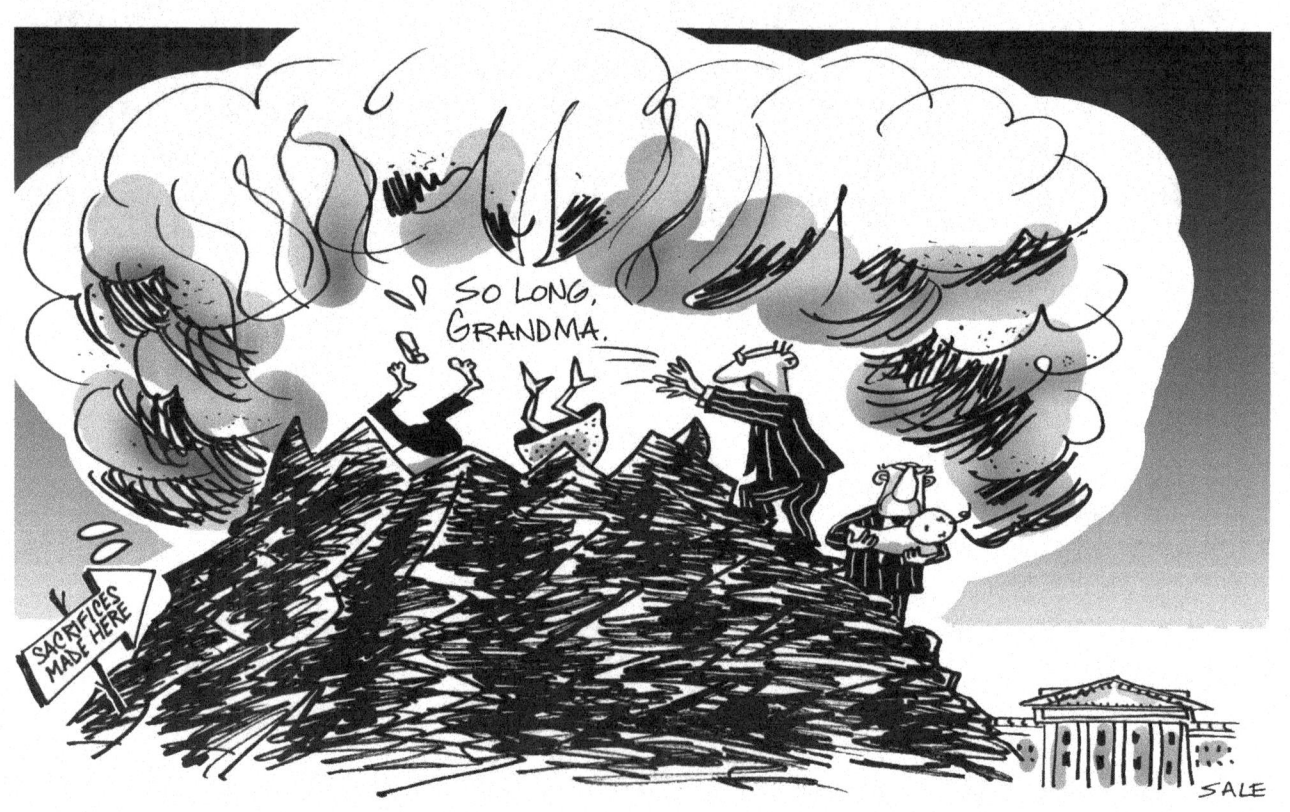

"Give us your sick and weak, your elderly and poor — the burdens on society,"
demanded the capitalist gods, and their political shills fell in line.

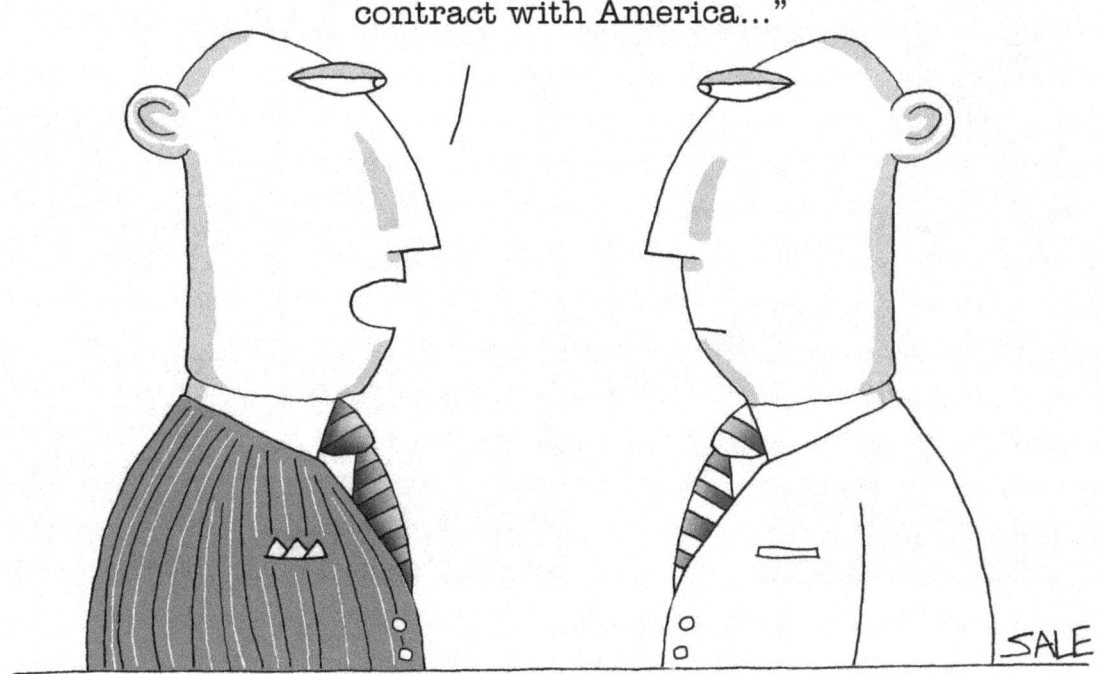

"...Not on it."

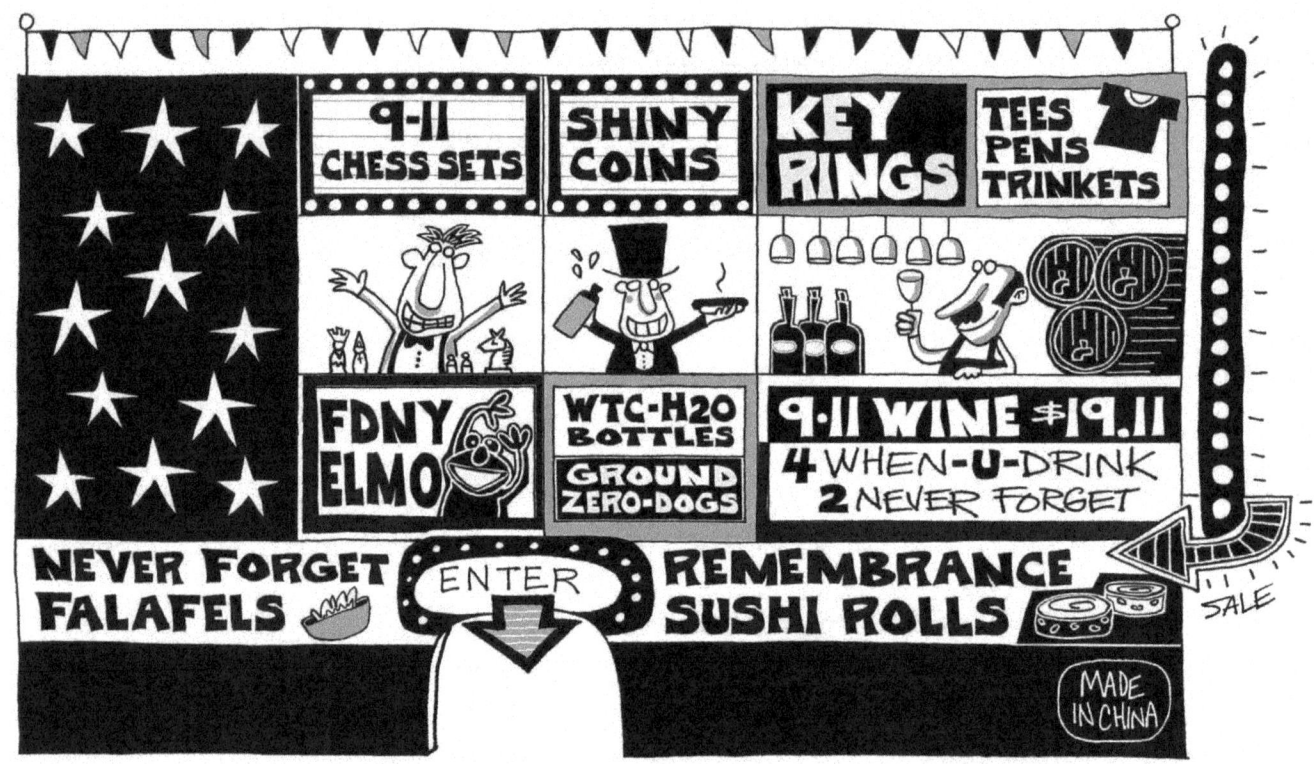

MISSING AN OPPORTUNITY TO EXPLOIT AN EVENT BY SELLING CHEAP NOVELTIES TO MAKE A QUICK BUCK IS UN-AMERICAN & MEANS THE TERRORISTS WIN.

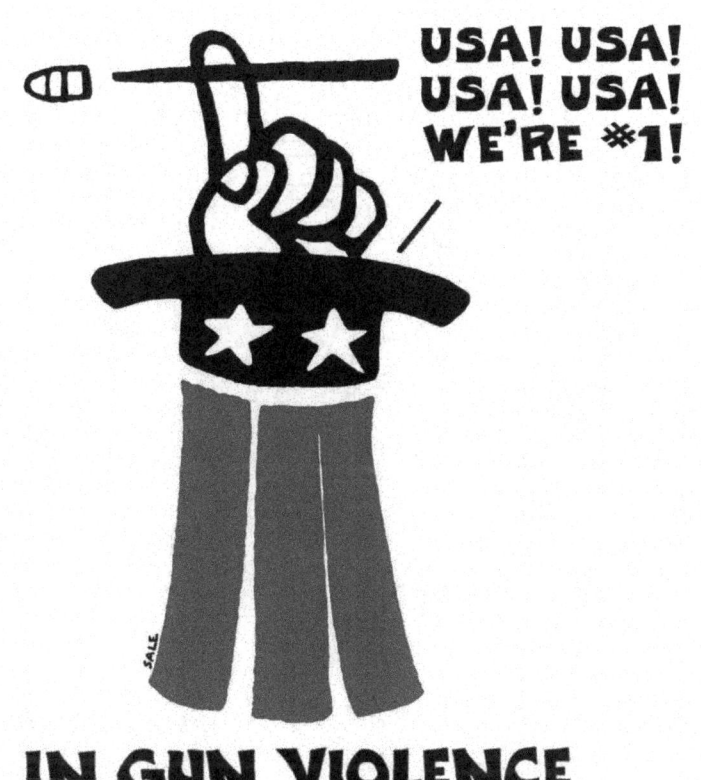

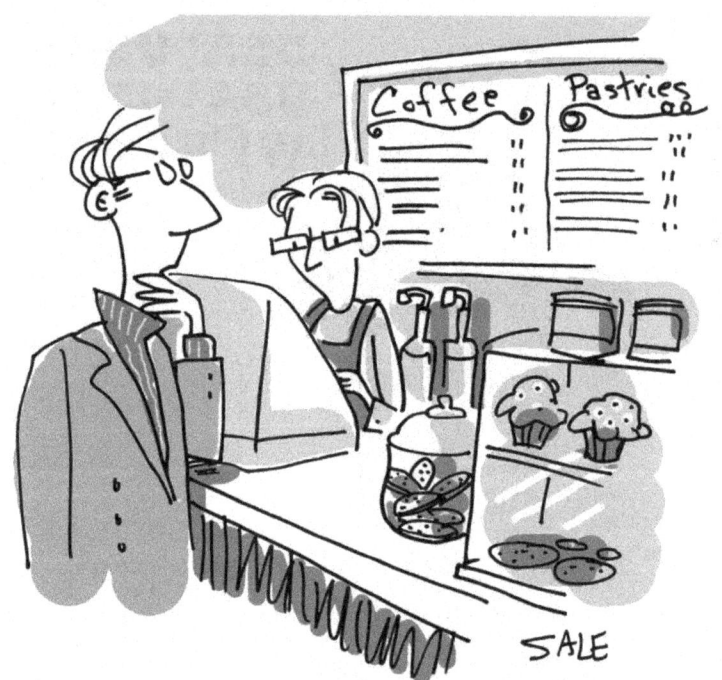

I'll have a cafe mocha-vodka-Paxil-marijuana-latte
to go and recreational size it, please.

Twits Twerk & Tweet.

SALE

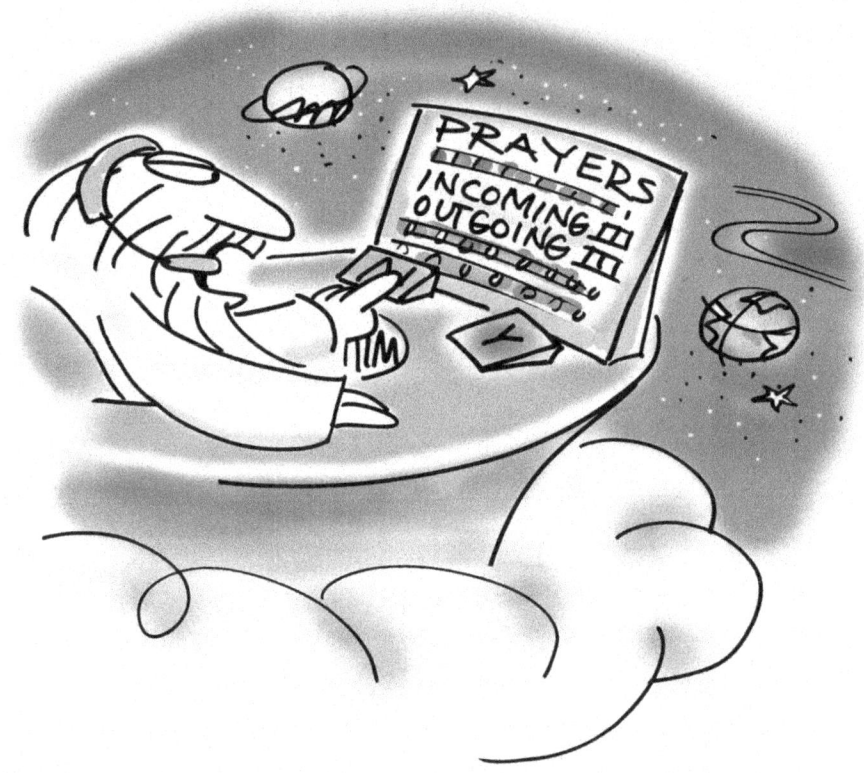

"Hello Peter, please change our voice-mail greeting to
reassure people that Oprah is ending this week — not the world."

God gets the last laugh.

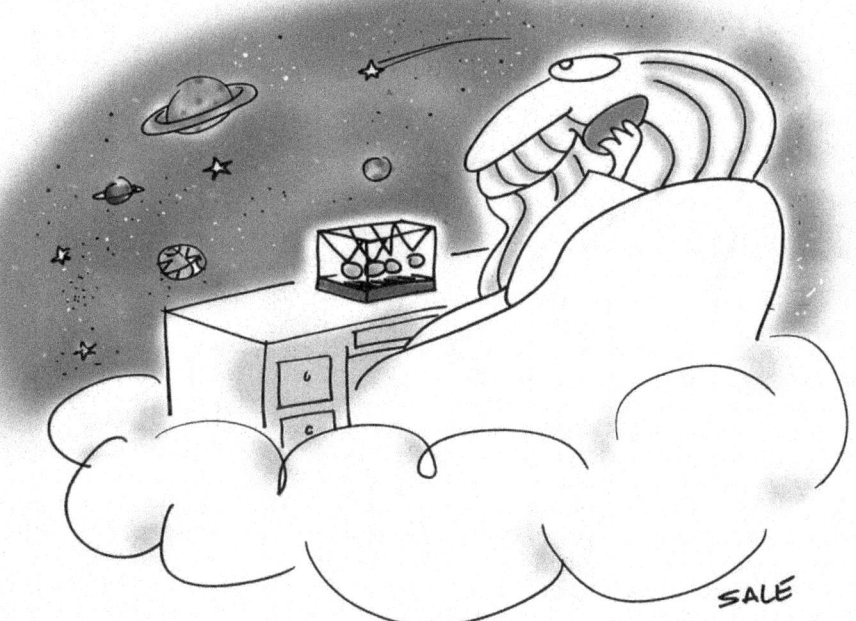

"This is the operator...You have a collect call from Hell, from a Mr. Oral Roberts, Will you accept the charges?"

11:59PM APRIL 14TH

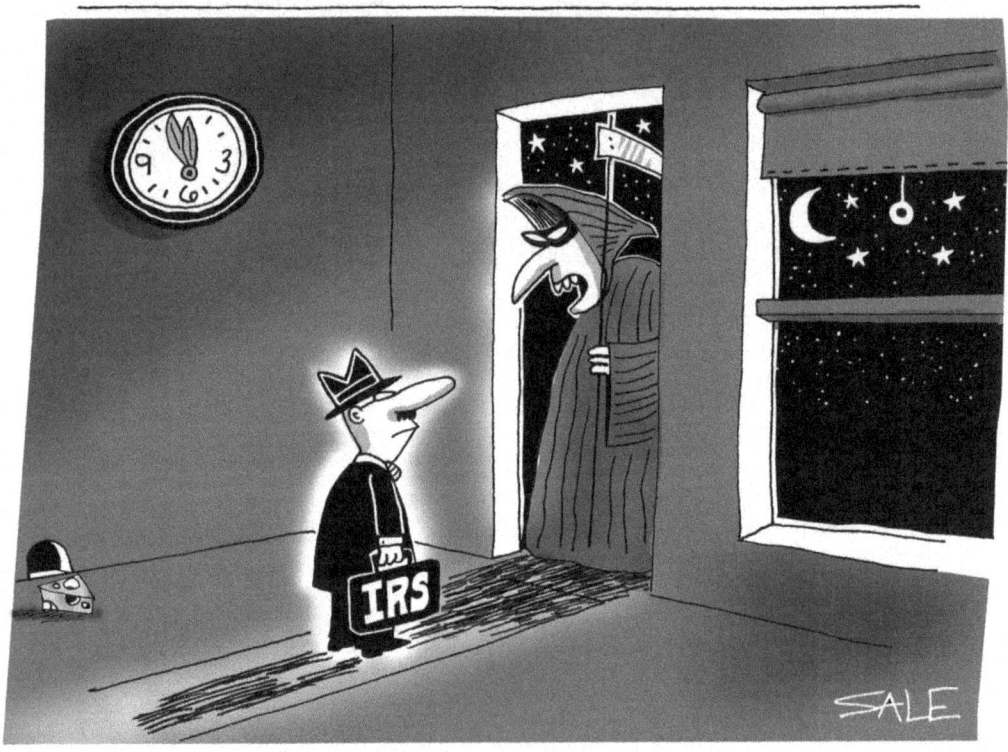

"Ready to kick some ass?"

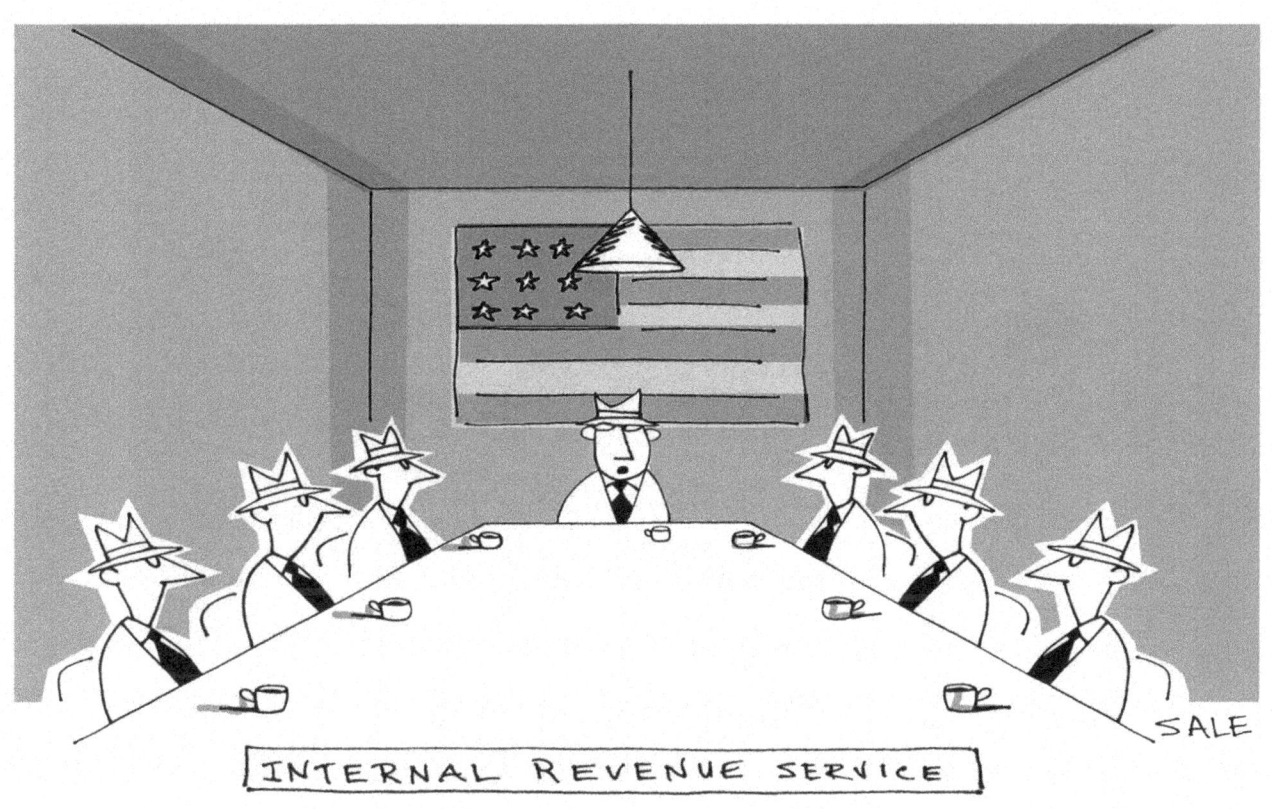

"*Fools and their money are soon parted, gentlemen.
It is our job to take the rest.*"

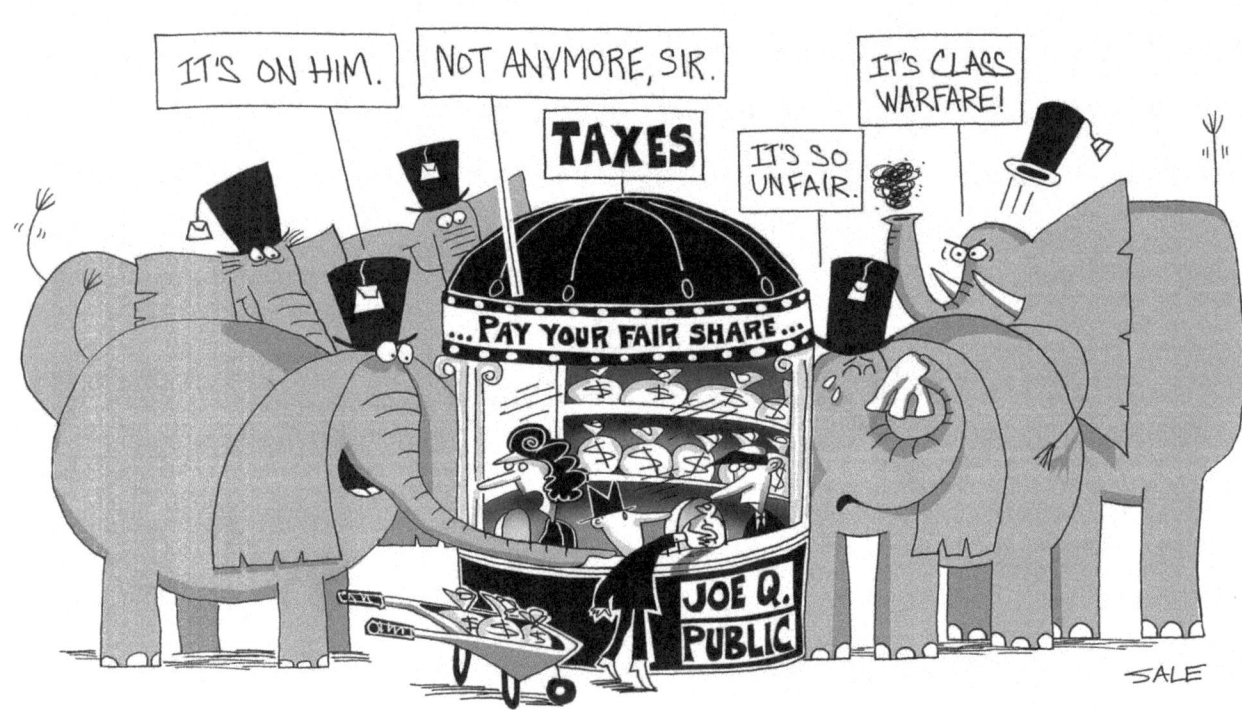

144

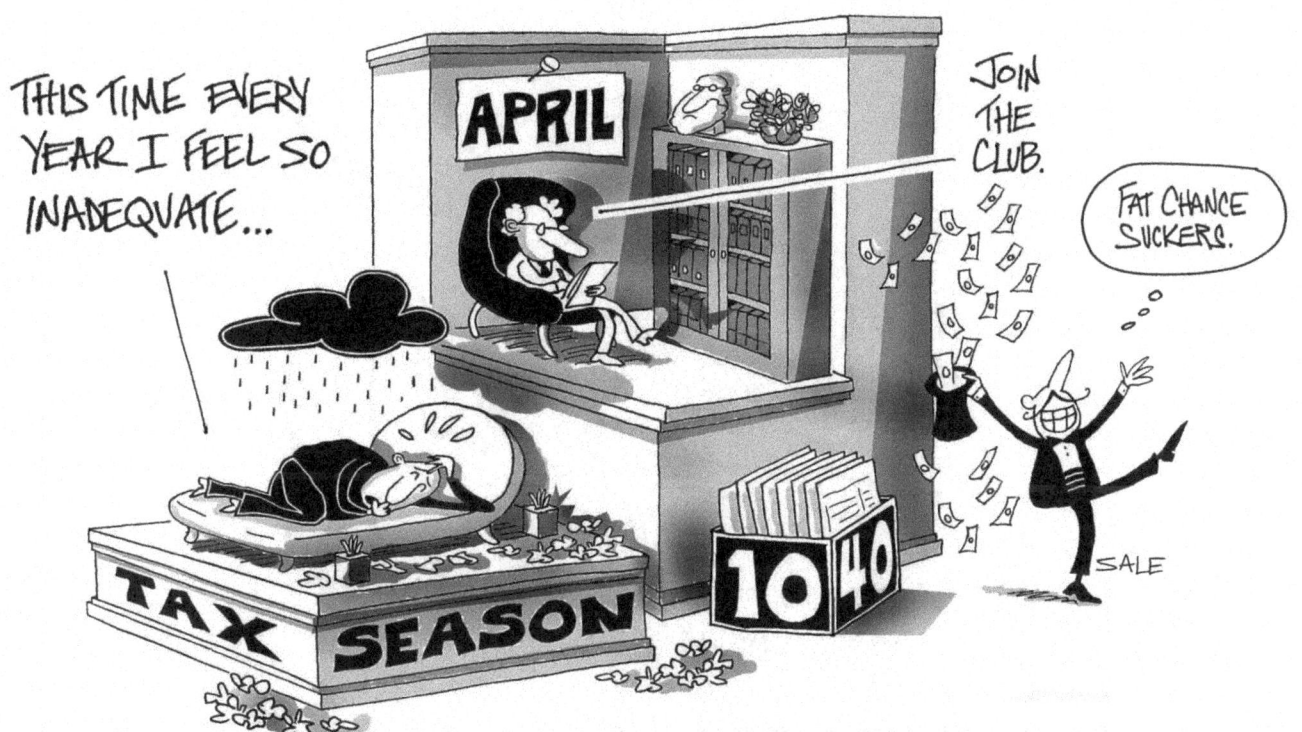

LOOPHOLE ENVY

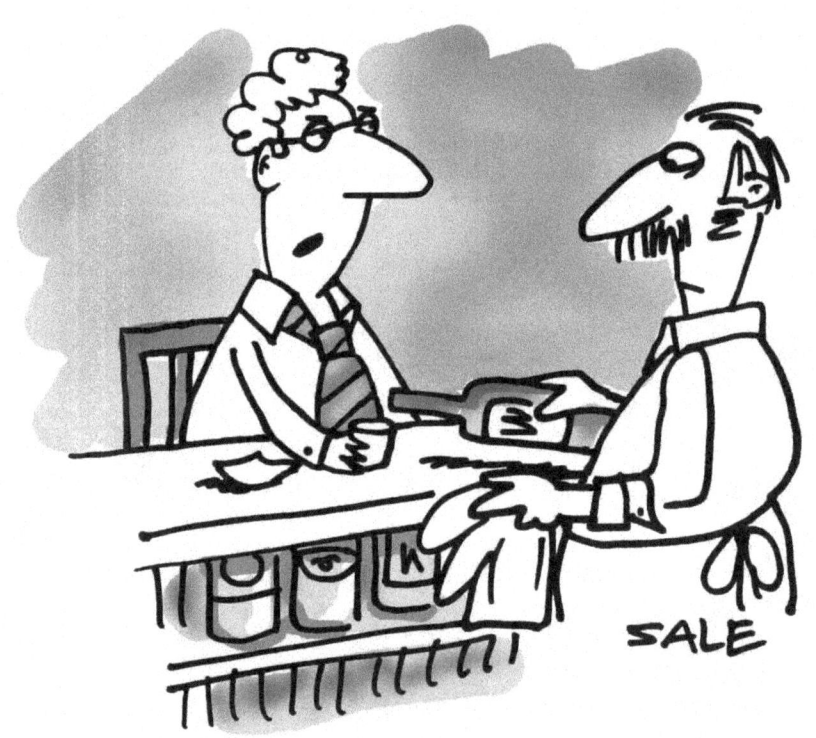

"*The wife and I had to postpone our divorce since neither of us can qualify for another mortgage.*"

The Recession Hits Heaven.

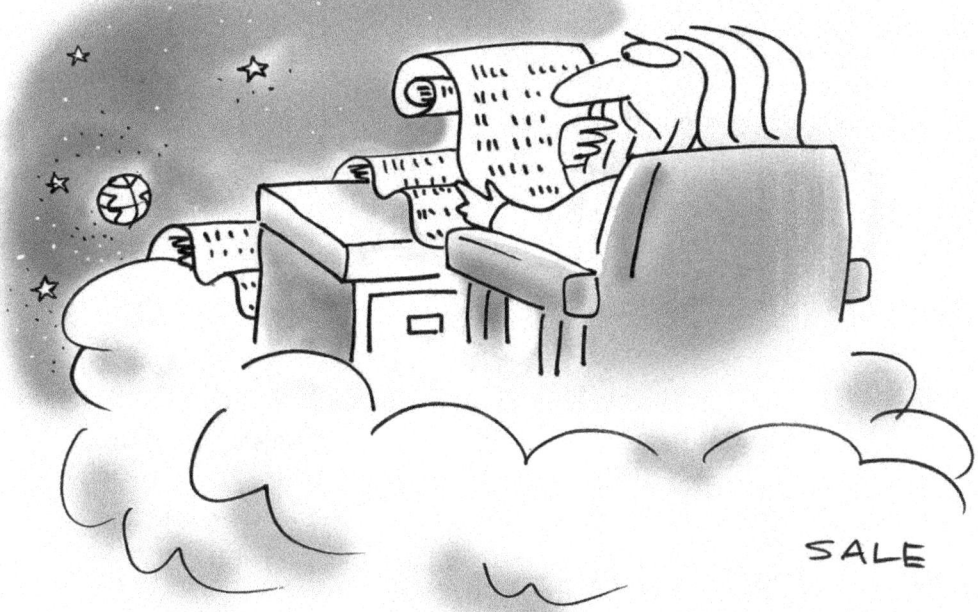

SALE

With a soaring deficit and the high cost of energy, God is forced to review his policy of opening a window whenever closing a door.

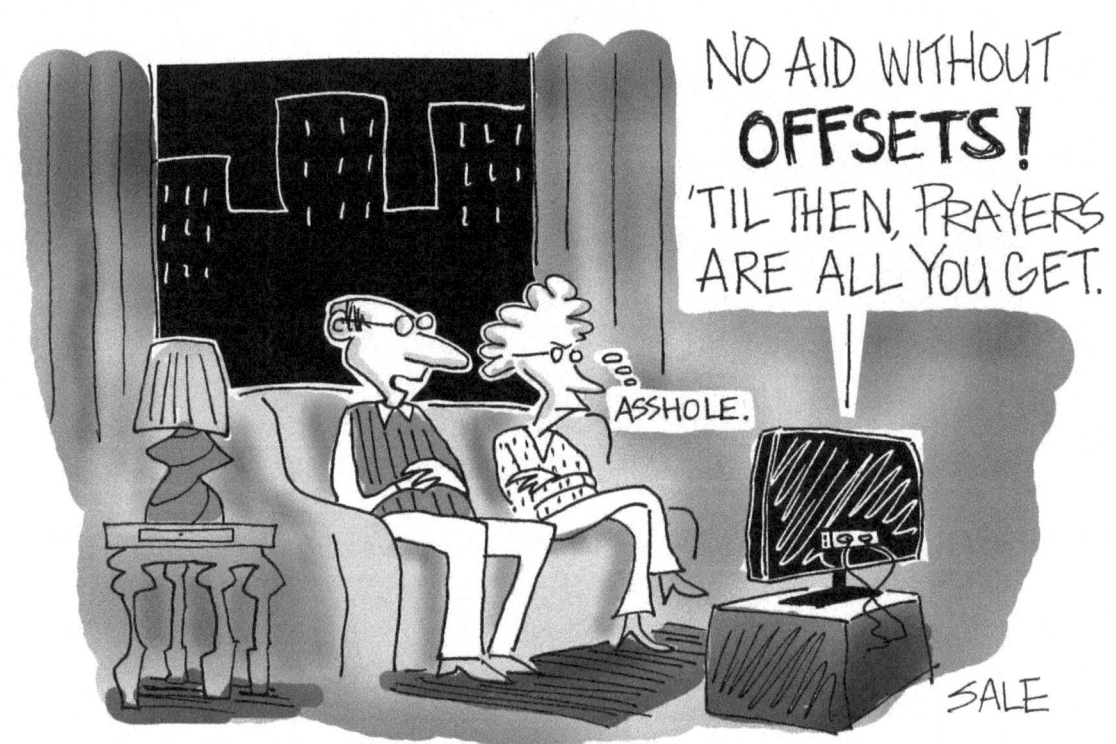

"What would Jesus offset?"

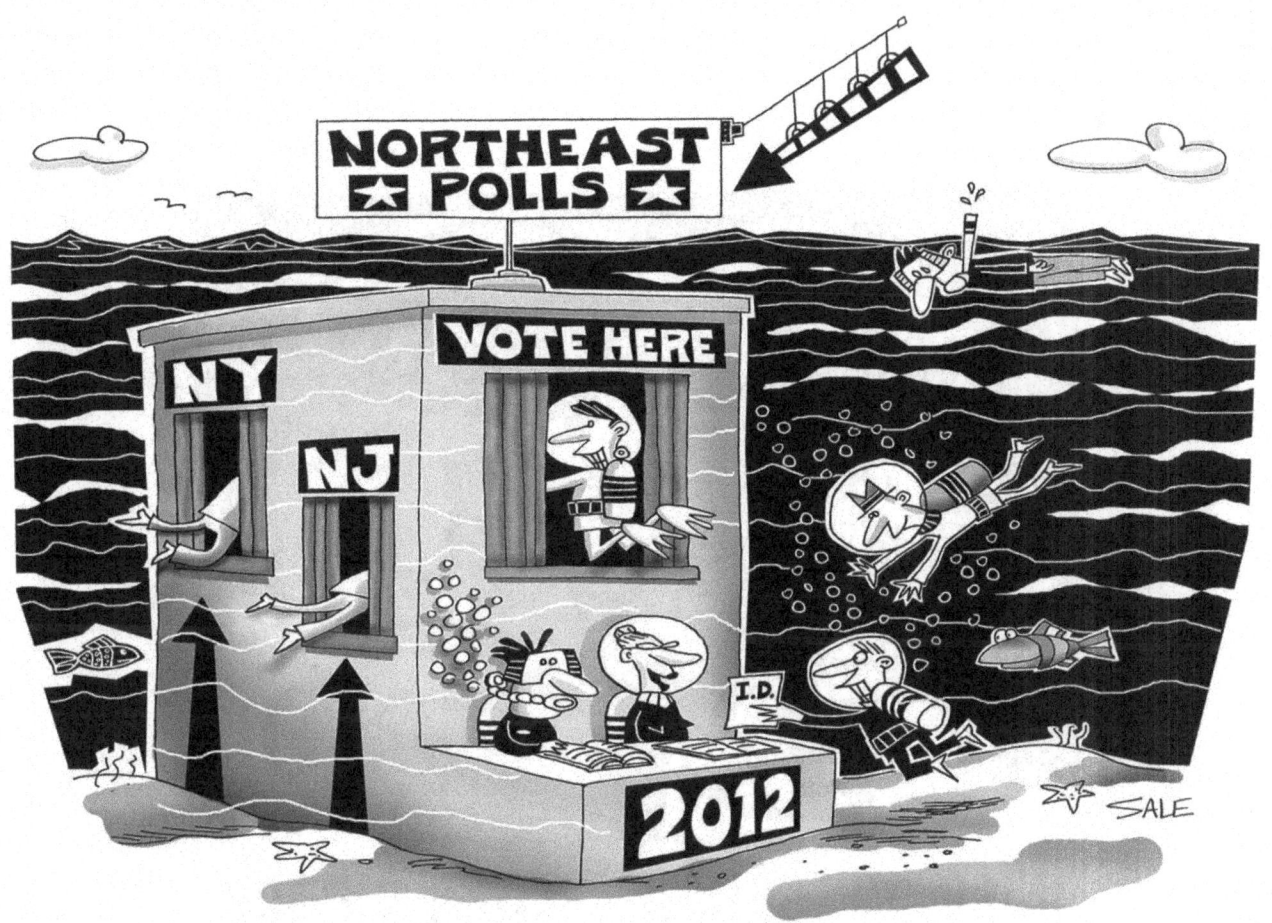

Hurricane Sandy.

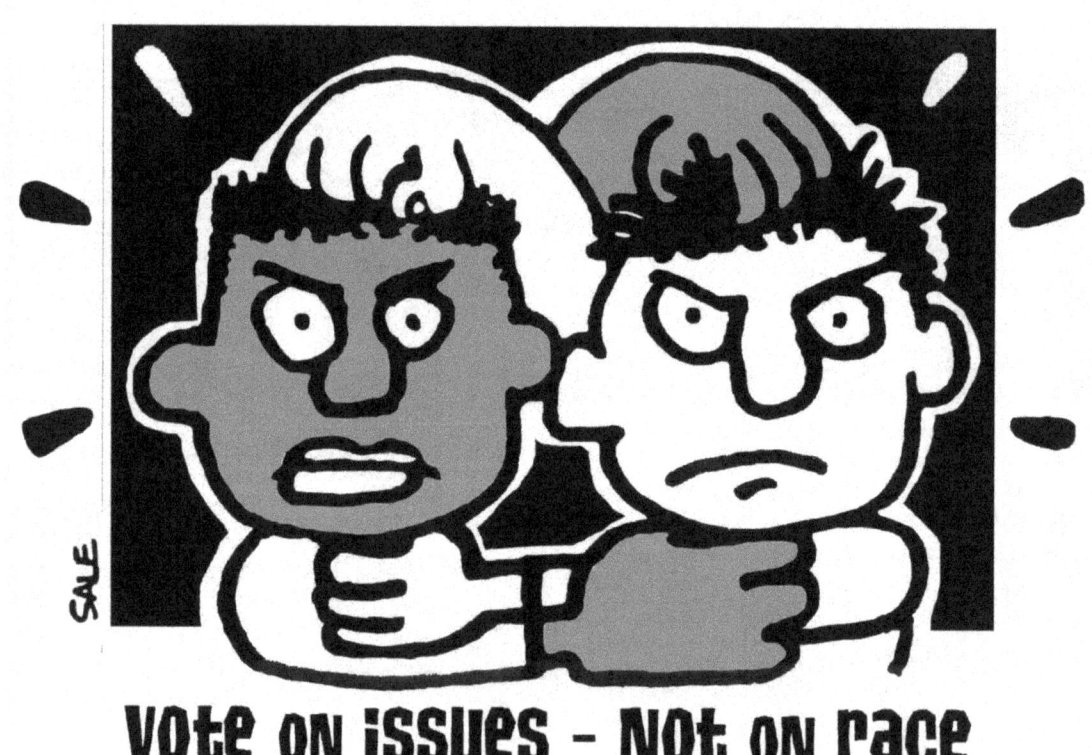

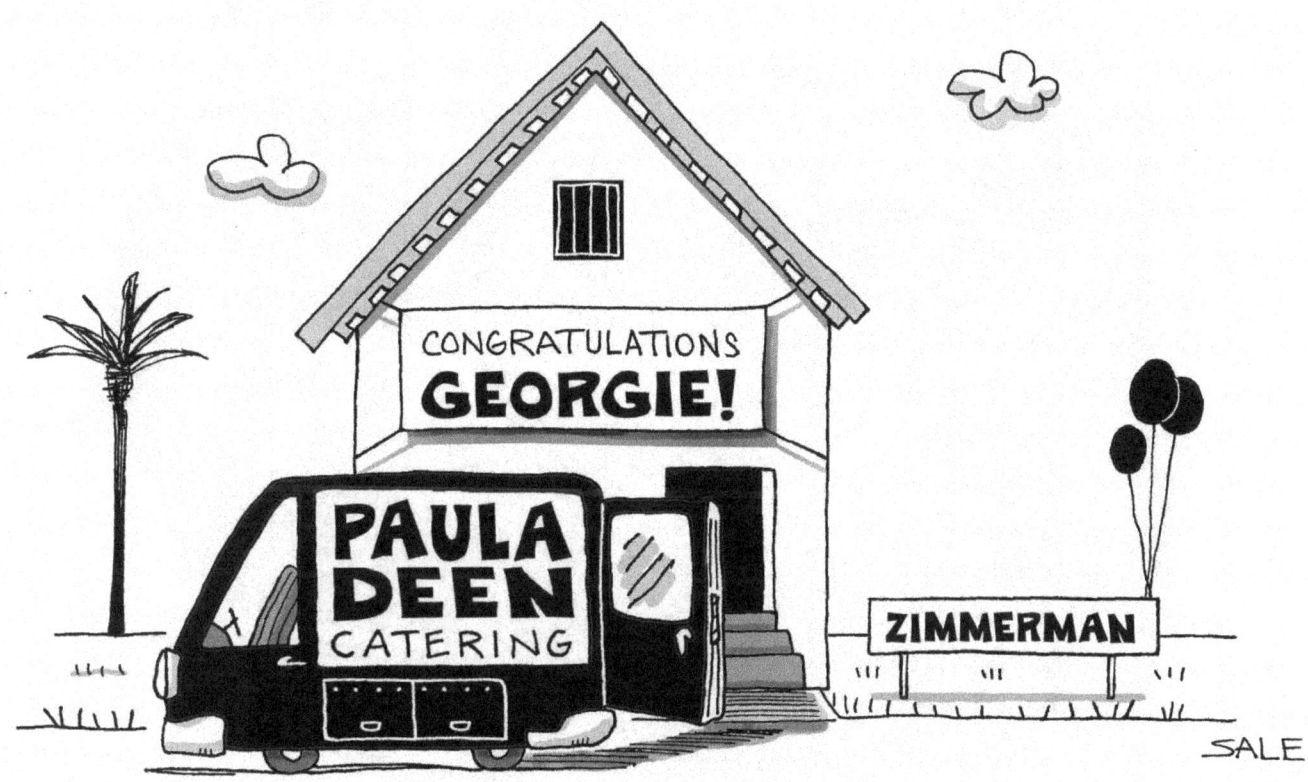

NO UNEMPLOYMENT EXTENSION.

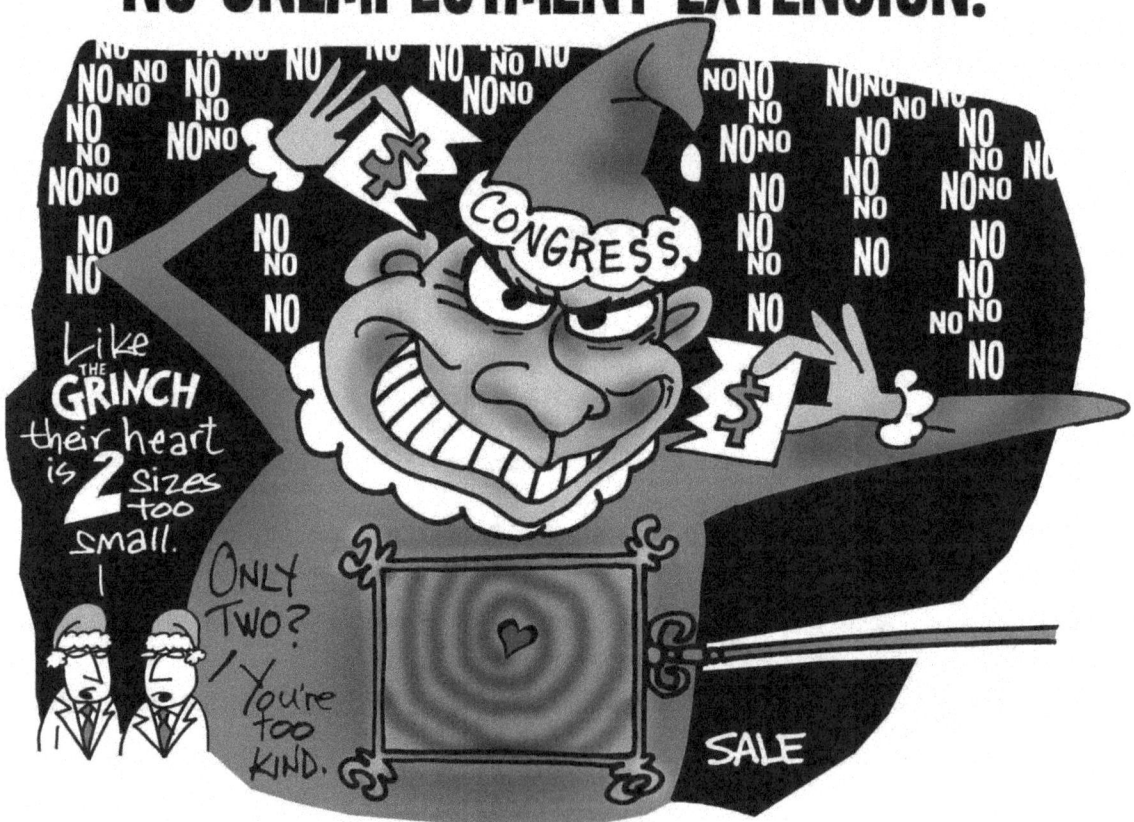

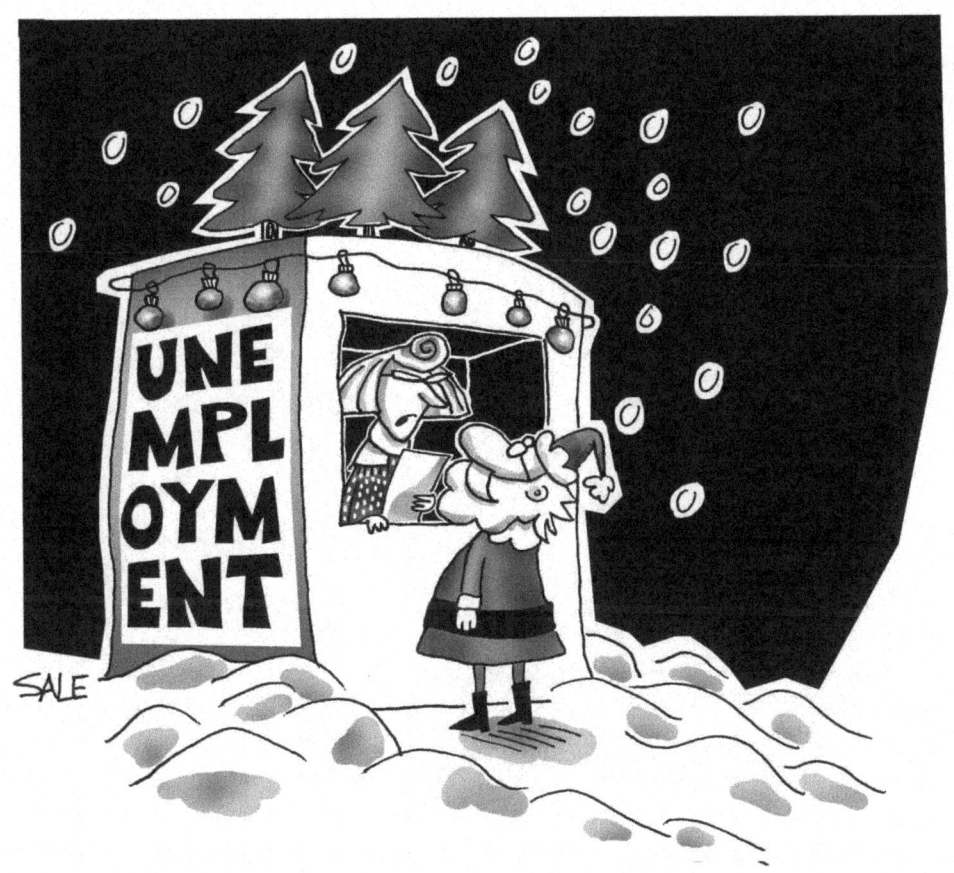

"Granted it is a lot of work sir, but one night of work a year does not qualify you for unemployment benefits."

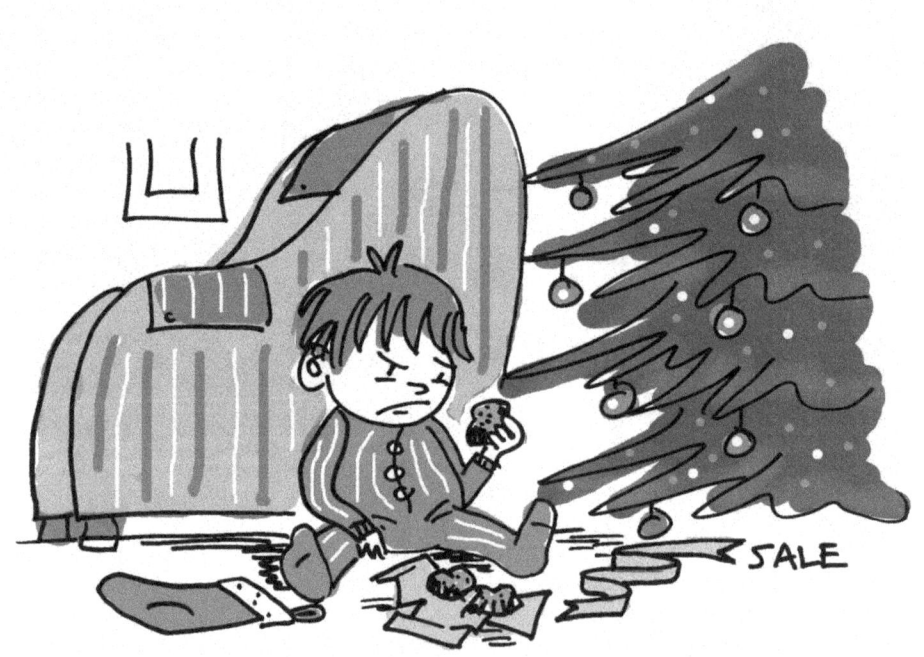

The bad news was Santa brought rotten Johnny coal
for Christmas. The good news was it was clean coal.

Peace

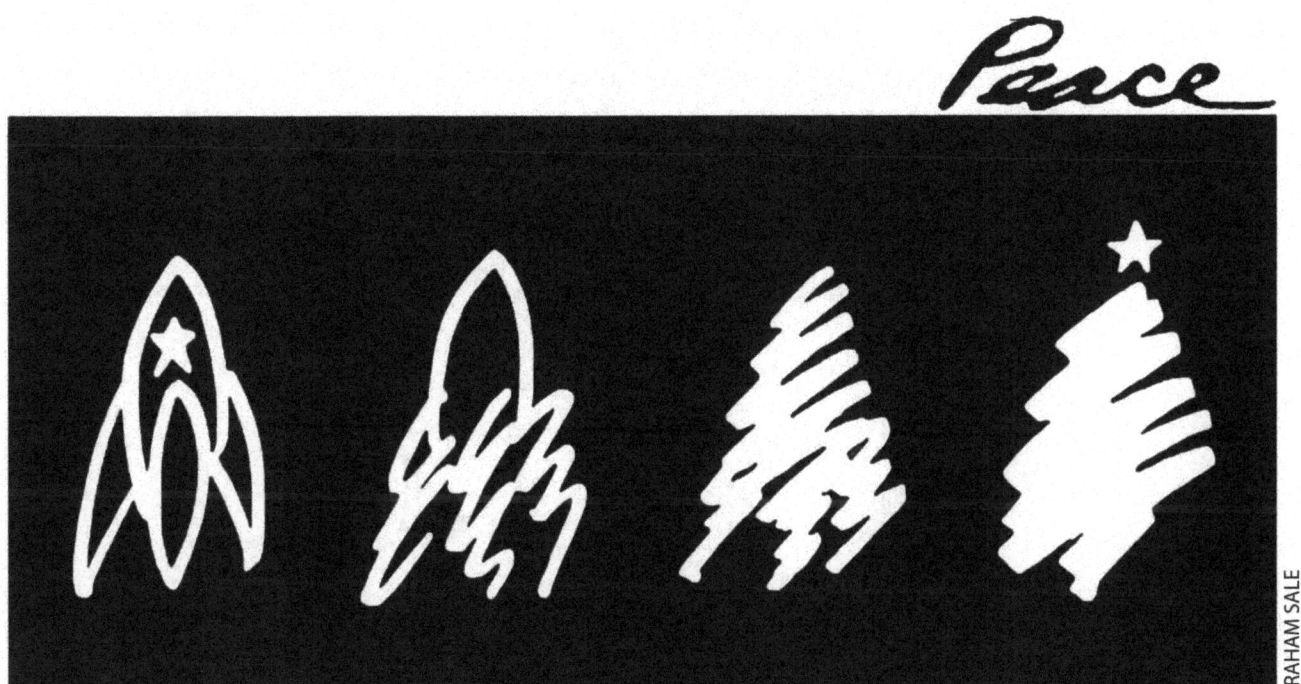

155

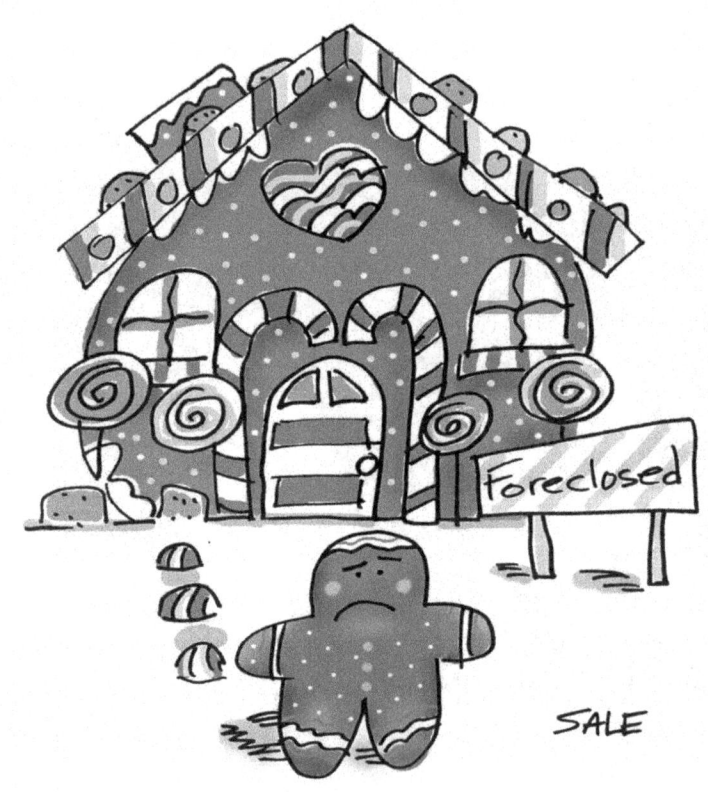

Christmas at the Gingerbread House.

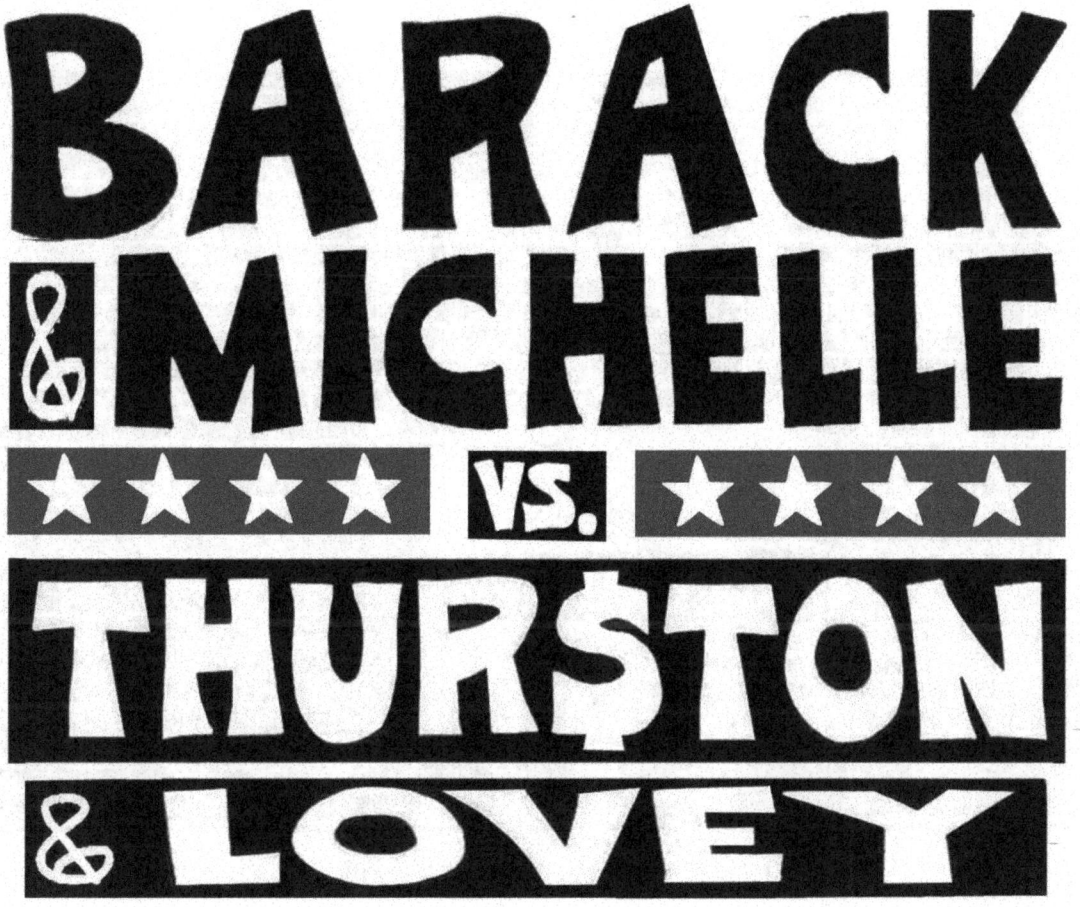

Co-starring: **Paul Ryan** as **'Gilligan"** and **Rush Limbaugh** as the **"Skipper."**

157

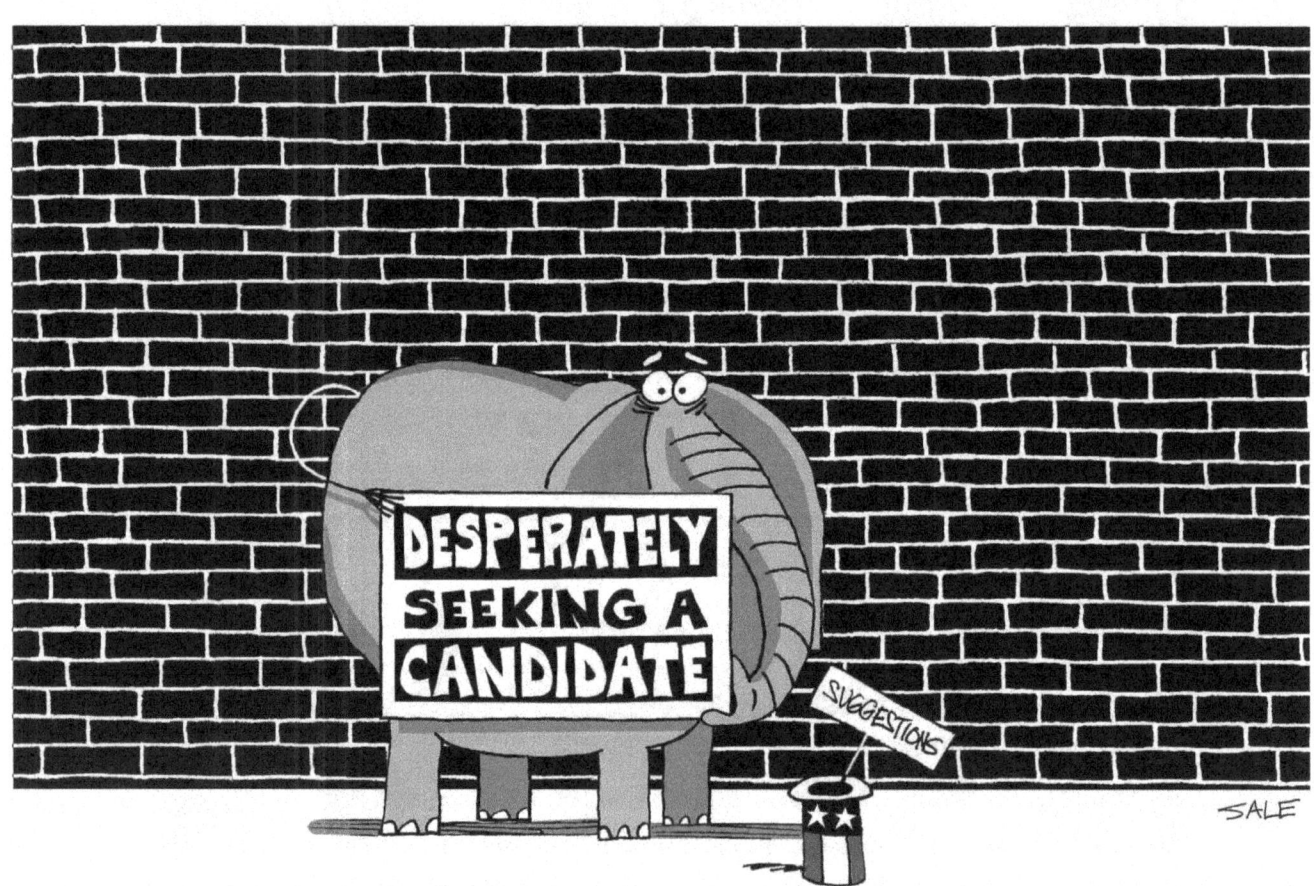

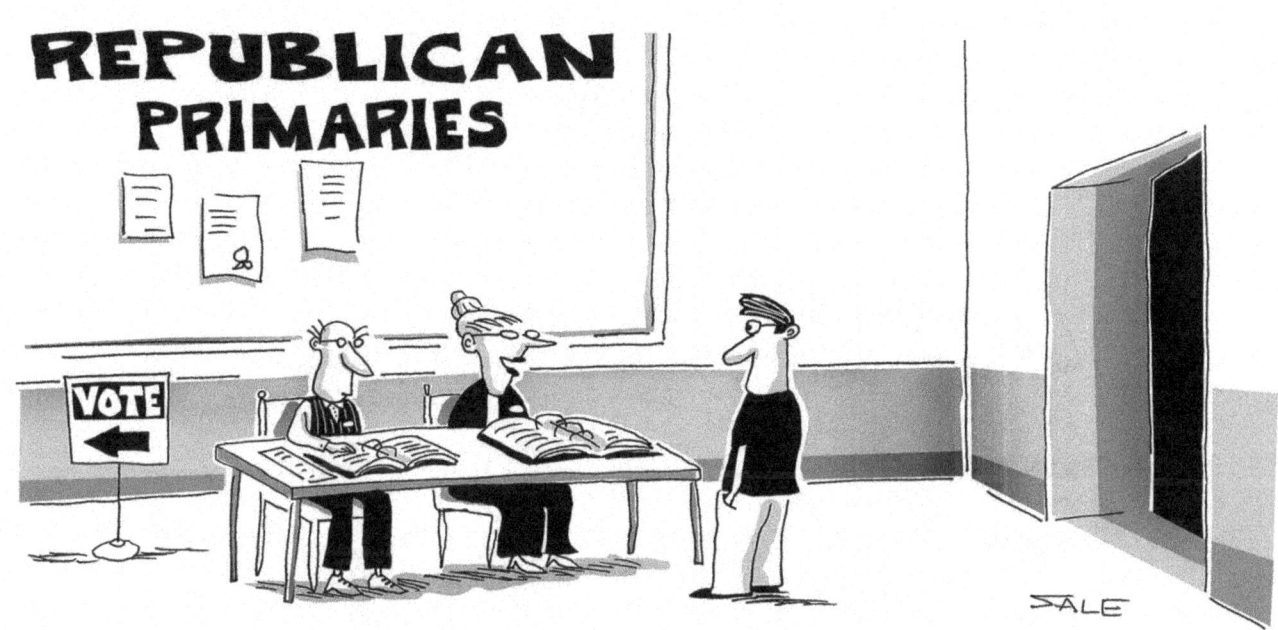

*"As you know, you've got to be crazy to run for president,
and boy have we got some candidates for you!"*

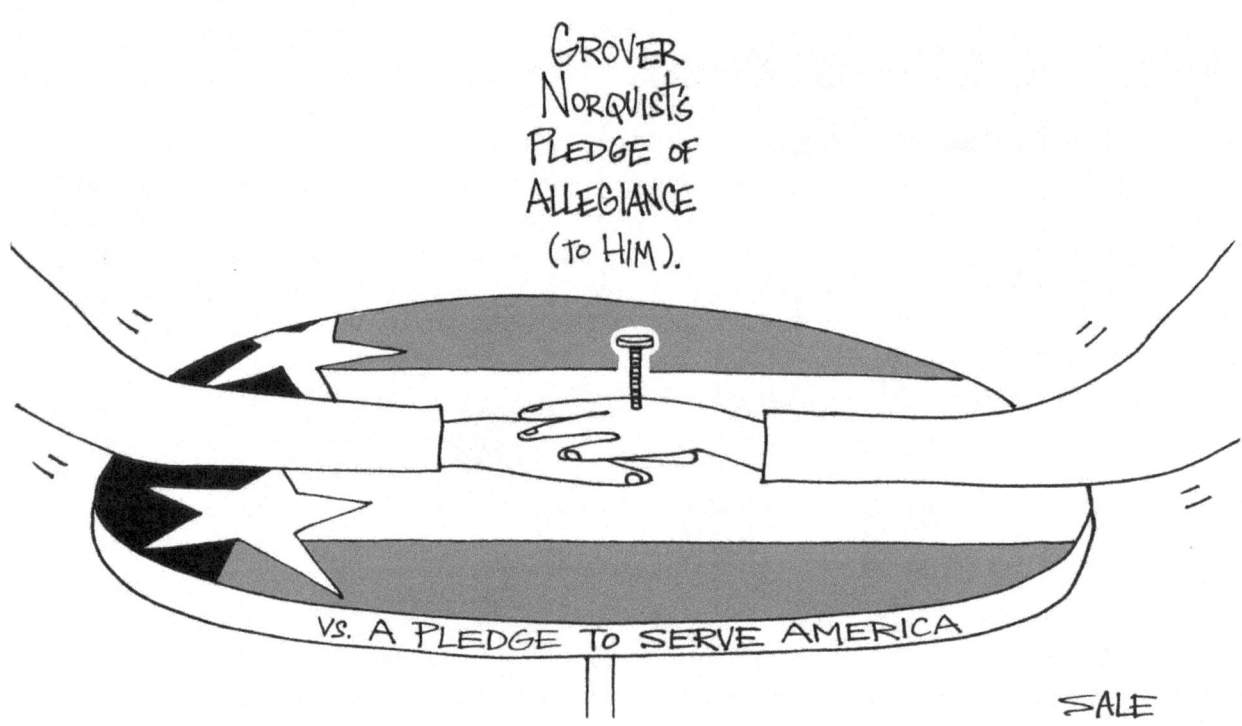

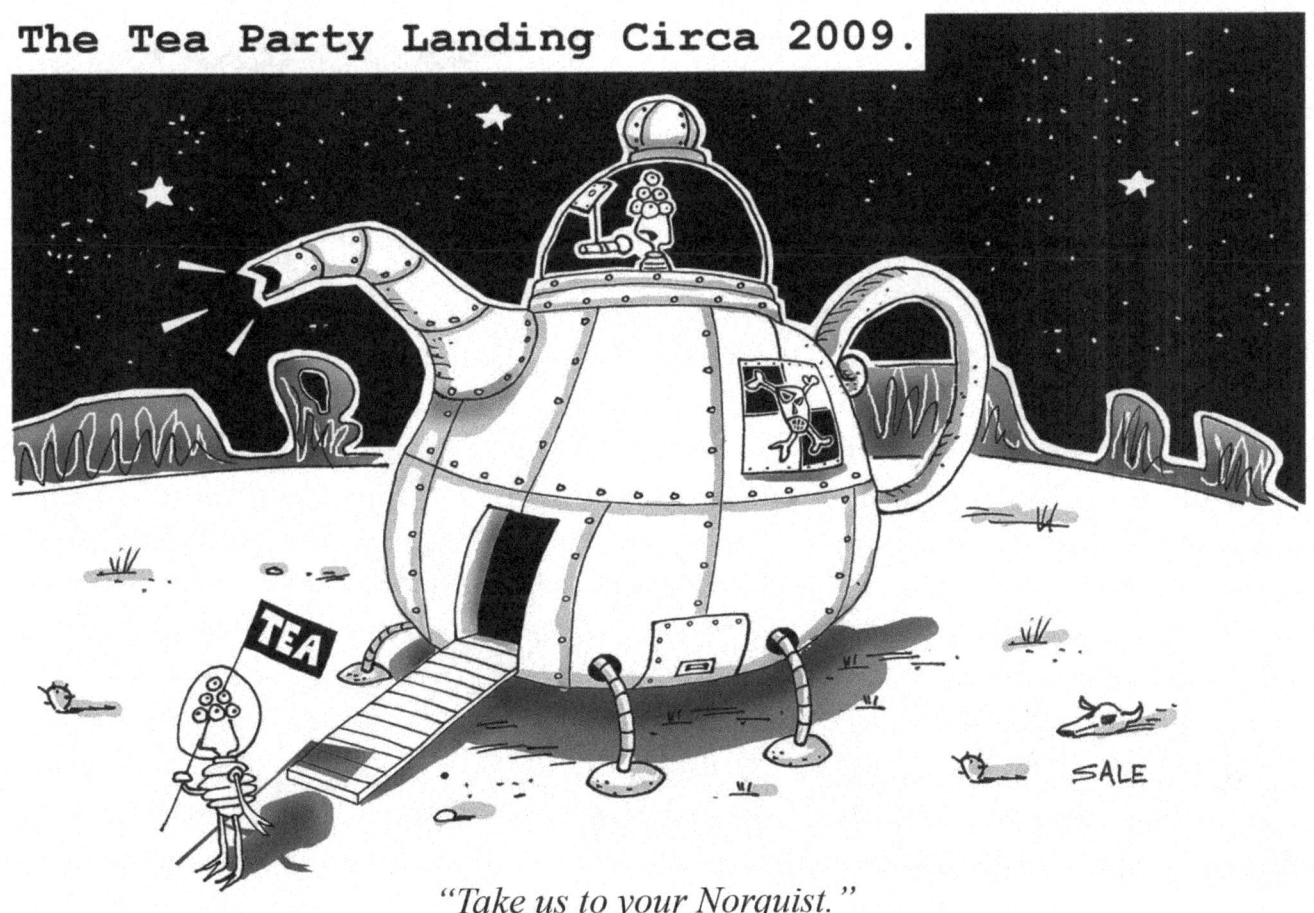

"Take us to your Norquist."

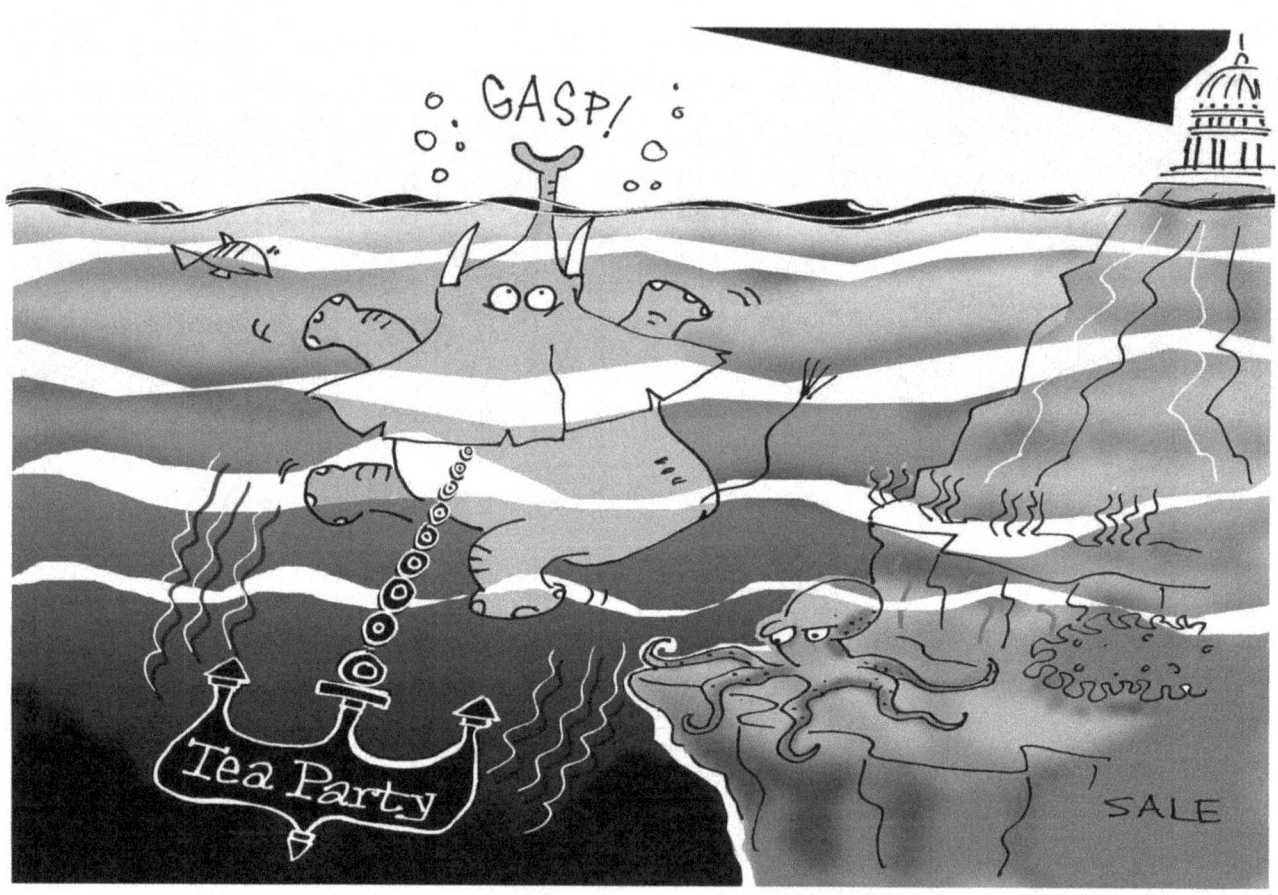

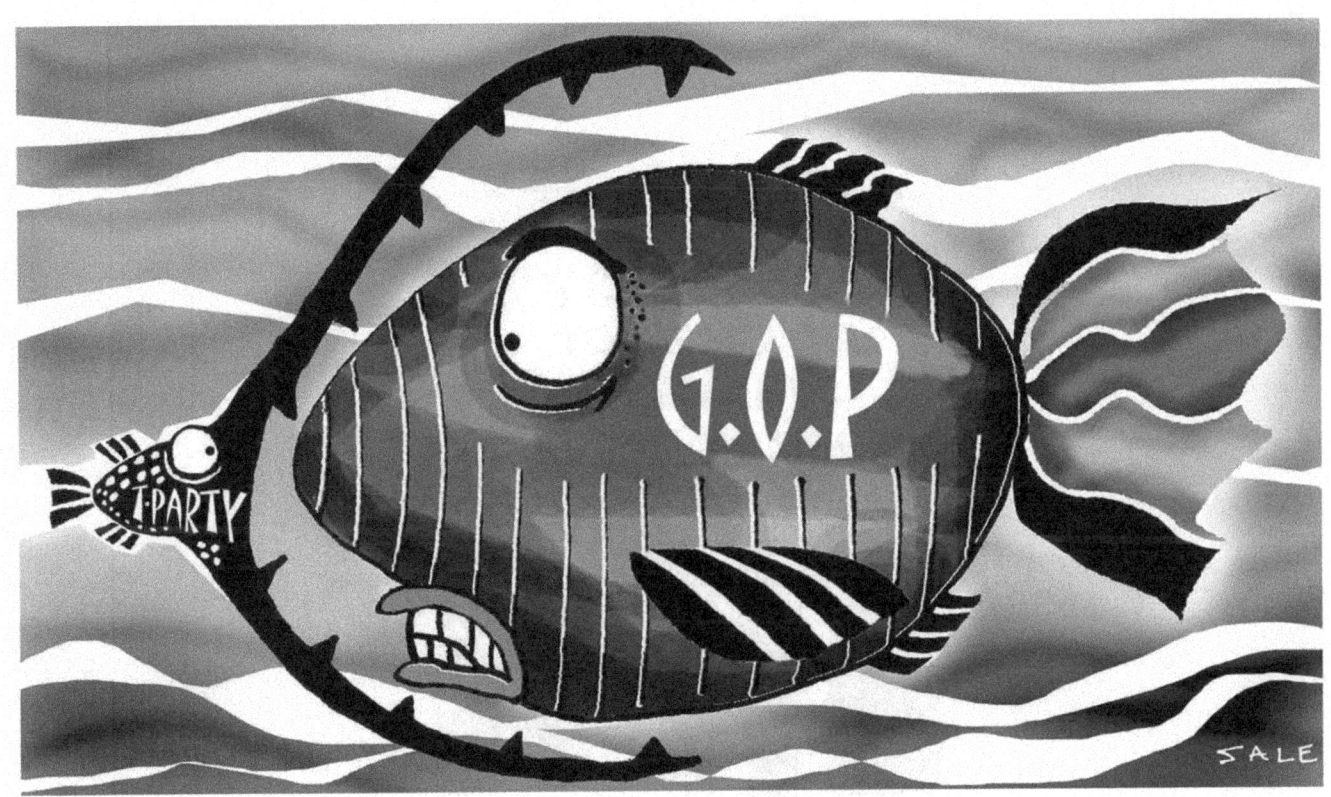

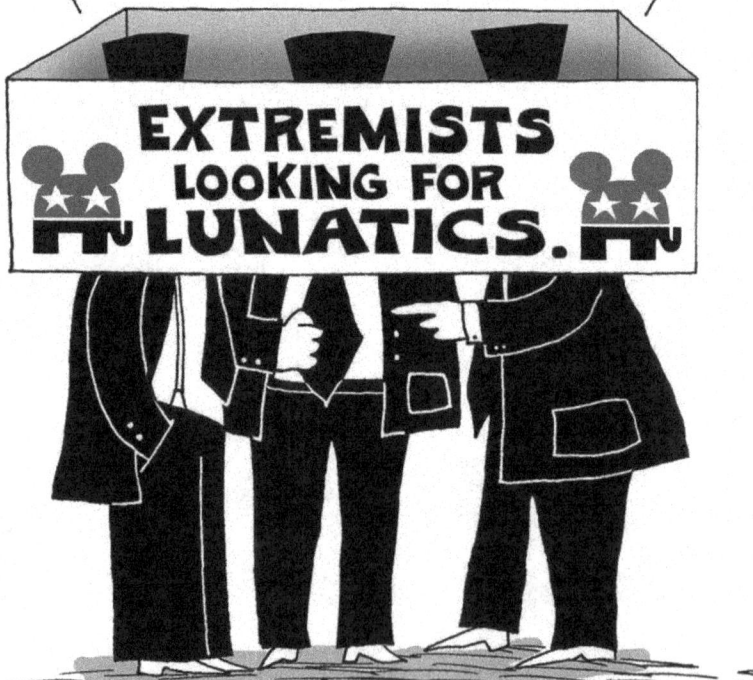

164

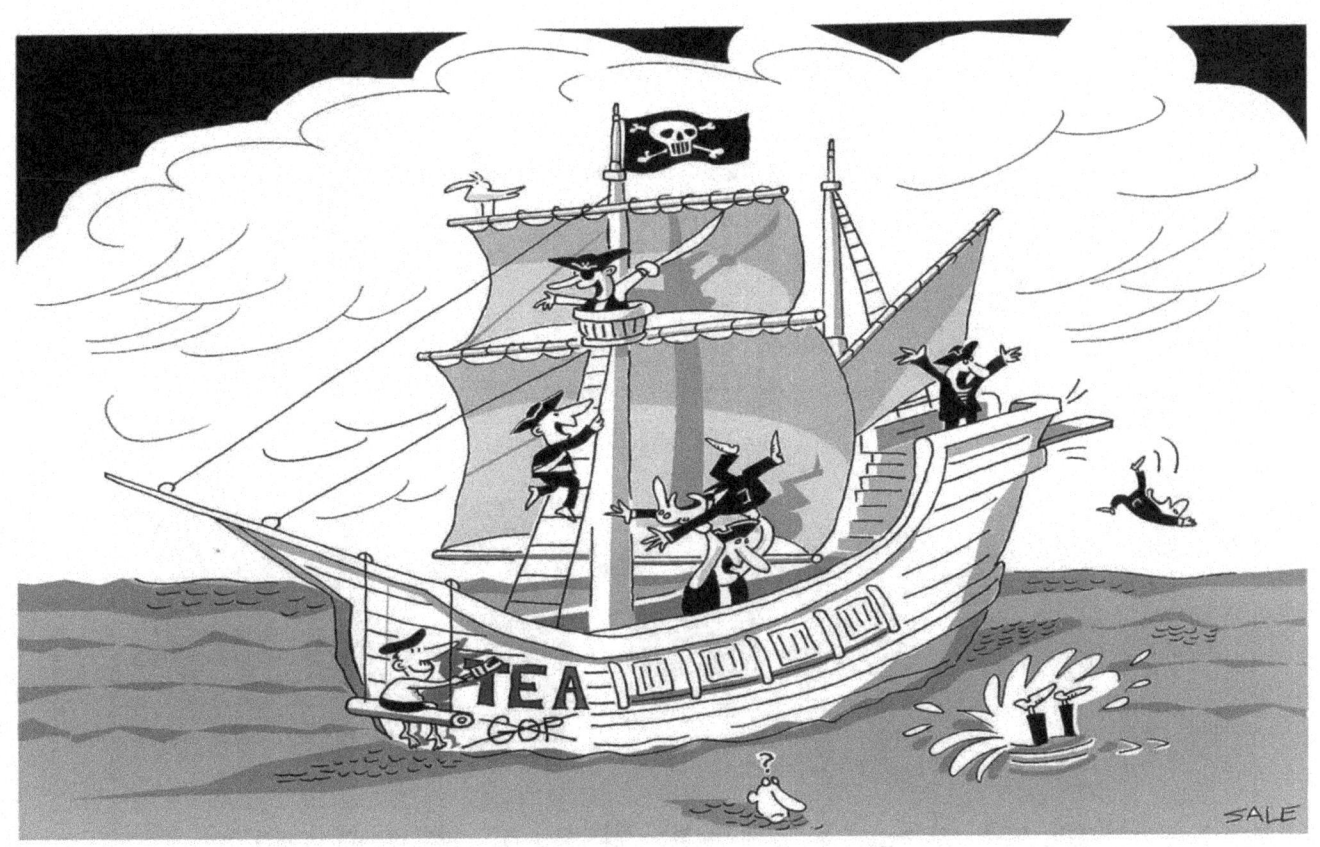

IS THE PARTY (G.O.P.) OVER?

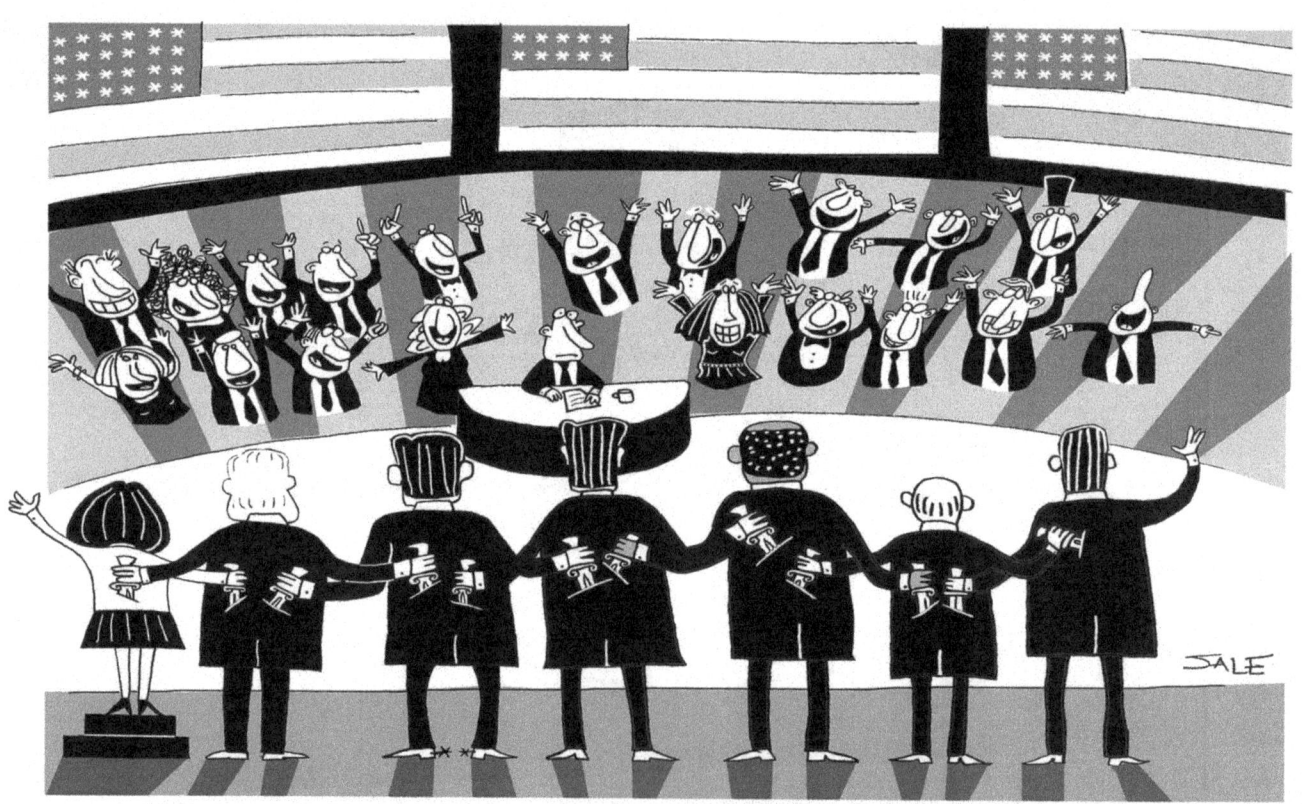

"BRAWL IN THE FAMILY"

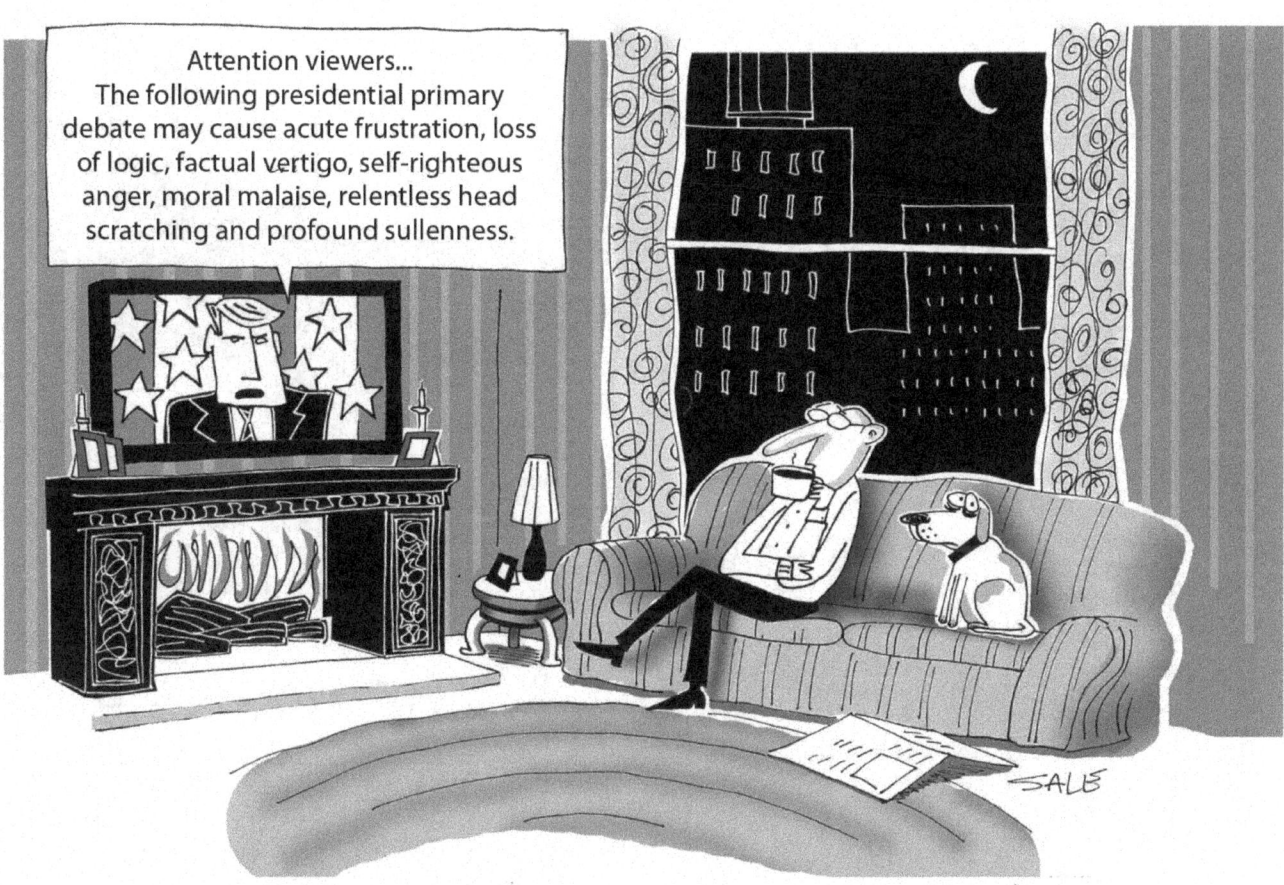

167

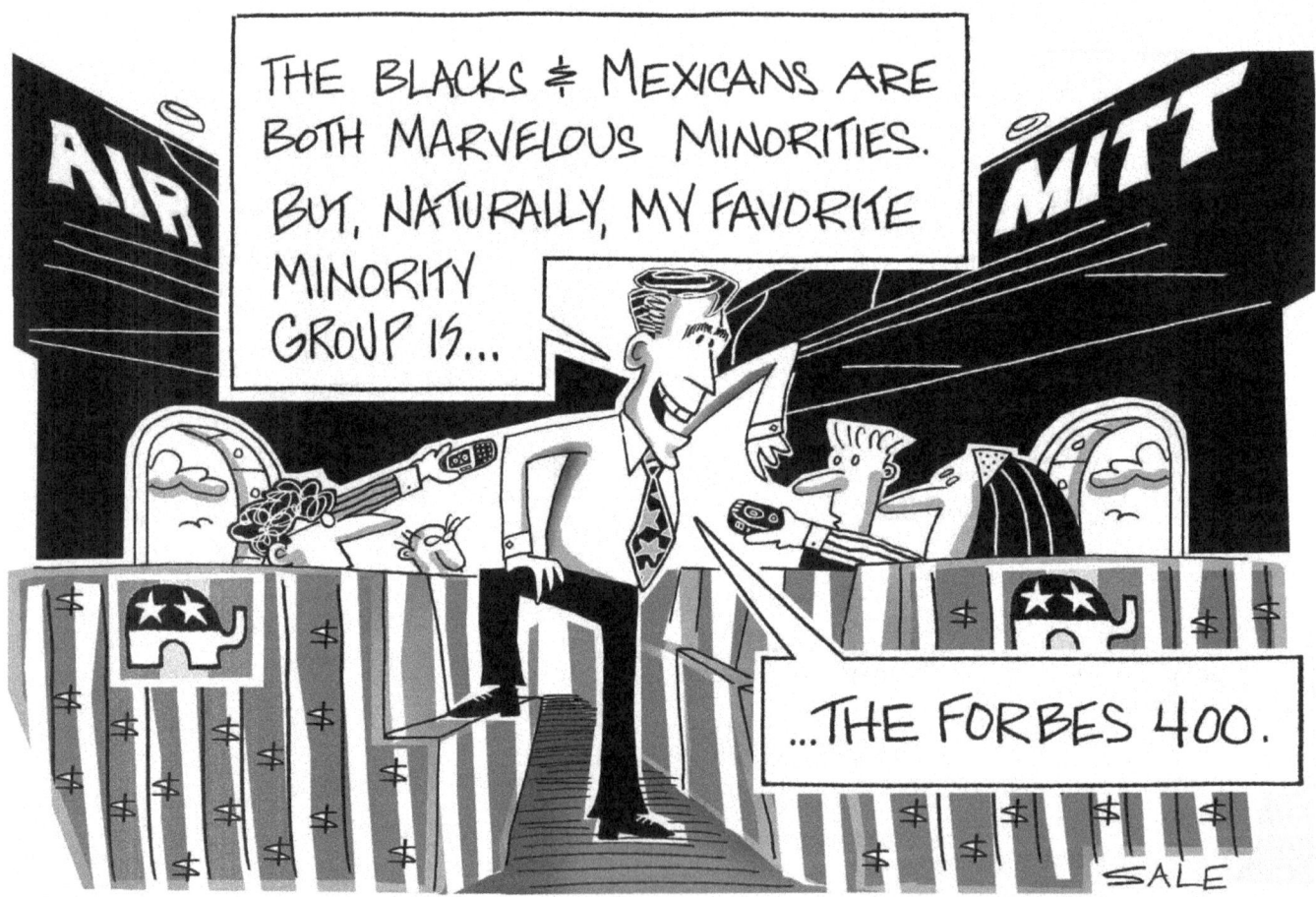

168

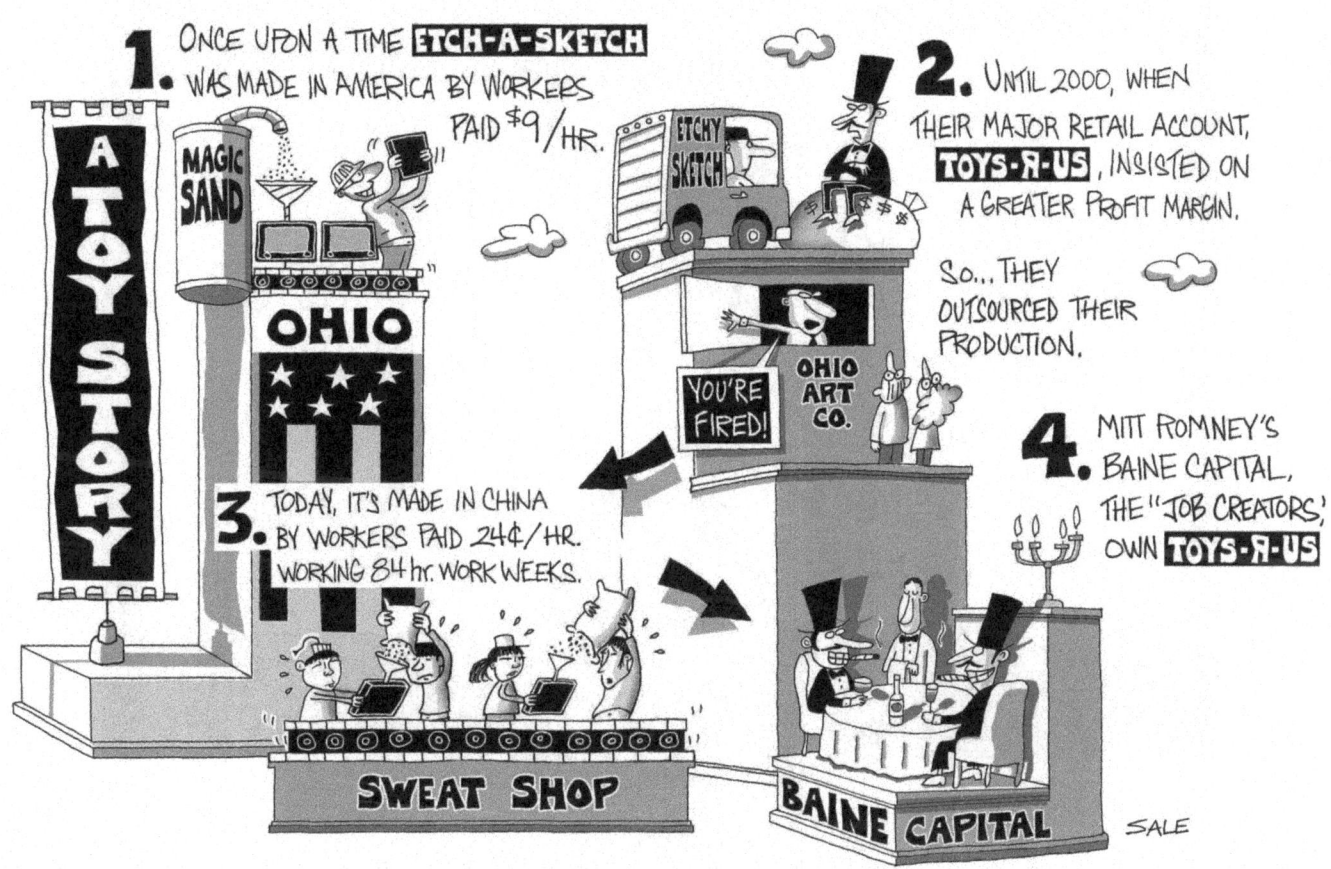

169

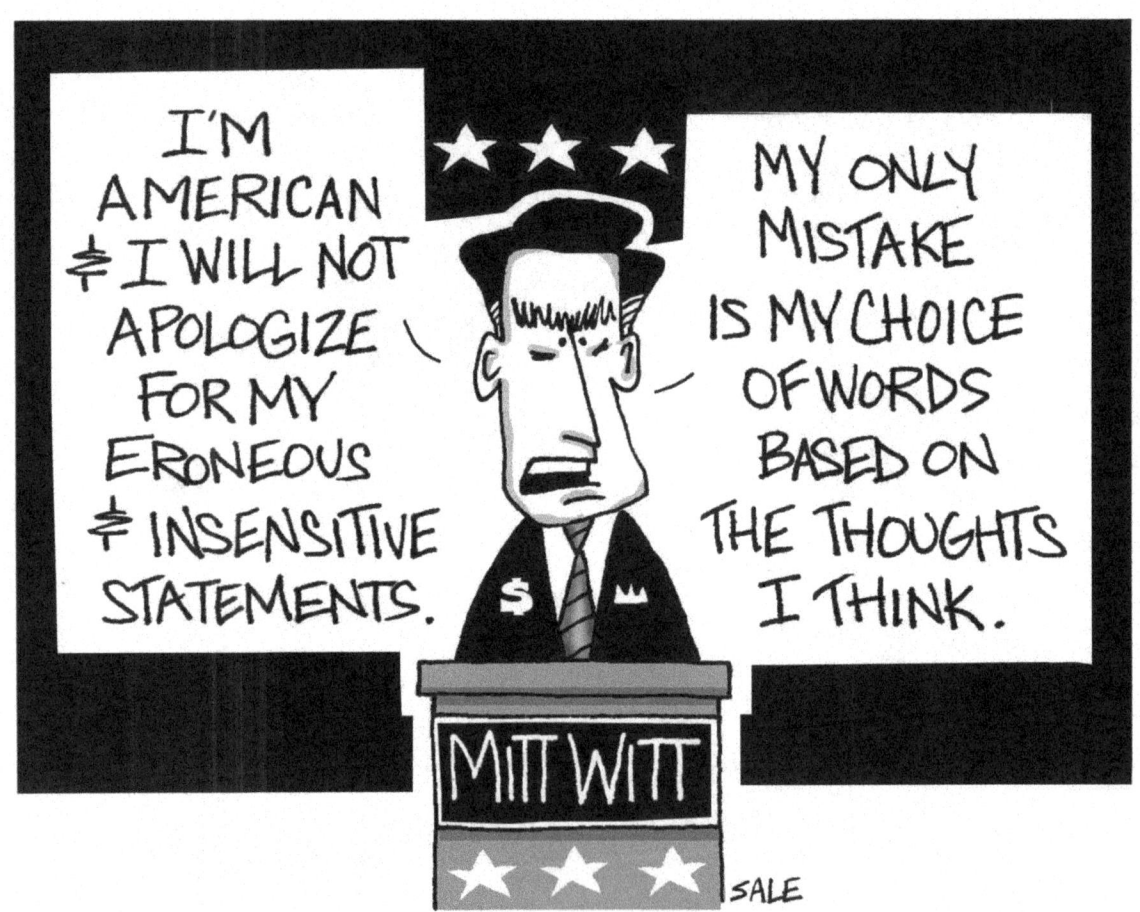

170

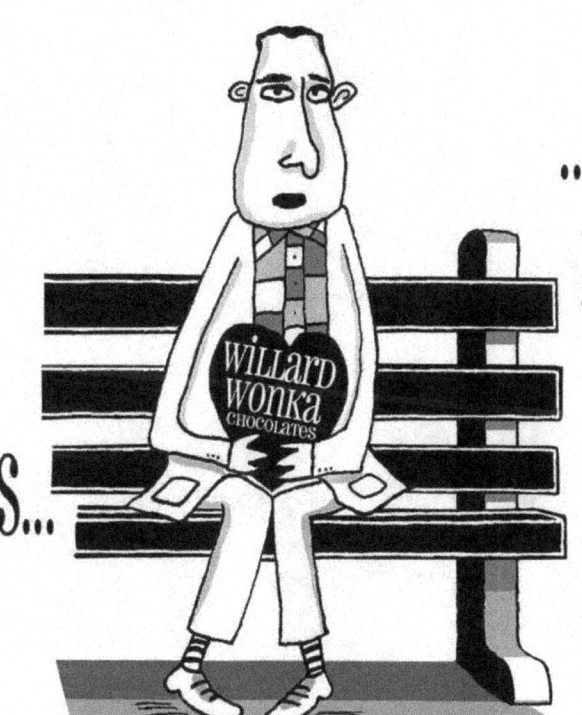

MaMa SaYS, MR. ROMNEY iS LiKE a BOX OF CHOCOLaTES...

... YOU NEVER KNOW WHAT YOU'LL GET.

171

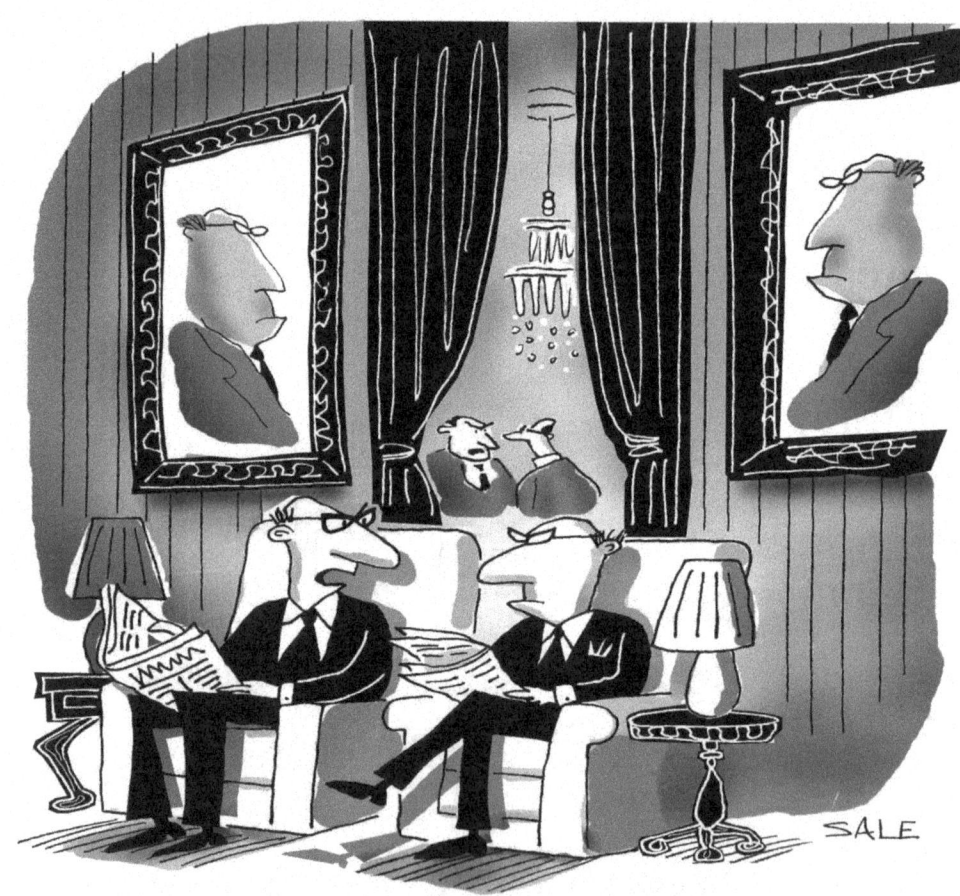

"It's finally happend...Romney has taken so many different positions
he just came out against himself."

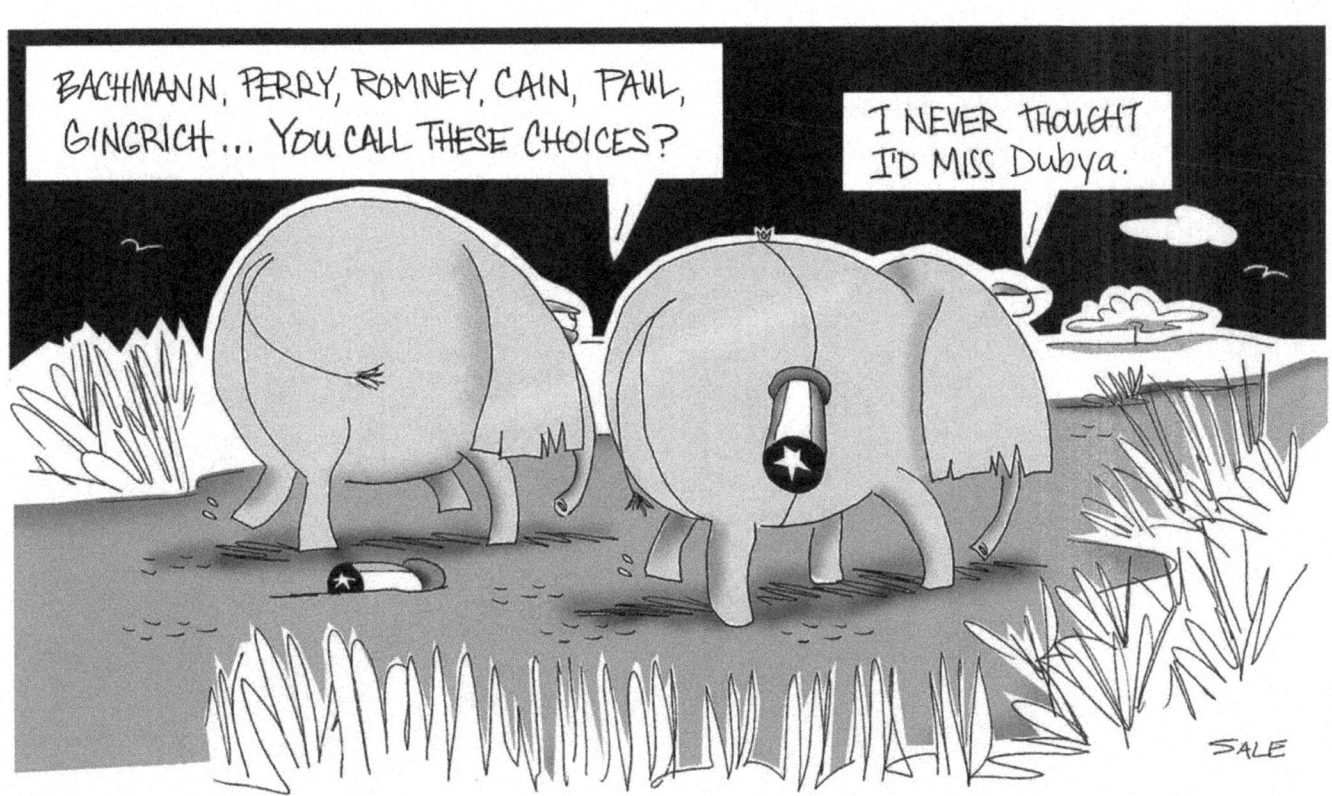

173

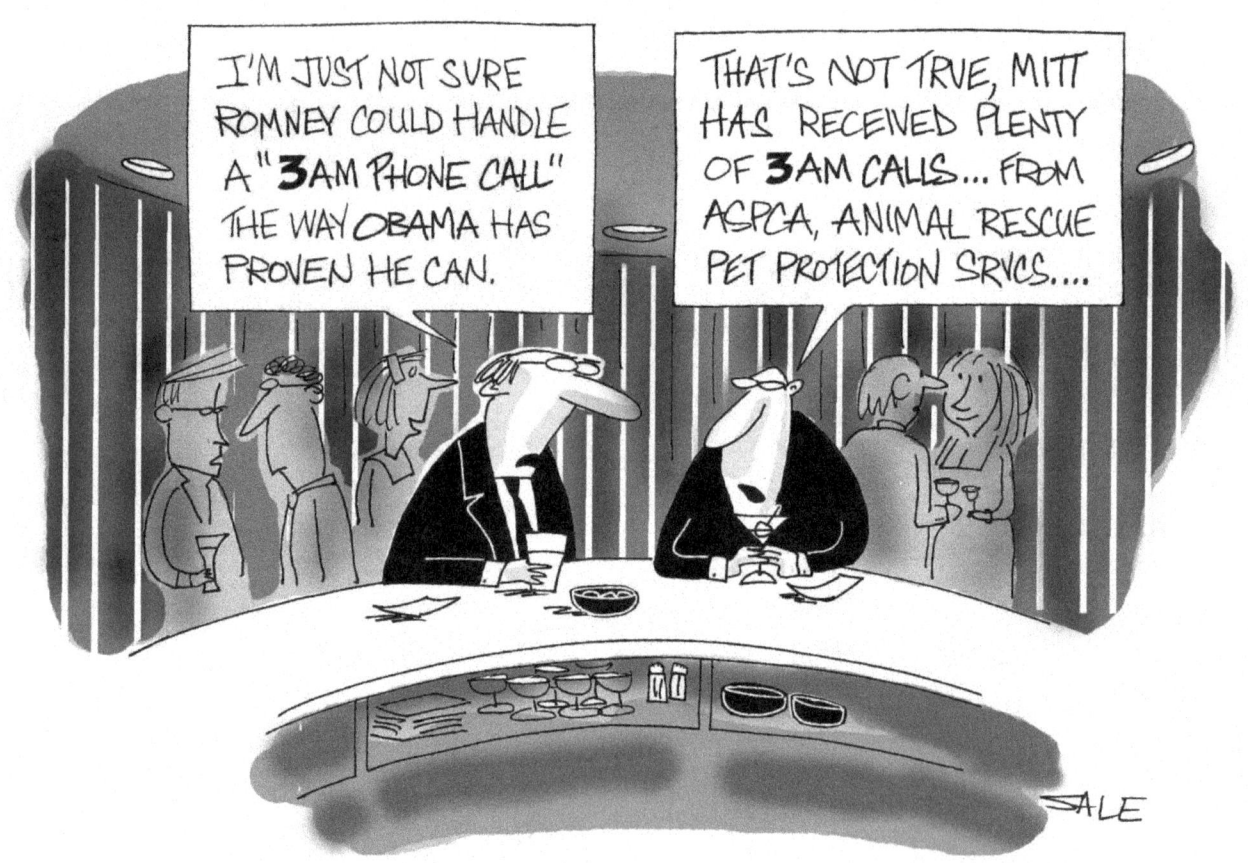

174

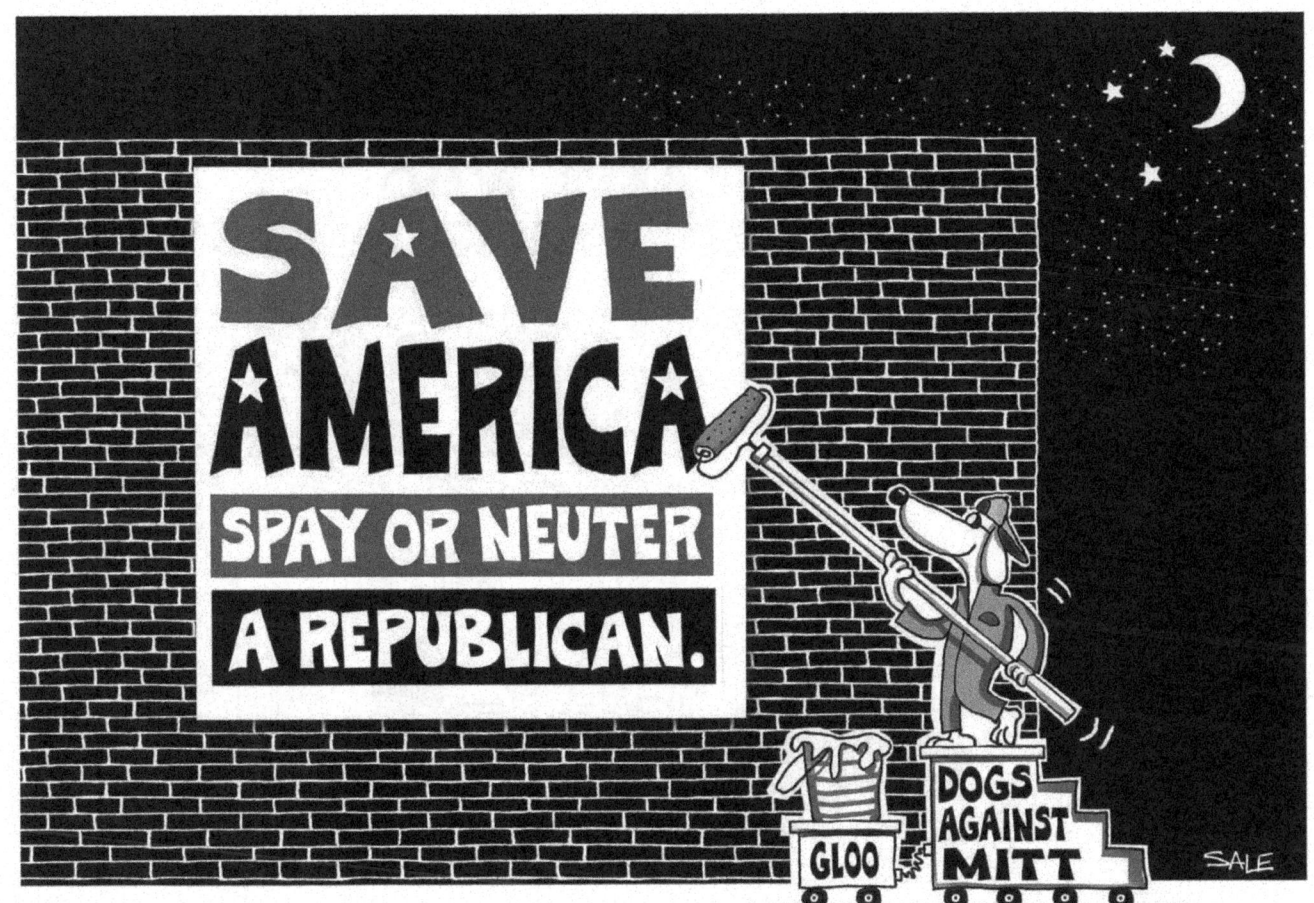

THIS AD IS APPROVED BY **DAM**, DOGS AGAINST MITT.

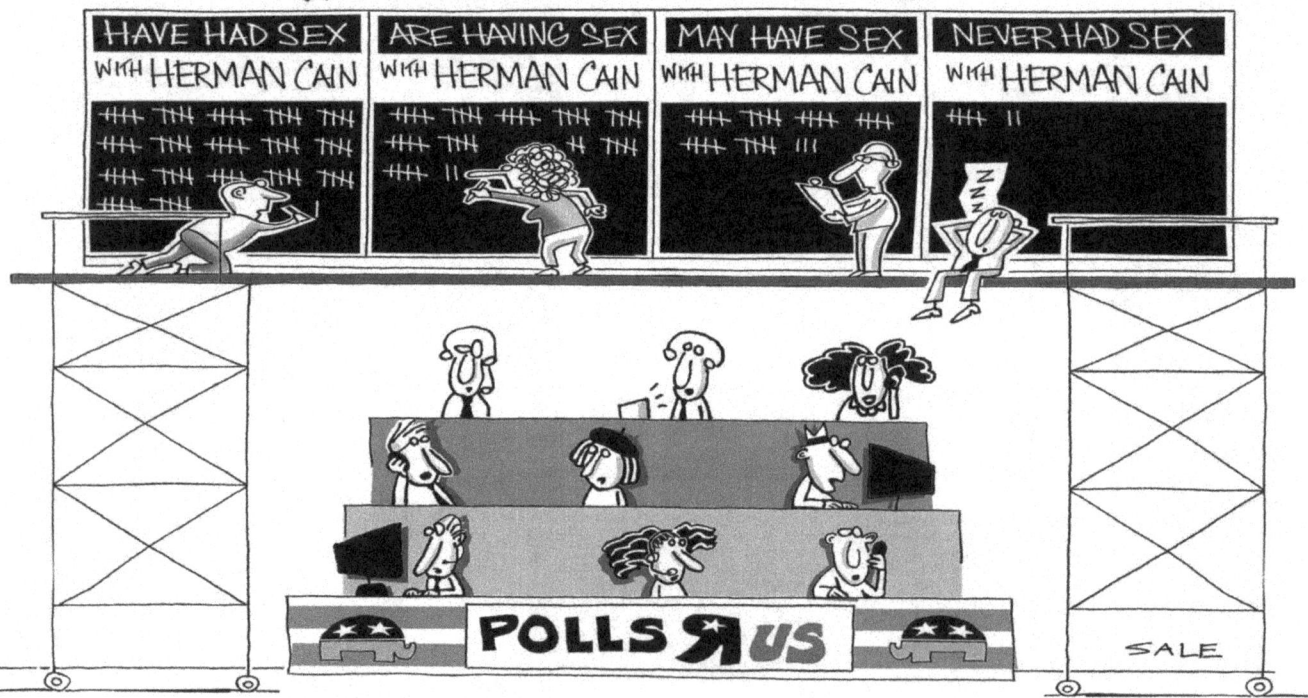

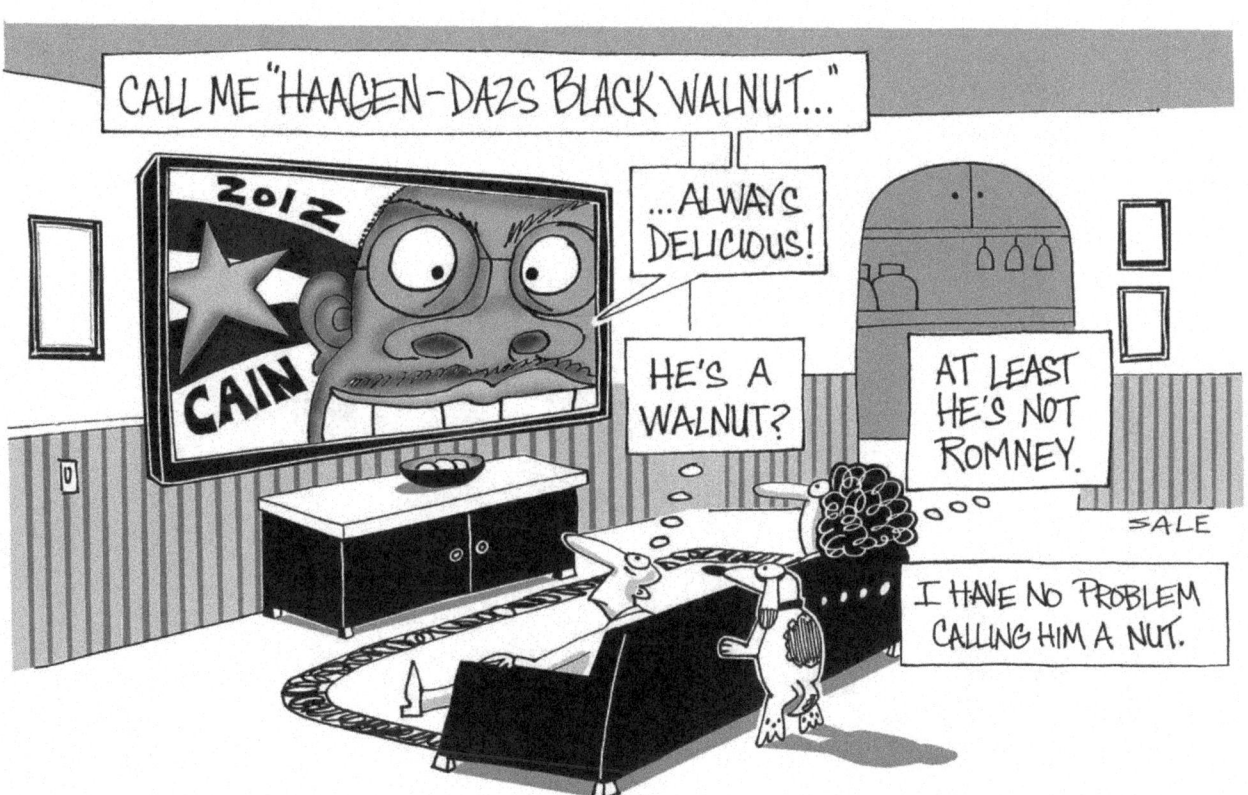

177

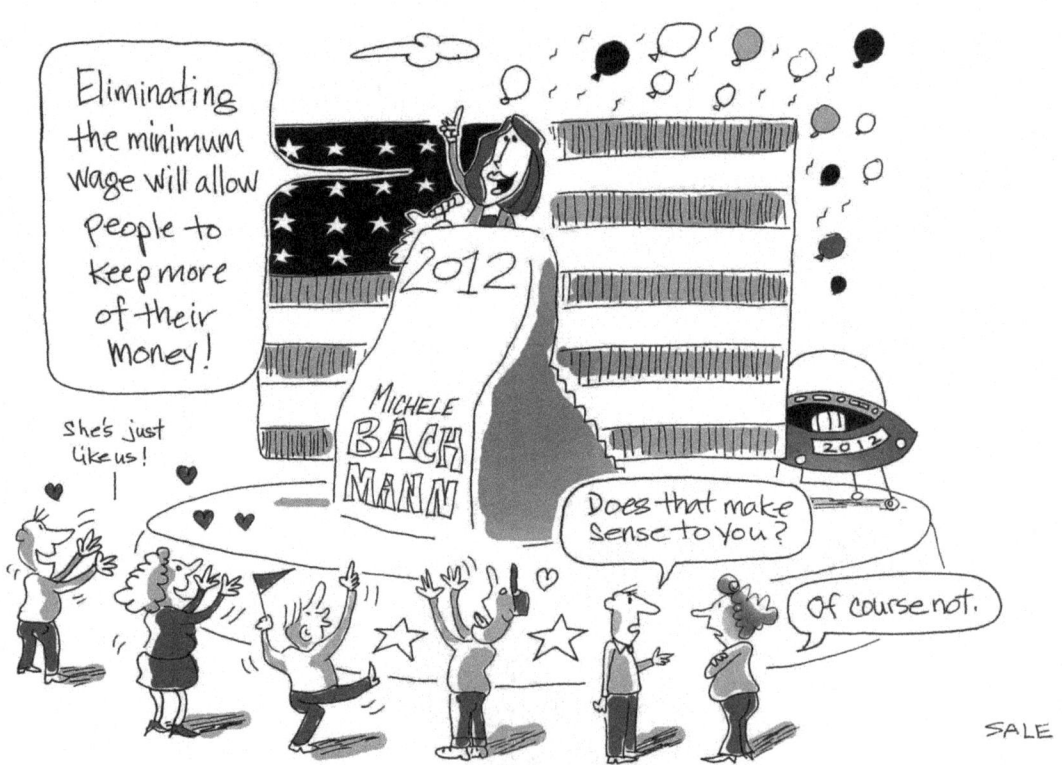

Hero of the stupid.

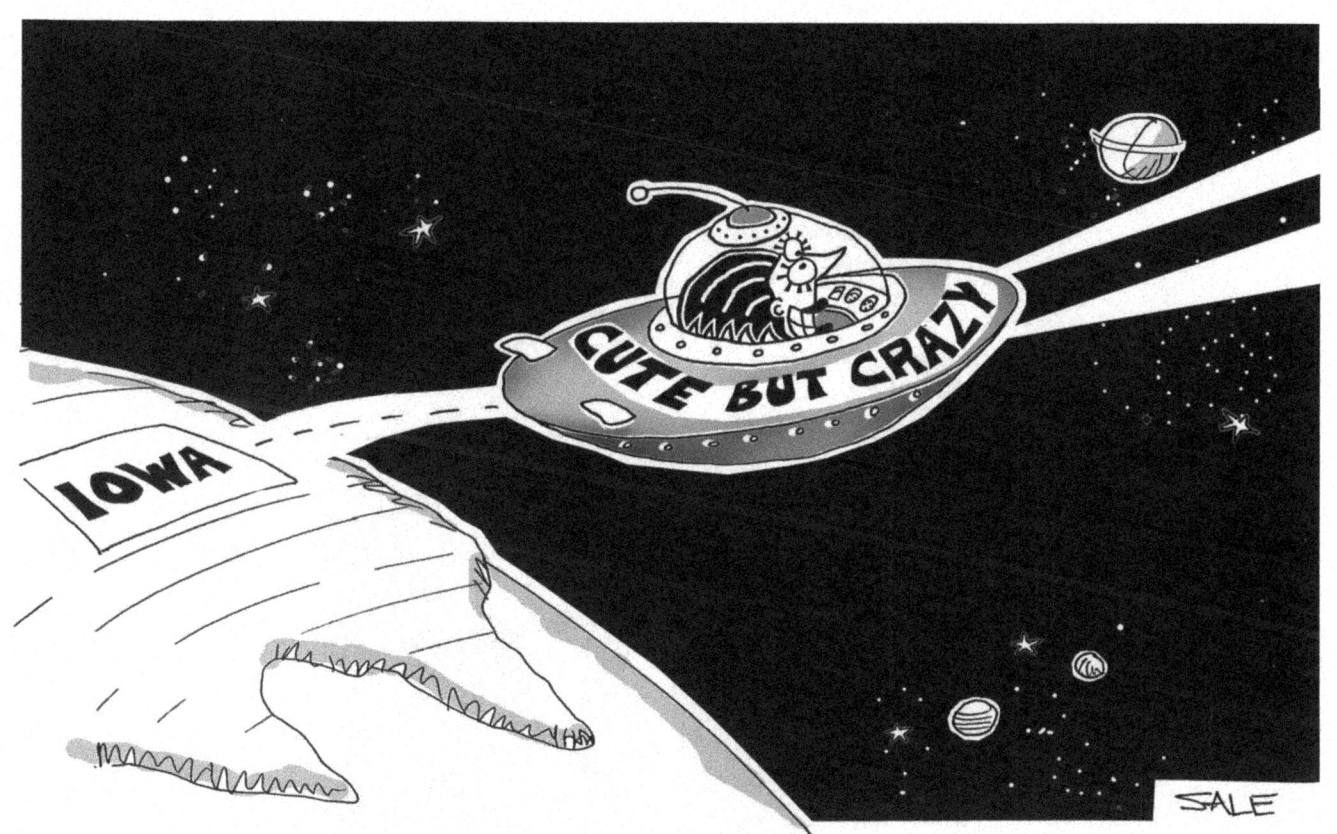

Michele Bachmann pulls out of the race after voters make it clear you can actually be too crazy even for a party who rejects science.

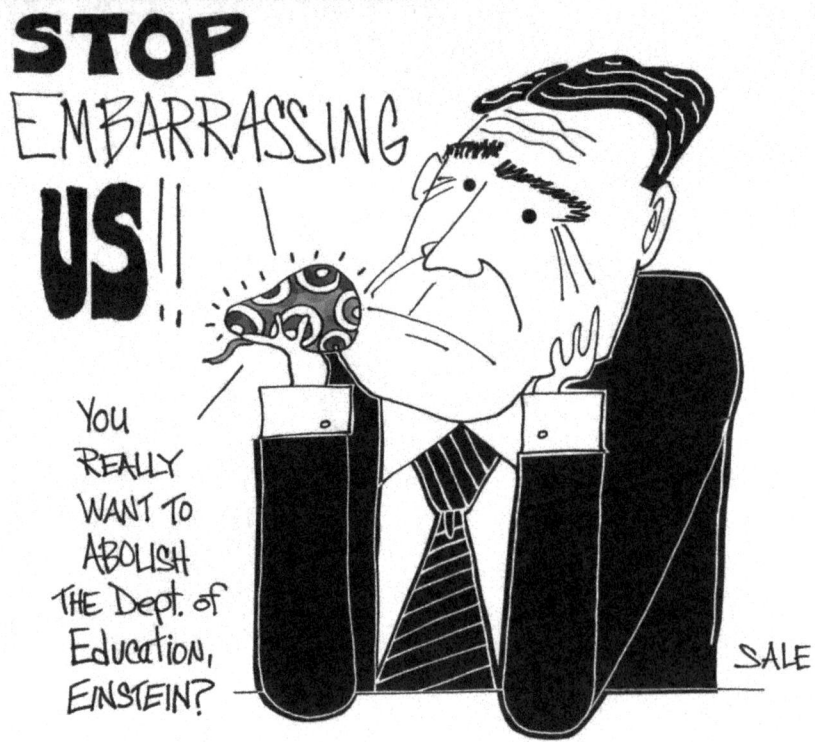

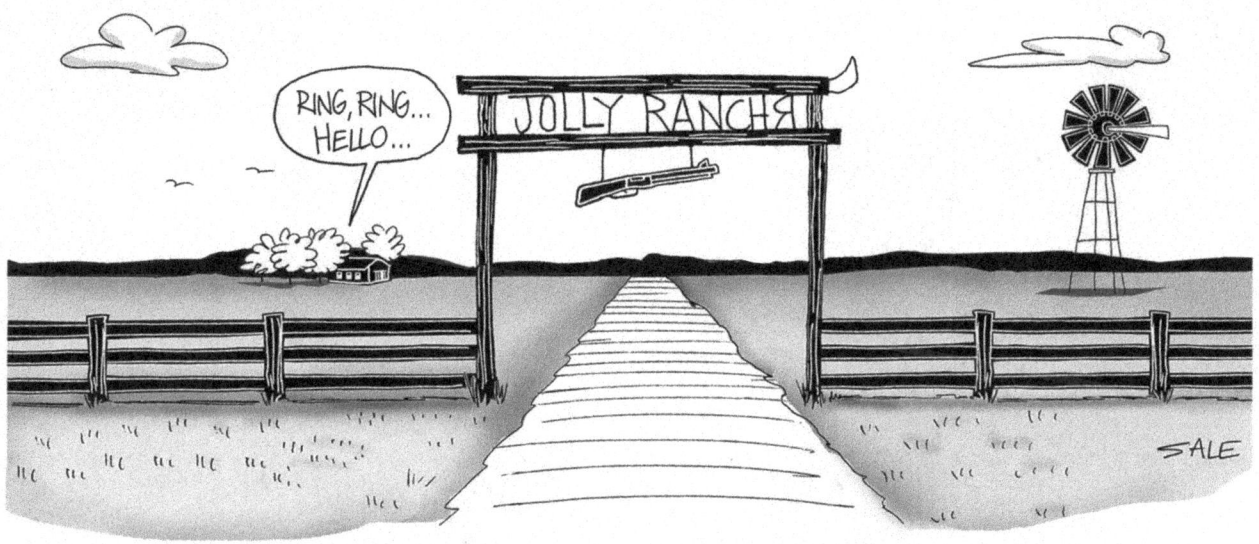

"By now you realize our Ricky is a child-like nincompoop. But, it isn't his fault. We let him watch TV while doing his homework and eat candy for dinner. Please tell him he can be president of Texas and send him home."

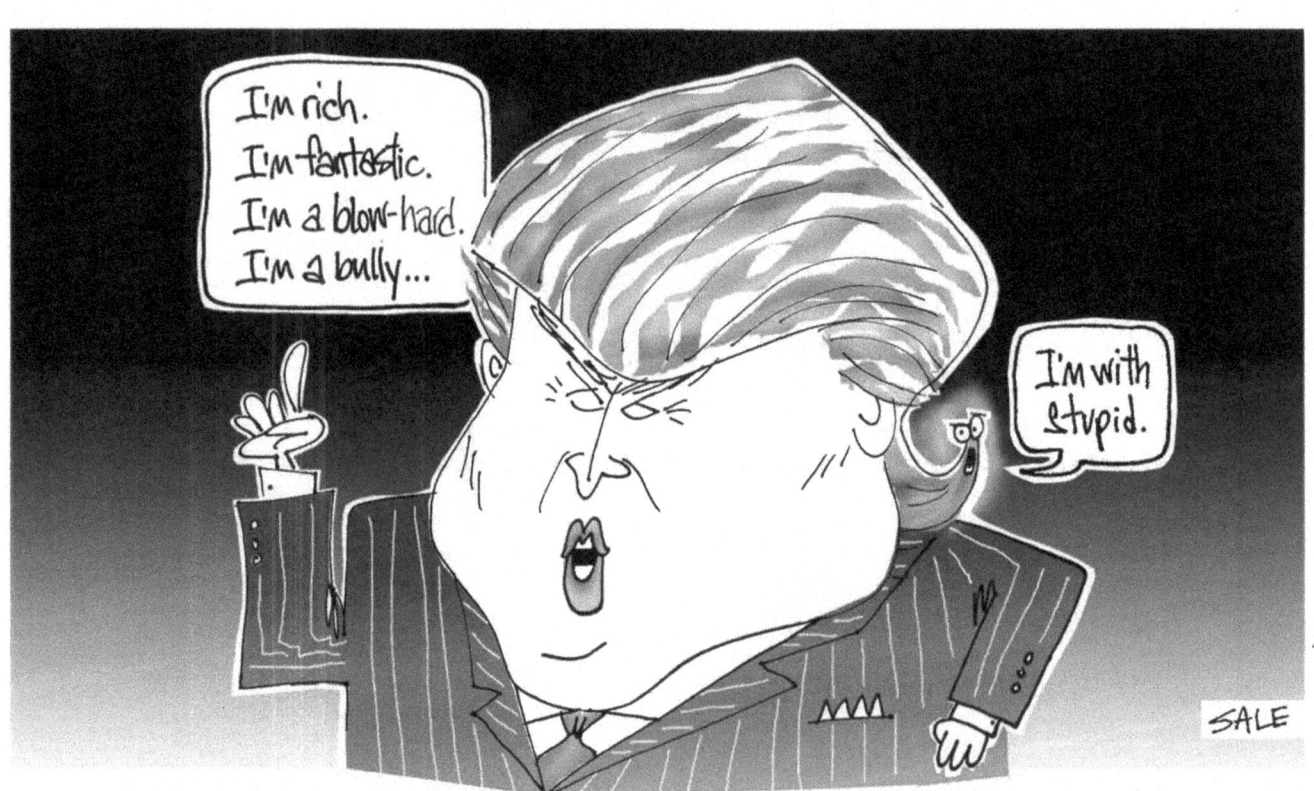

All Trumped up with no place to go.

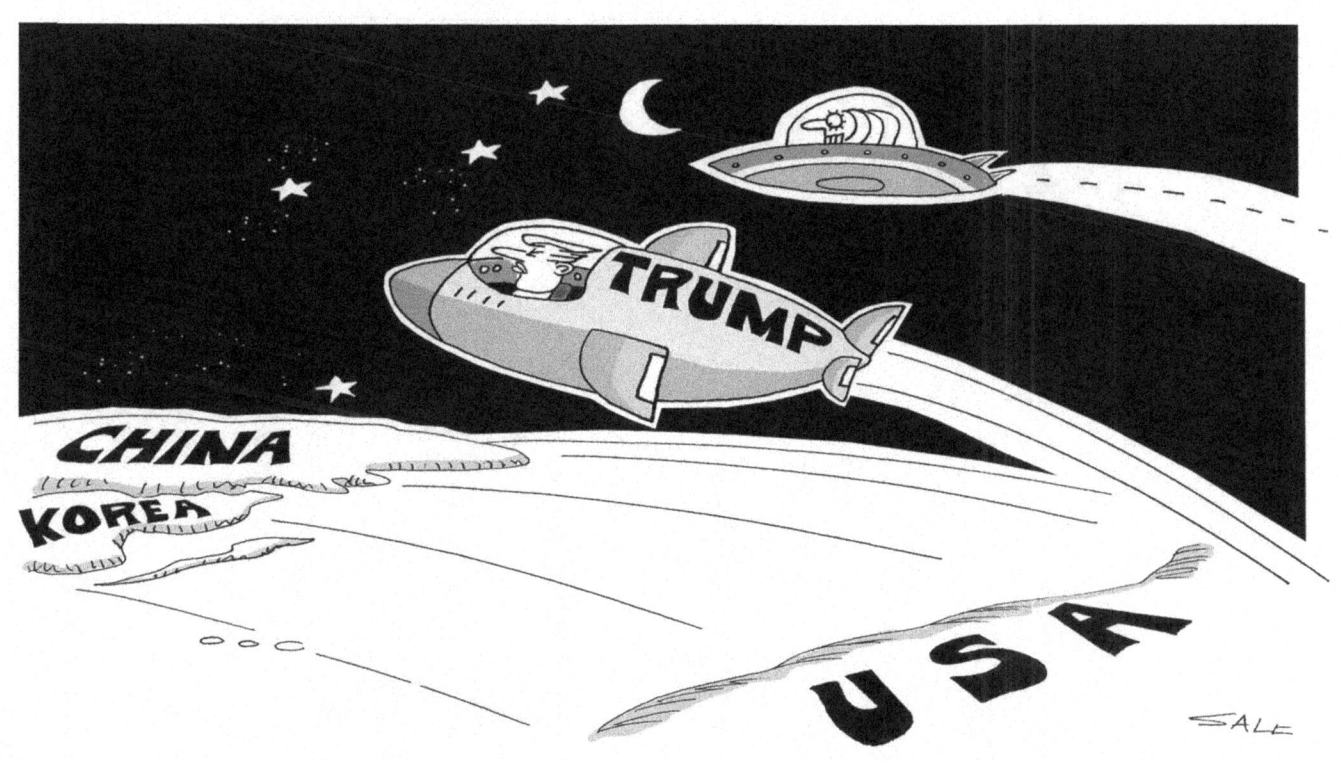

Upon learning of Kim Jong Il's death, Donald Trump and Michele Bachmann immediately left for North Korea announcing their candidacies for dear supreme leader declaring, "They like crazy? We invented crazy!"

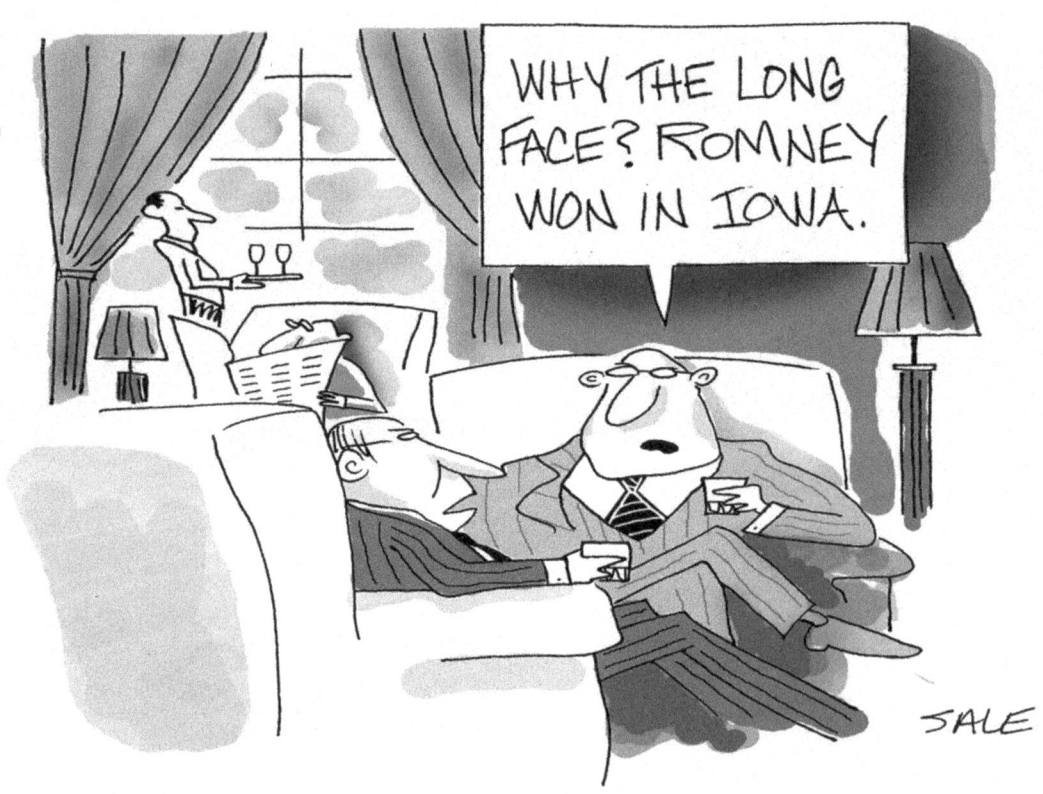

"True, but it took him four years and millions of dollars to beat Santorum, a war mongering, religious nut job, who polls in the single digits — by eight votes. Woo-hoo."

A foolish parent violates President Santorum's, "All Thou Needest to Know and Nothing More," home schooling curriculum by demonstrating a science experiment.

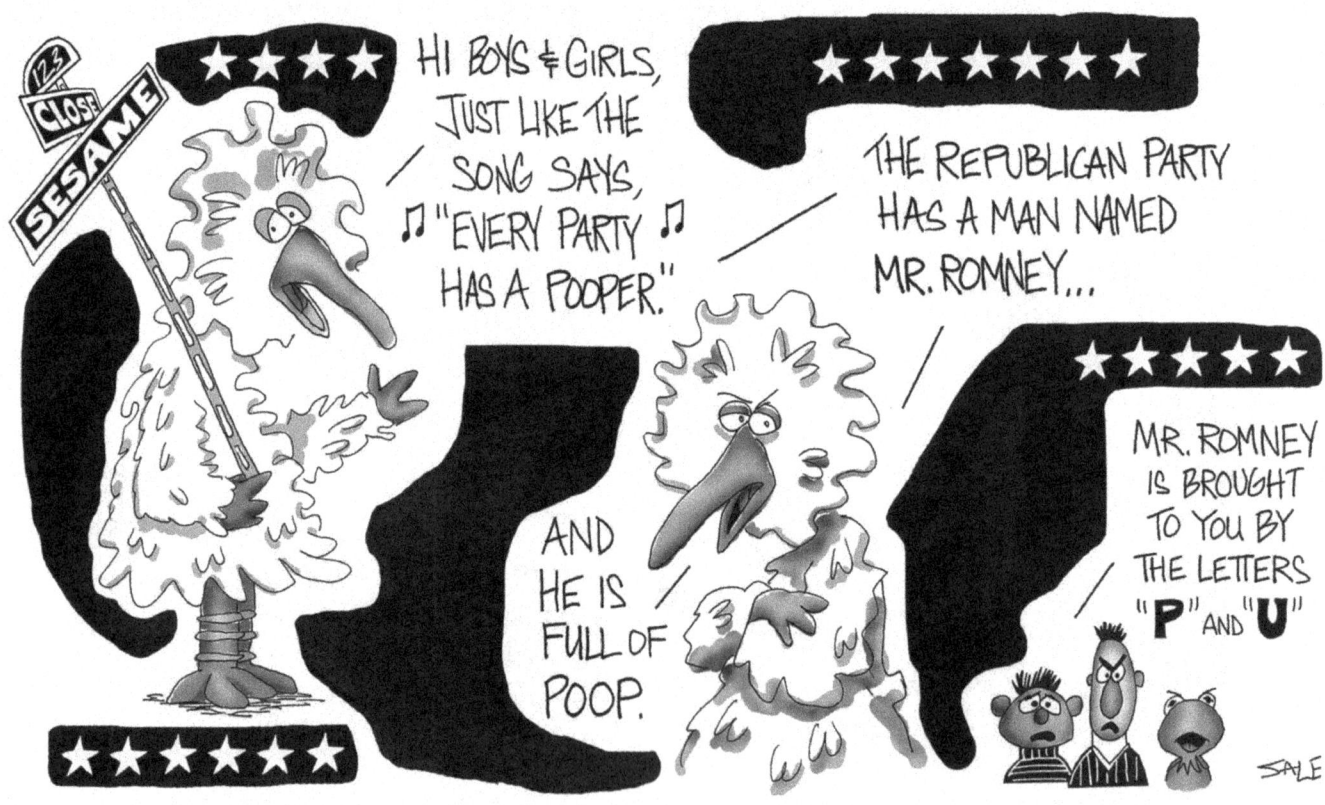

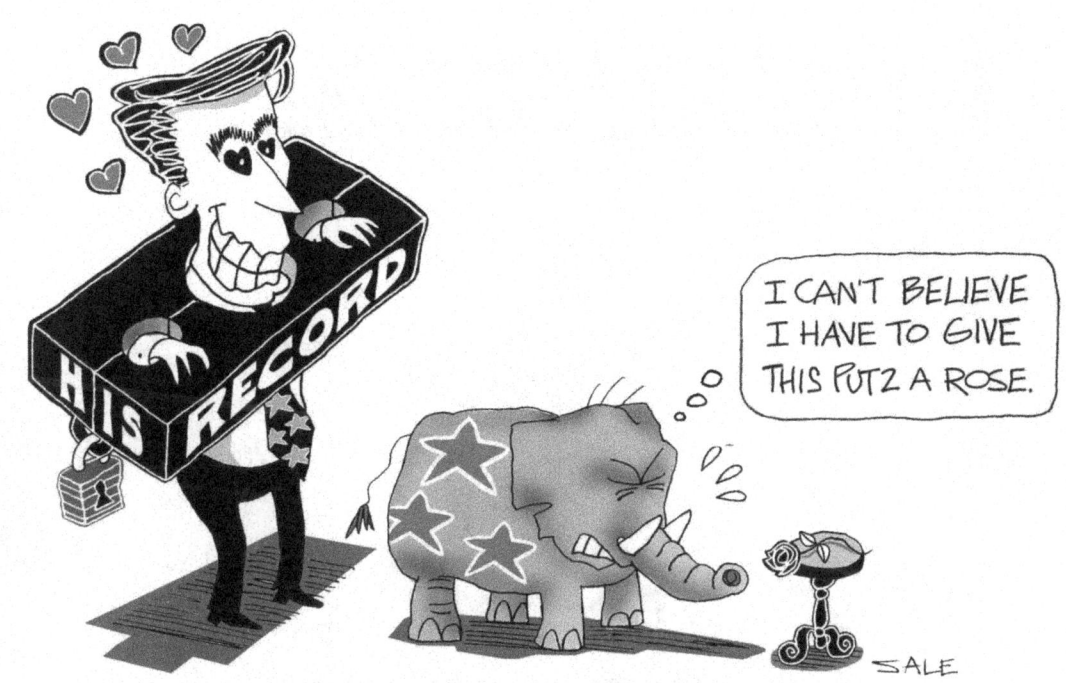

THE TROUBLE WITH MITT.

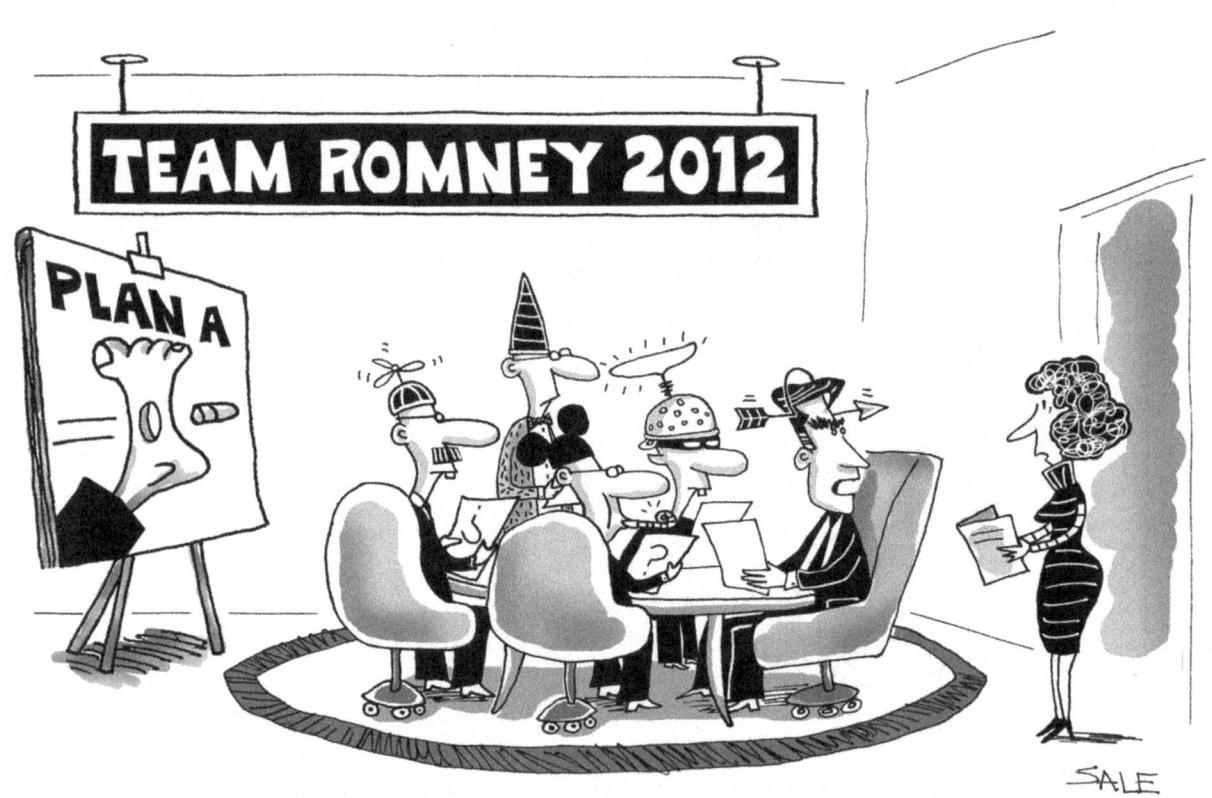

"Not now, Miss Krugerrand. Can't you see we're strategizing?"

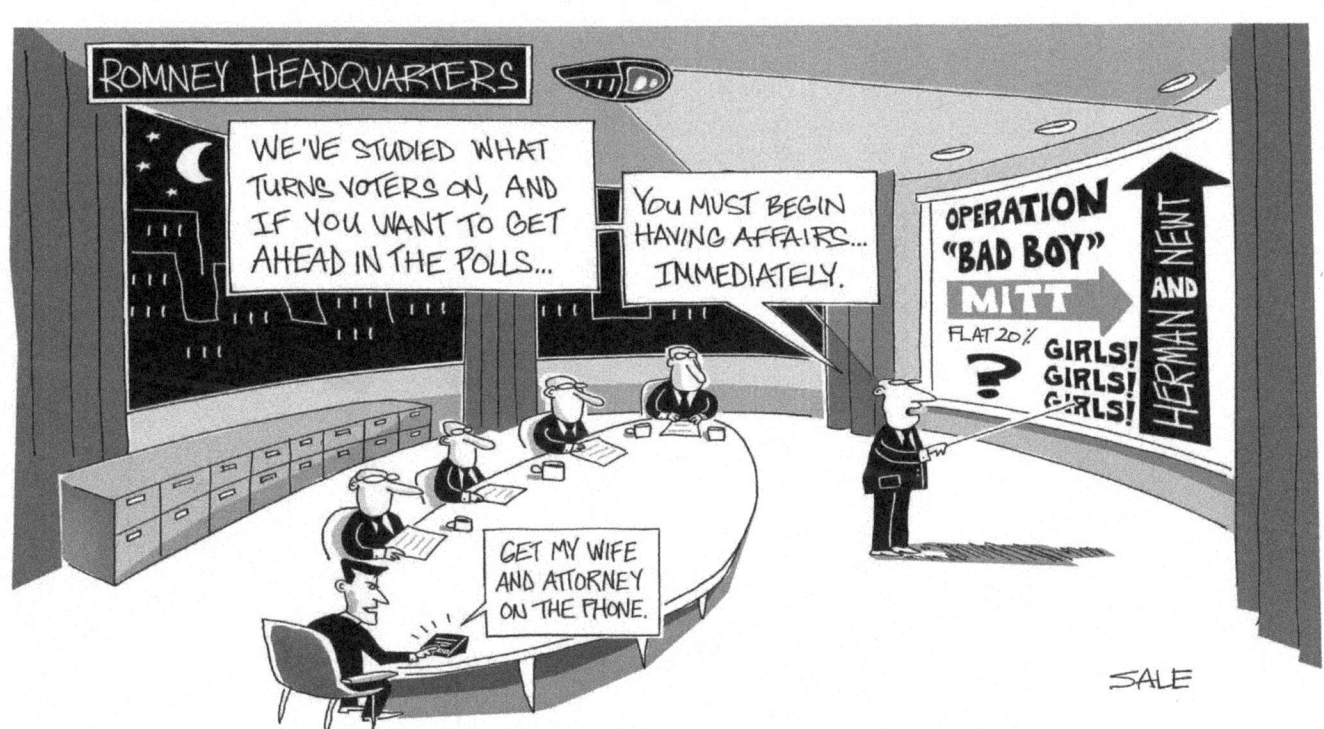

REPUBLICANS & FOX NEWS EXPLAIN MITT'S POOR POLLS.

POLLS ARE JUST A BUNCH OF STATISTICS.

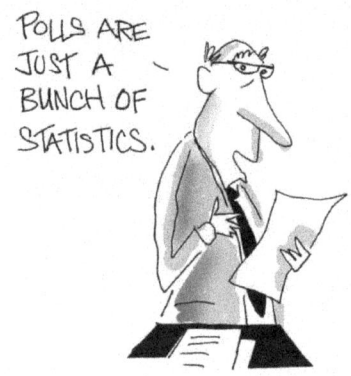

REFLECTING THE REALITY OF WHAT PEOPLE THINK. (SIGH...)

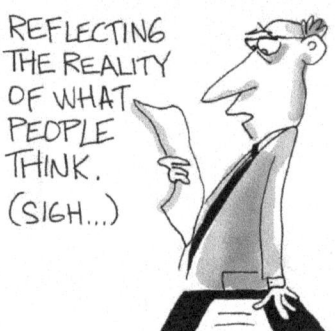

BUT, STATISTICS ARE BASED ON <u>MATH</u>...

WHICH IS PRACTICALLY <u>SCIENCE</u>!

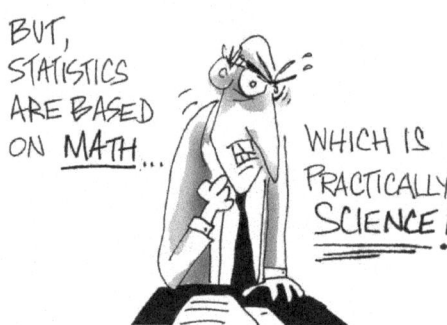

THEREFORE, POLLS ARE A <u>HOAX</u>.

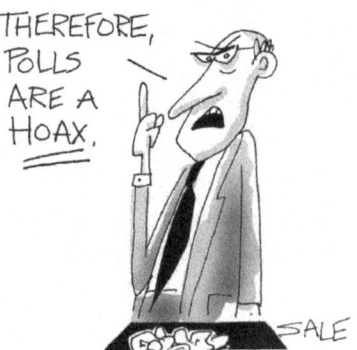

SALE

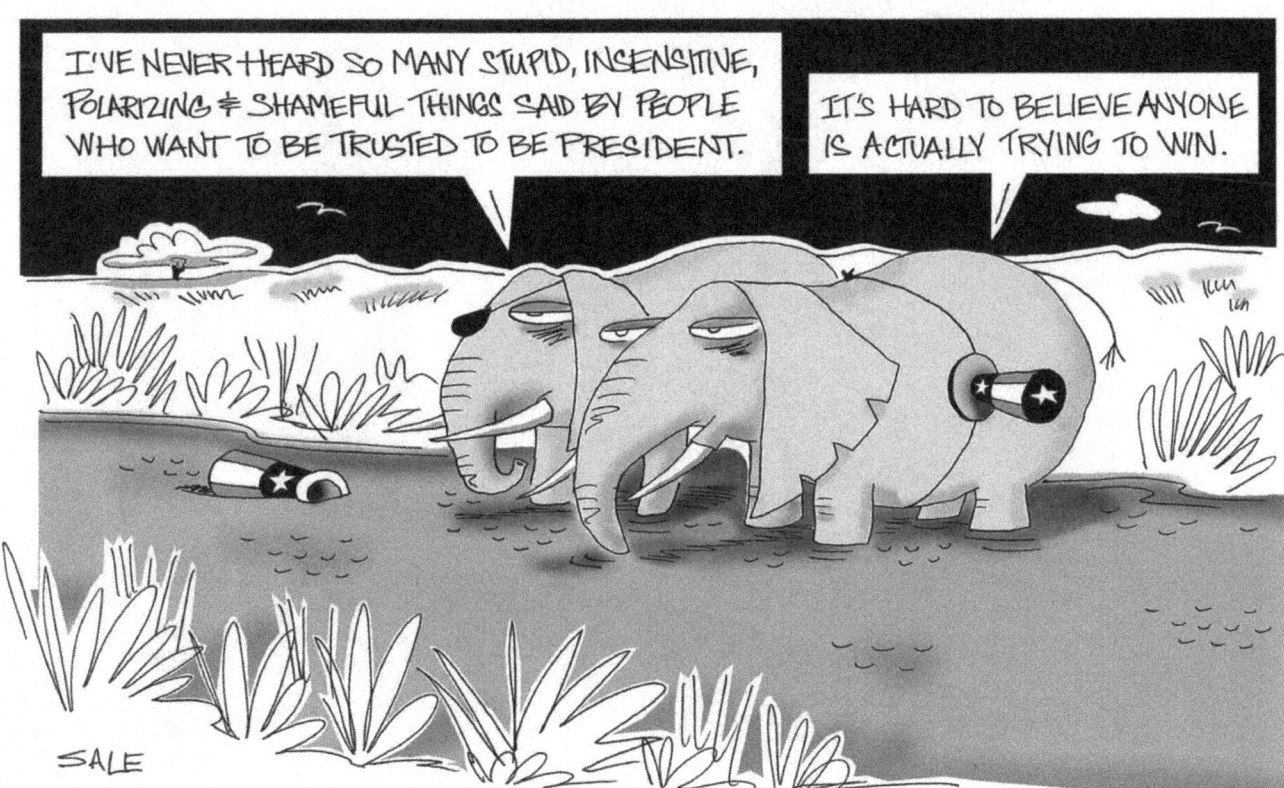

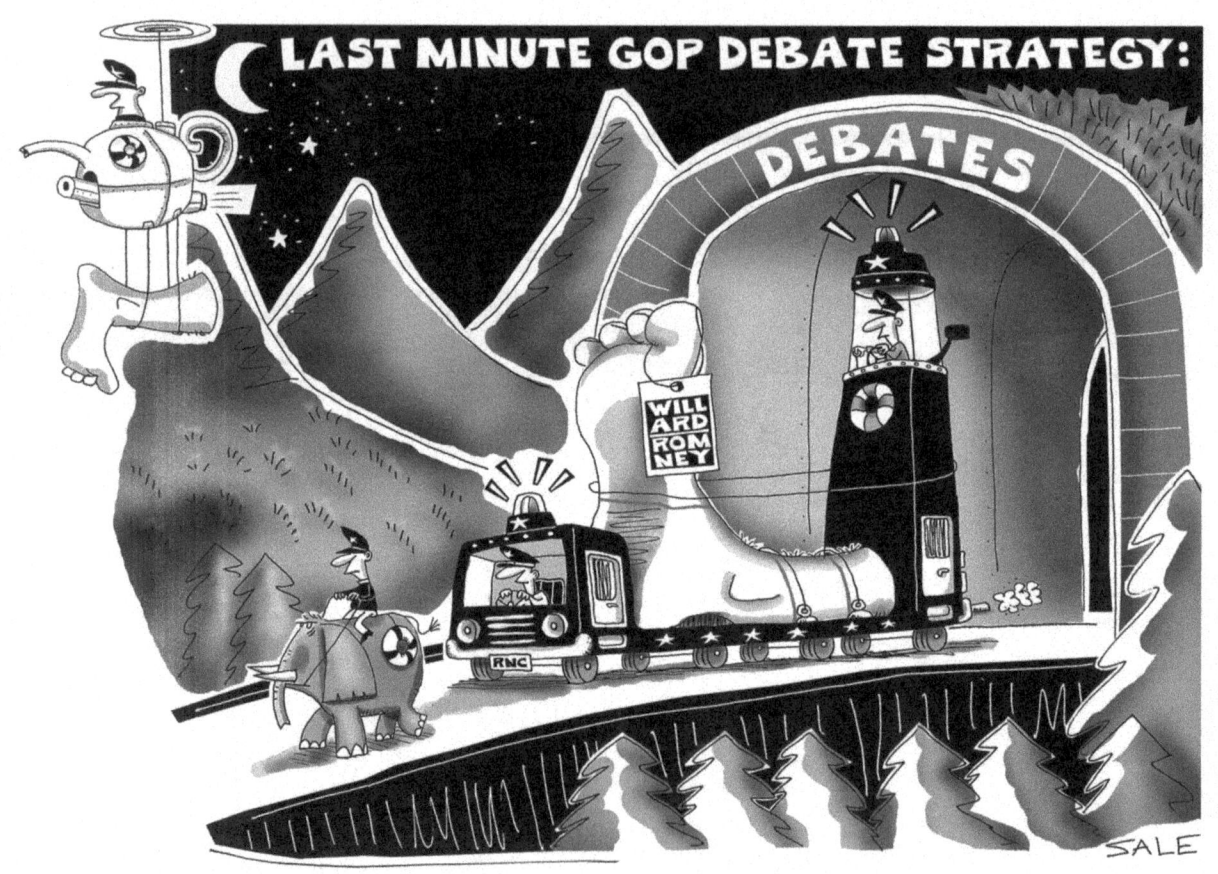

Mitt's feet are dispatched to separate locations to ensure they stay out of his mouth.

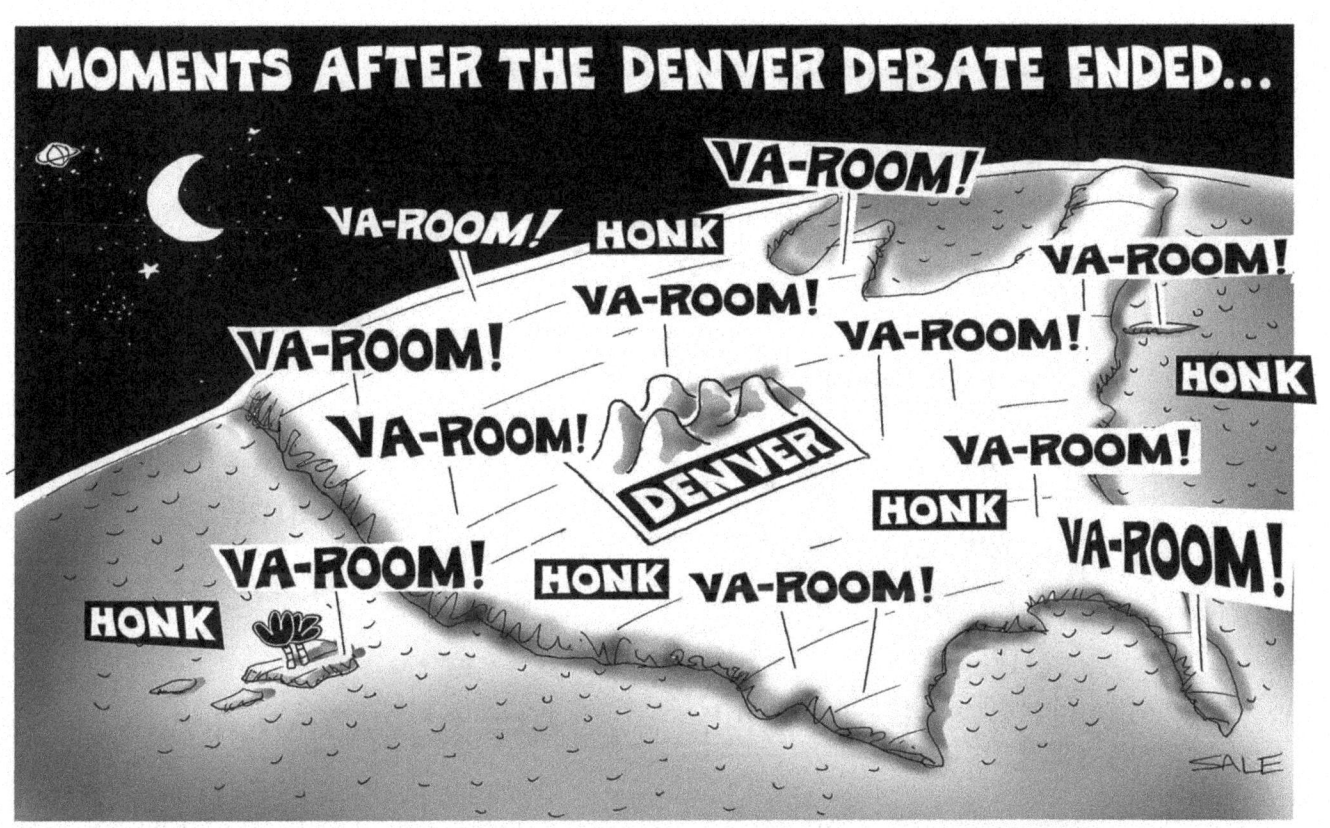

"Republicans across America could be heard restarting their clown cars."

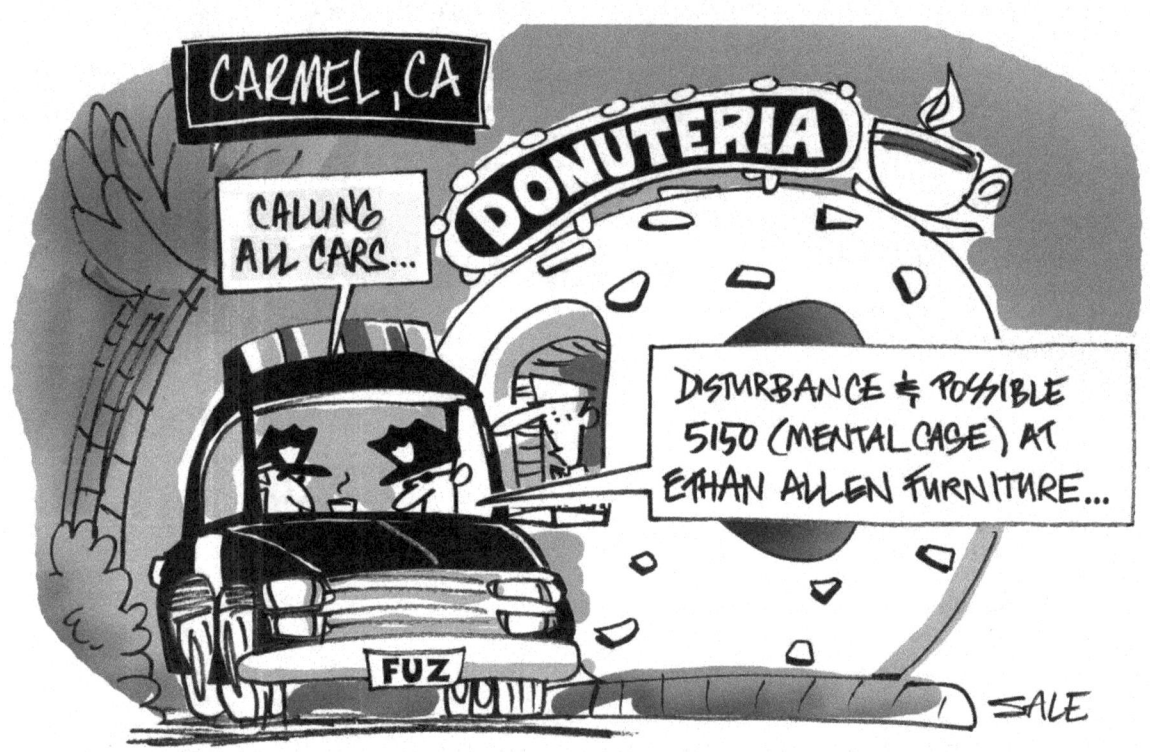

"*Former Mayor Eastwood is engaged in a confrontation with a dining room set and wicker patio arrangement. Advise bringing butterfly net.*"

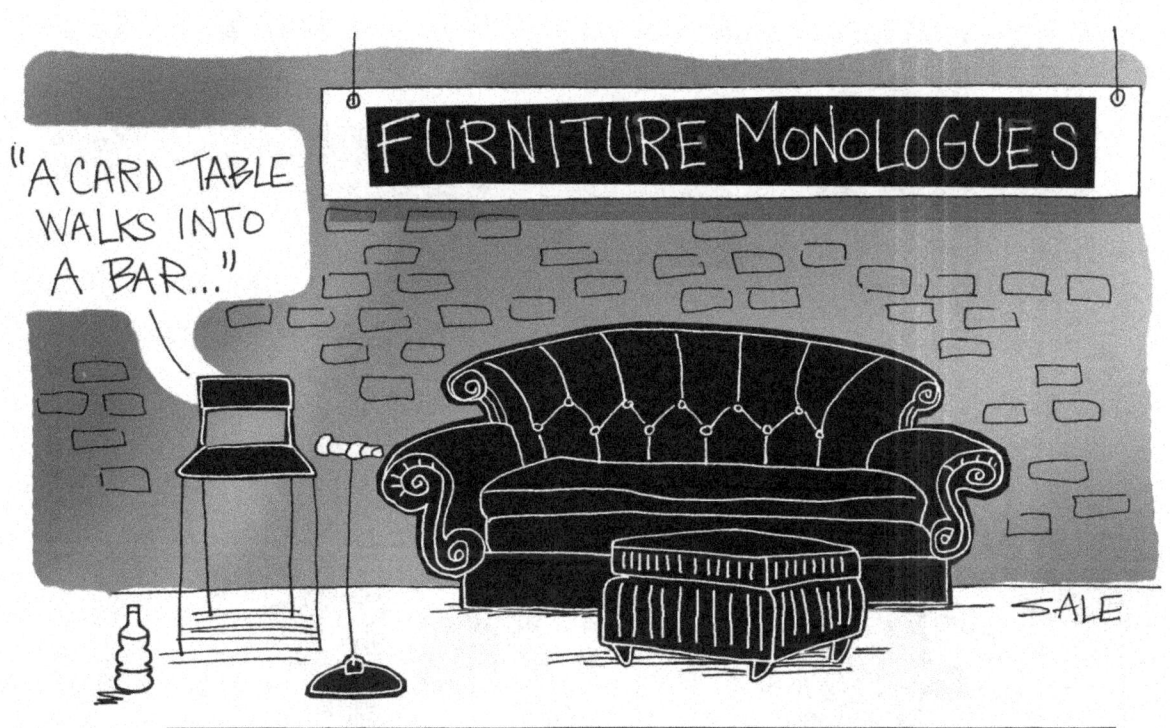

Starring: Clint Eastwood's Republican Convention chair,
Dick Van Dyke's ottoman and the sofa from Friends.
Spring 2013. Call Ticketmaster.

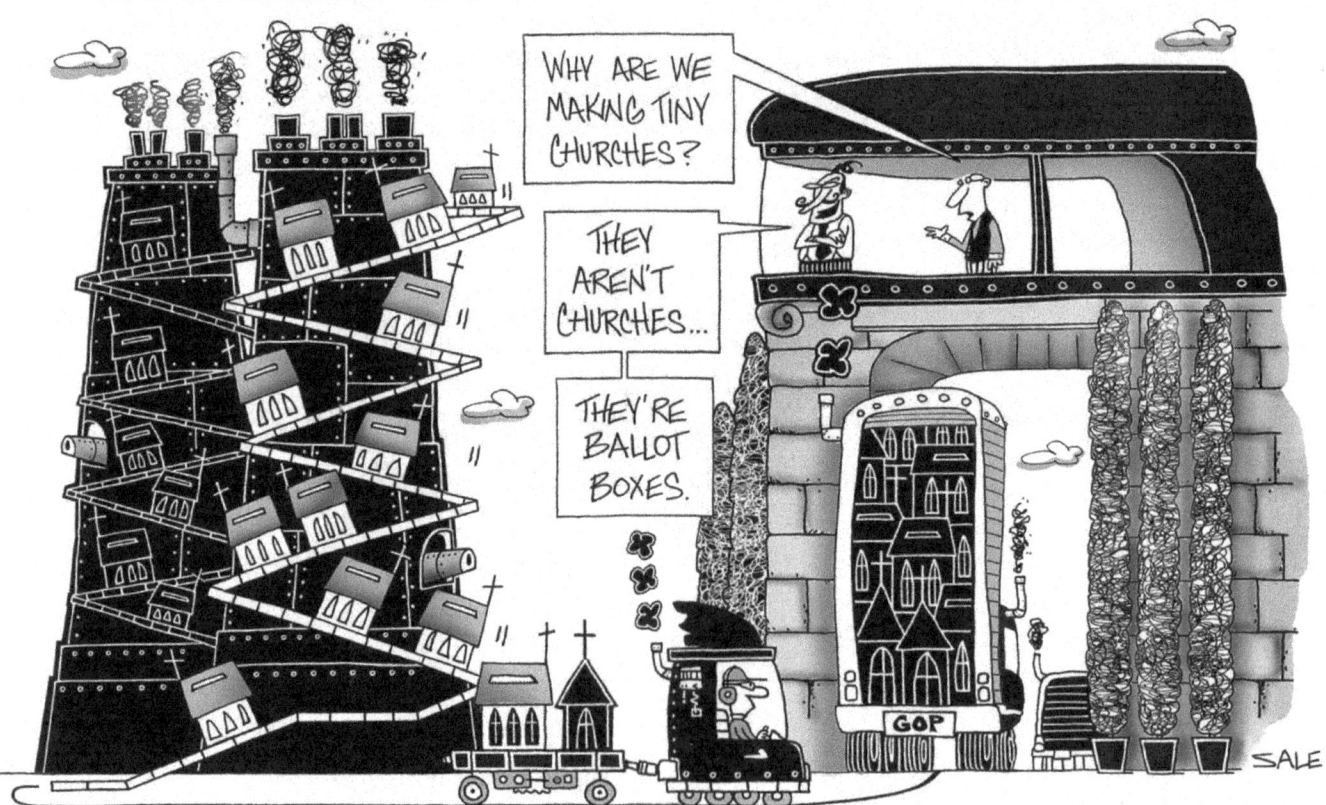

196

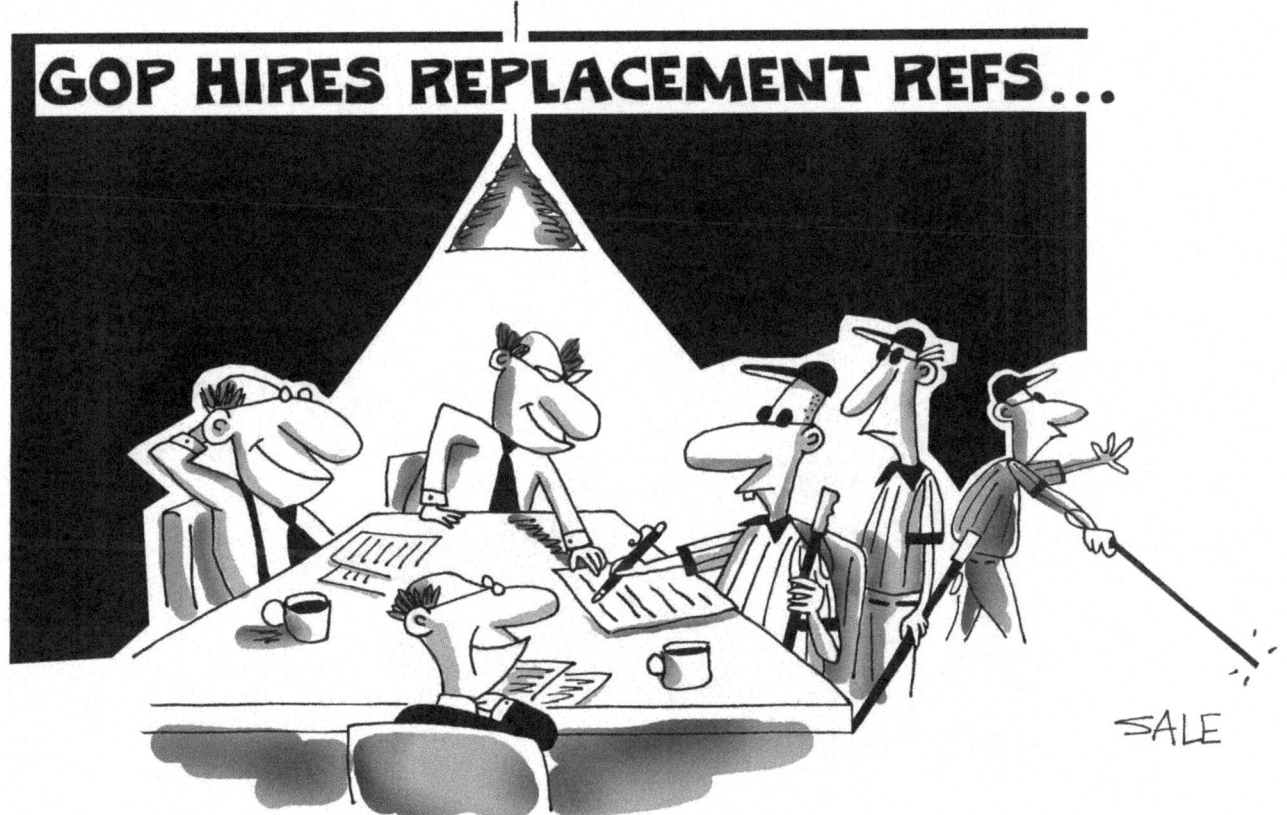

"To count ballots in swing states."

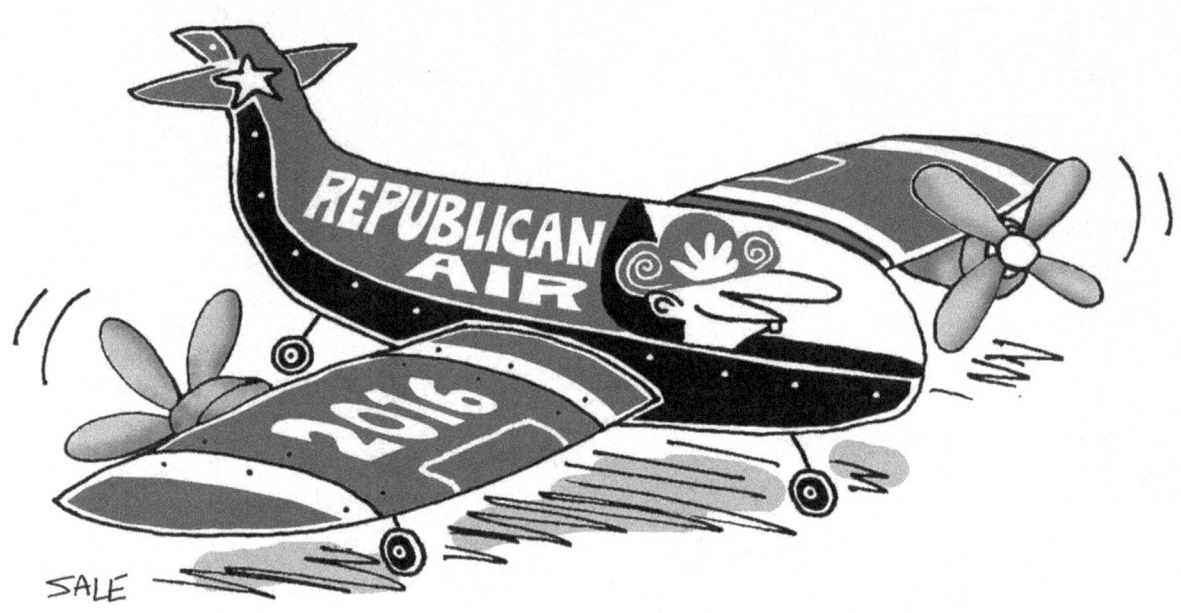

BONUS STUFF

ANATOMY OF A CARTOON

MEN IN HATS

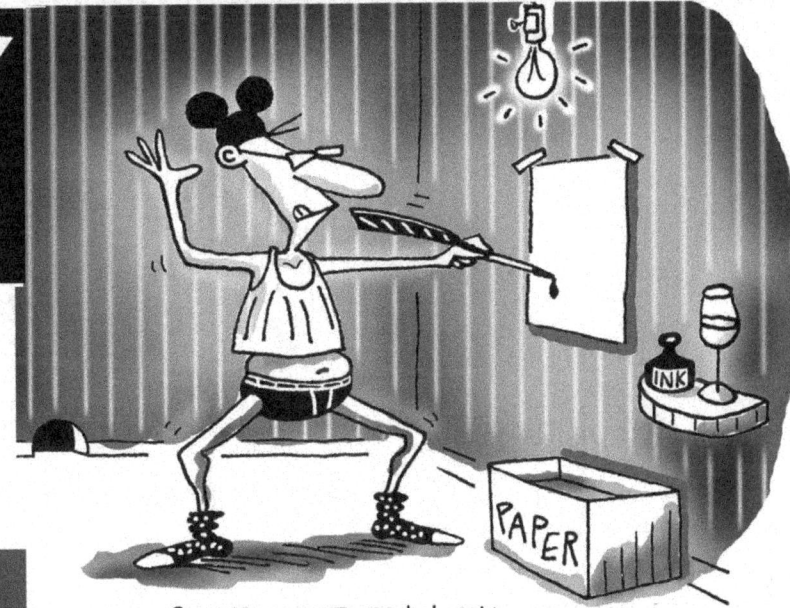

CARTOONIST AT WORK.

INK

PAPER

Anatomy of a Cartoon...

Have you ever wondered how an idea turns into a finished cartoon? Here are some of the key sketches that went into creating the "The Petroleum Club" cartoon.

1

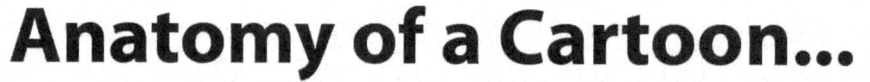

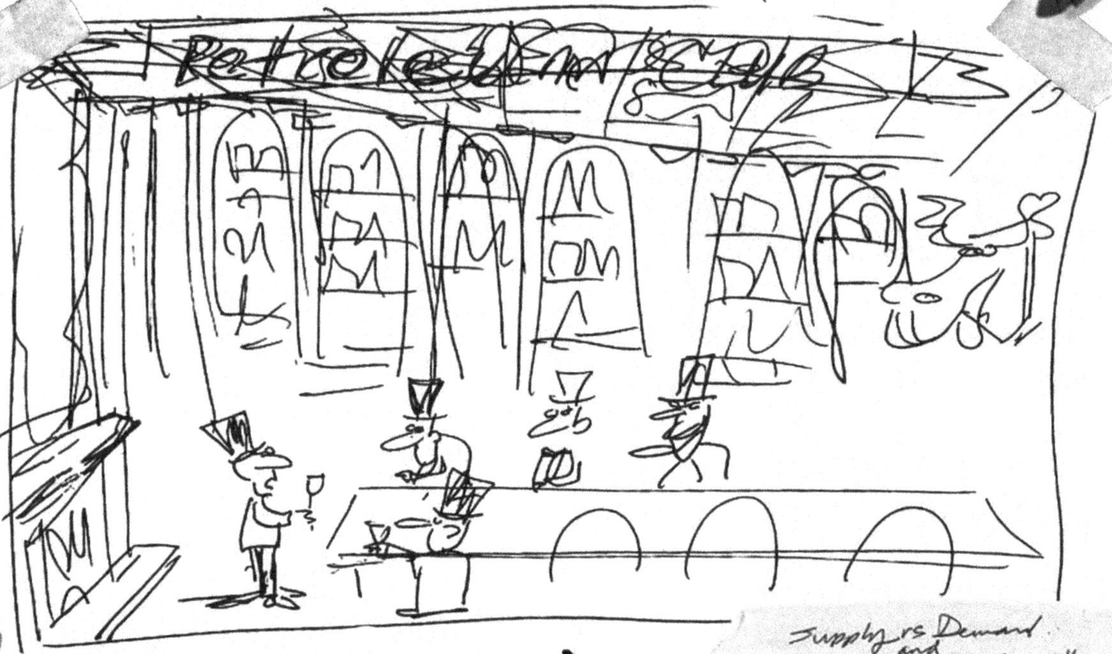

The original idea I jotted down.

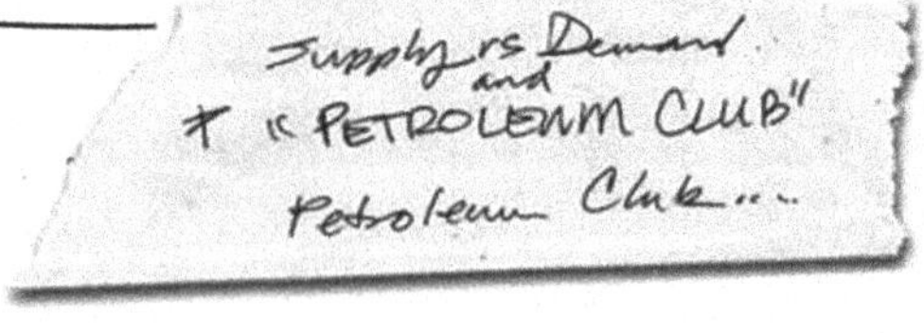

Supply vs Demand
and
× "PETROLEUM CLUB"

Petroleum Club...

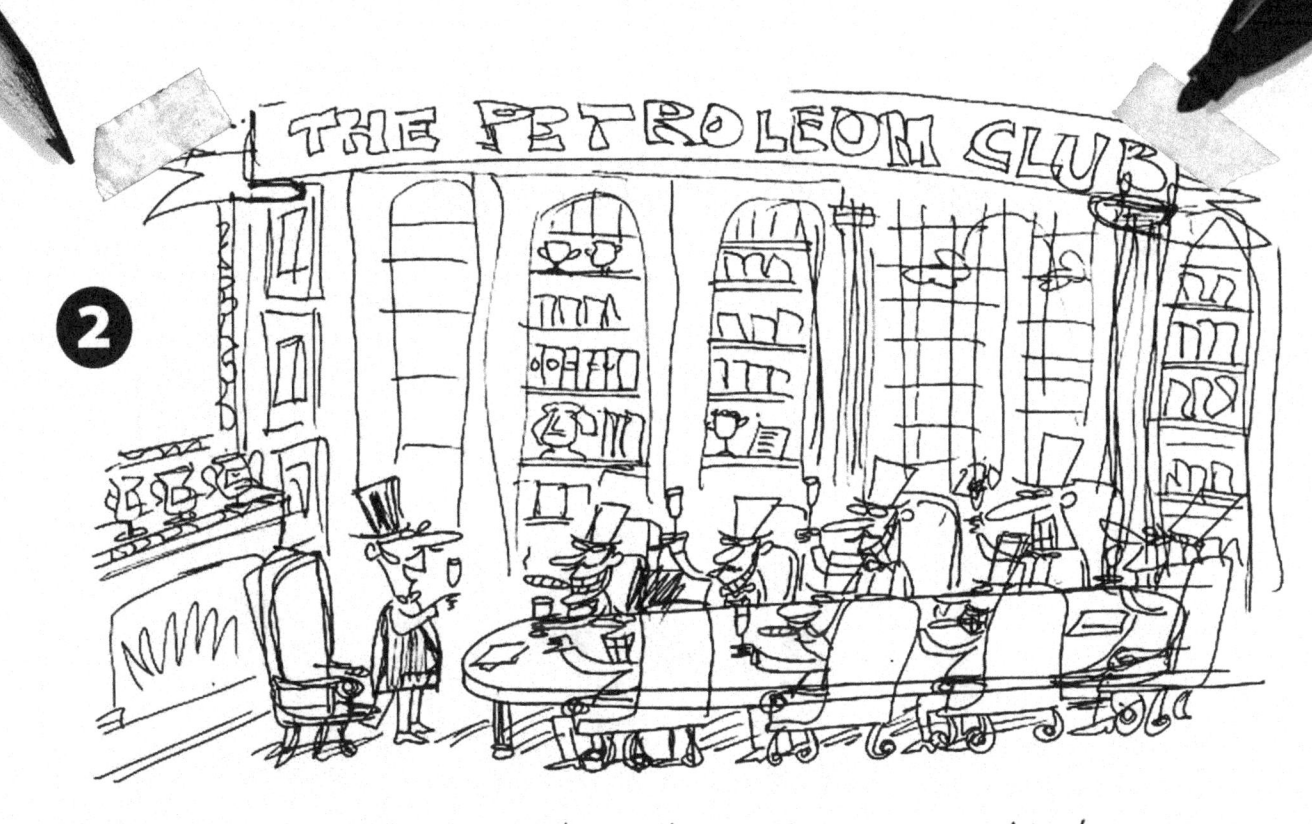

Gentlemen, I am pleased to announce that once again, inspite of a poor economy we show record-breaking profits, ...

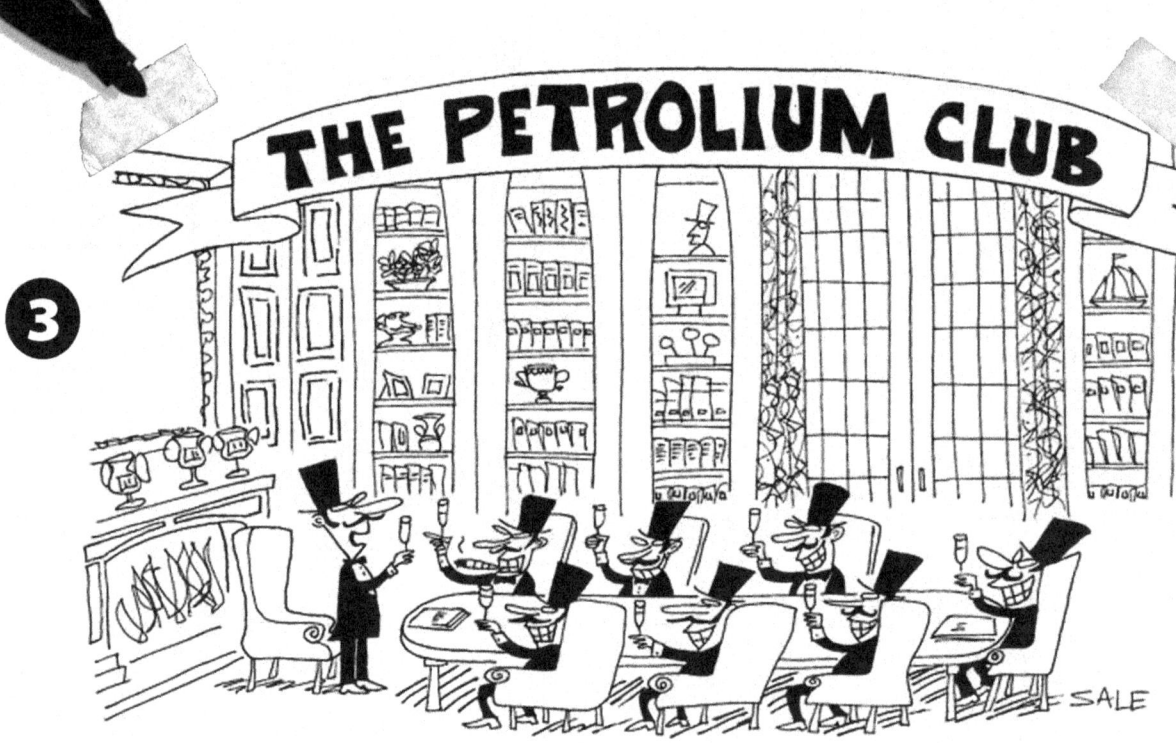

"Once again, despite a poor economy, we show record-breaking profits. So let us toast that wonderful law of supply and demand...."

Now it is time to add some gray tones...

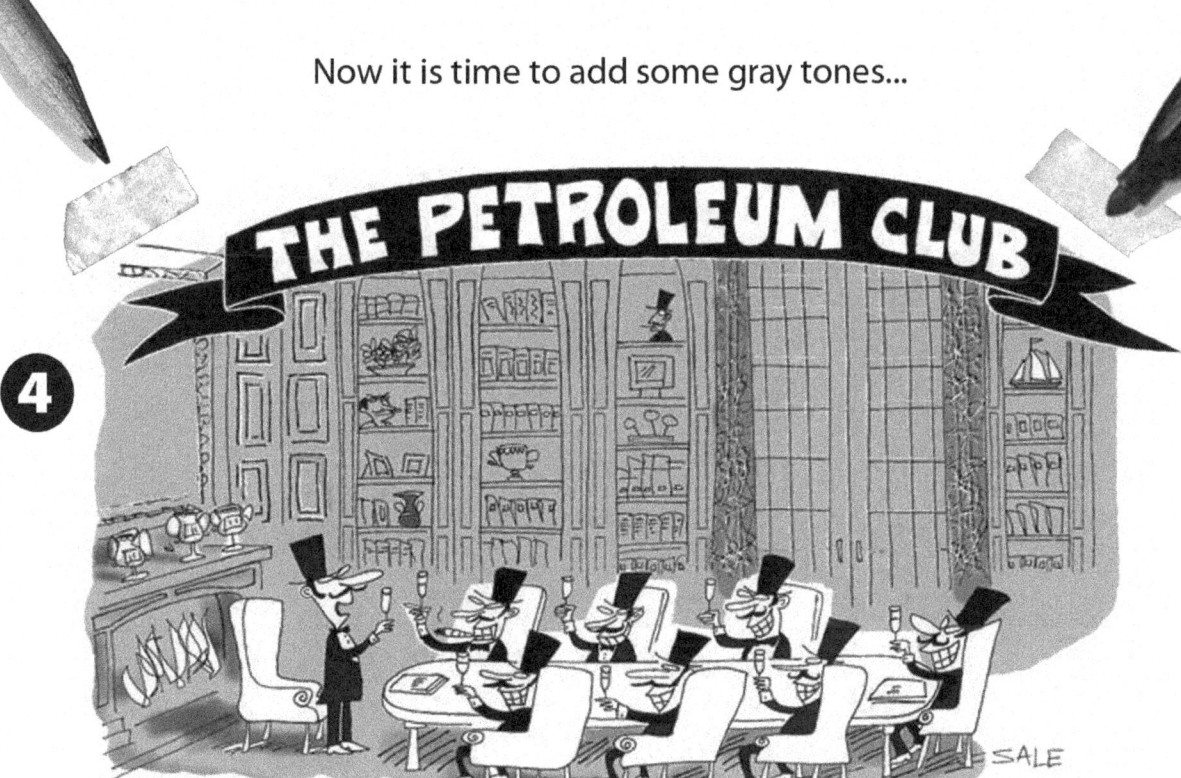

"*Once again, despite a poor economy, we show record-breaking profits. So let us toast that wonderful law of supply and demand....*

5 Lastly, I enhanced the gray background details and changed the caption. *The Petroleum Club* was now ready to go to print!

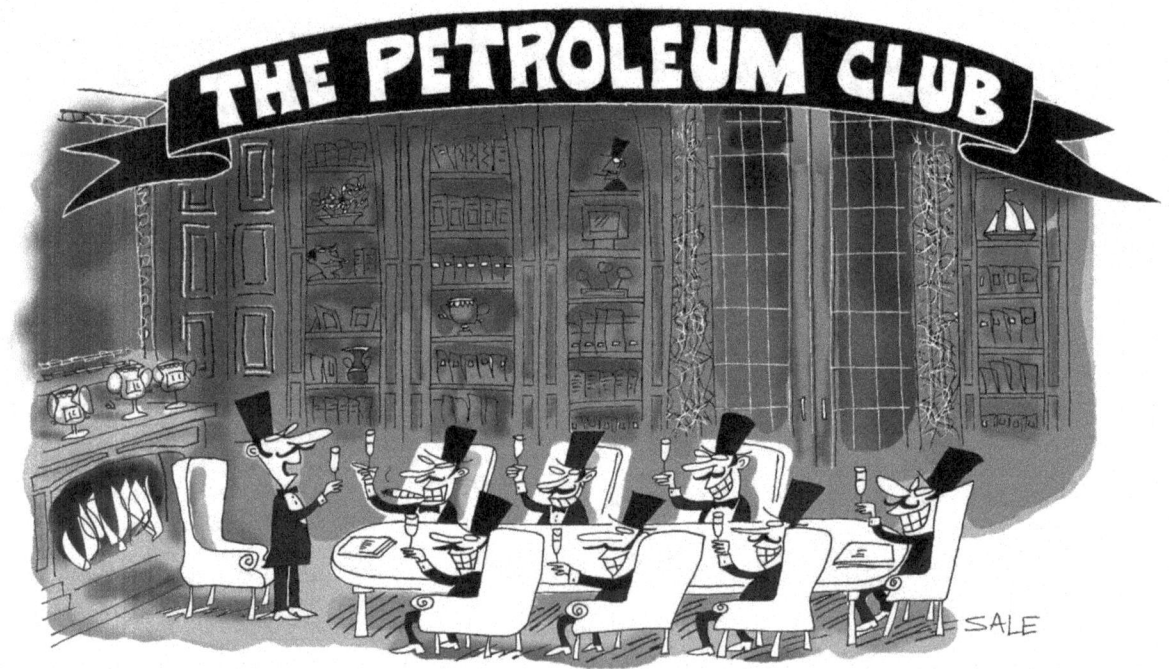

"Let us toast that wonderful law of supply and demand.
When you control the supply you can demand whatever the hell you want."

Welcome to MEN IN HATS...

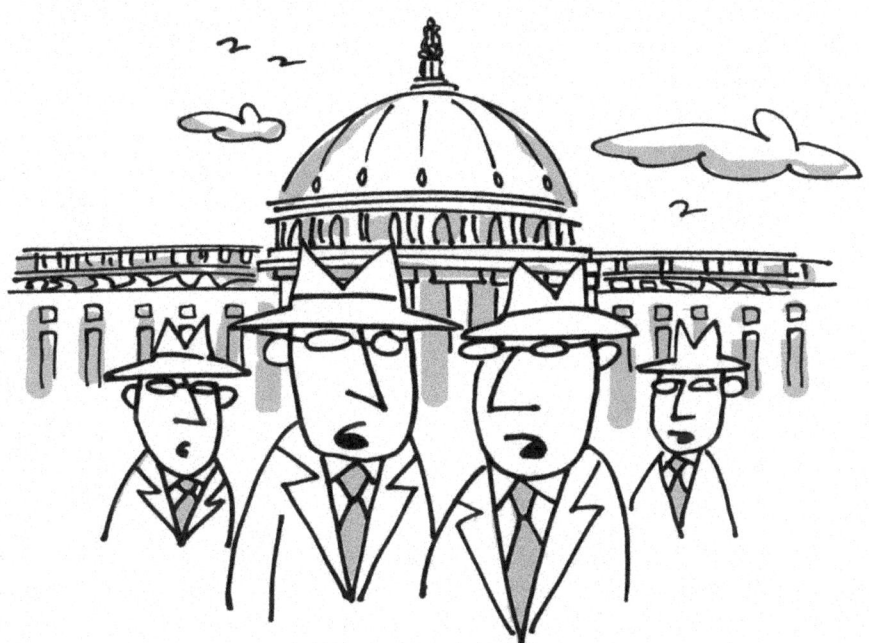

"If idiots could fly - this place would be an airport."

MEN IN HATS

MEN IN HATS began as a doodle I drew on the corner of an envelope that I threw away and then saved, and rediscovered years later. They had a conservative, Stepford Wives, clone-like quality that I thought might be funny if juxtaposed with silly or esoteric text. I began creating them solely for my own amusement.

I never could've imagined they'd get me a job as an editorial cartoonist or that they'd become a controversial socio-political cartoon, featured in one of the country's oldest newspapers, during arguably the most important election in history.

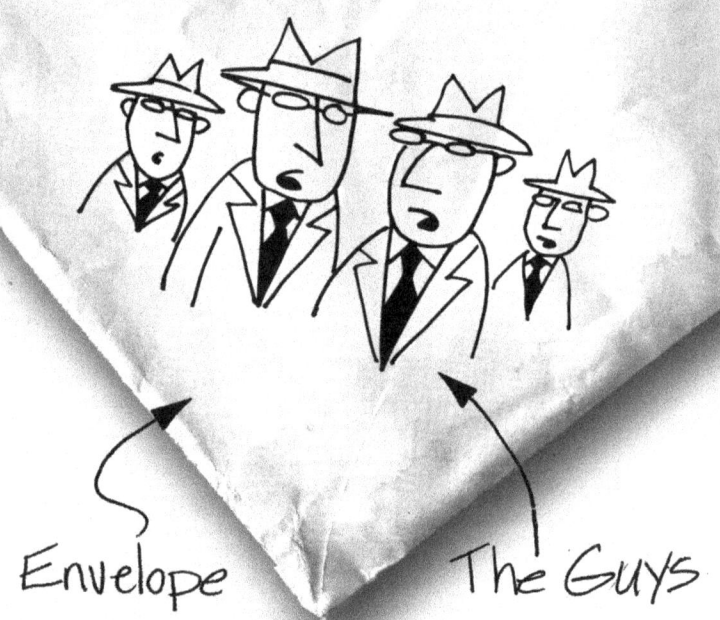

Envelope

The Guys

Risky Vision

Men In Hats became what it is today because of the vision of Chris Peck, then editor of the Commercial Appeal. After we agreed I'd contribute daily editorial cartoons to the newspaper, he asked if there was anything else I wanted to show him. I said I had something new I was working on and gave him a handful of Men In Hats cartoons (I made up the name on the spot). He looked at them and told me that if wanted to develop them, he would feature the cartoon every Saturday in the newspaper's editorial section— beginning that weekend. I was stunned.

I felt Chris was taking a big risk. How would people react to a cartoon that never changed? People like cartoons because they are simple and quick to read. Would readers put up with all the text in Men In Hats? And to be frank, I was just a teeny-weeny bit concerned about having to draw both a daily cartoon along with transforming *Men In Hats* into an editorial cartoon. Then there was the fact that I'd never been an editorial cartoonist before. Chris was patient and supportive, but I didn't sleep for two years.

Fortunately, Chris's risky vision paid off. I am proud of the body of work I created while working for him. The following are examples of *Men In Hats* as they first began and what they became as editorial cartoons. *Men In Hats: If Idiots Could Fly* is is a book of their cartoons that is available on my website: **grahamsale.com.** If you are unfamiliar with the guys, I'm certain you will enjoy them!

"Men in Hats" is something new in a profession that has grown dangerously predictable. Graham has a different take on political cartooning. Not the same old gags. Not the worn formats of old. I saw the difference the first day we met. It is one of the most creative, new concepts I've seen in editorial cartooning.

The Commercial Appeal needed to try something new in terms of political cartoons. Graham's "Men in Hats" series captured my imagination. So, in 2010 *The Commercial Appeal* began publishing "Men in Hats" every Saturday. The distinctive panel immediately became a high-interest feature of the newspaper. It has its fans and detractors, but remains one of the most talked-about features on *The Commercial Appeal's* editorial page.

Graham's cartoons wickedly point out the hypocrisy spewed by many politicians these days. "Men In Hats" make you think. It's not about a cheap gag. It is fresh and original. We need that in our political discourse these days."

- Chris Peck, Editor, The Commercial Appeal, Memphis

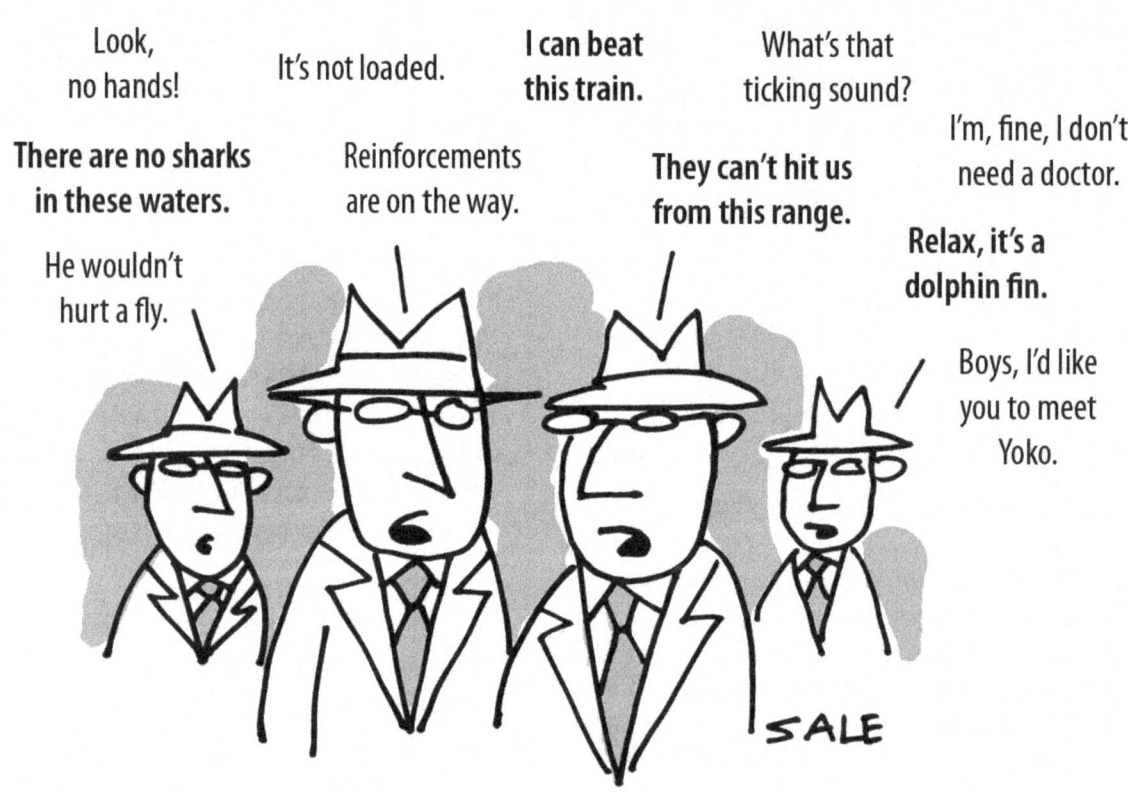

Famous last words.

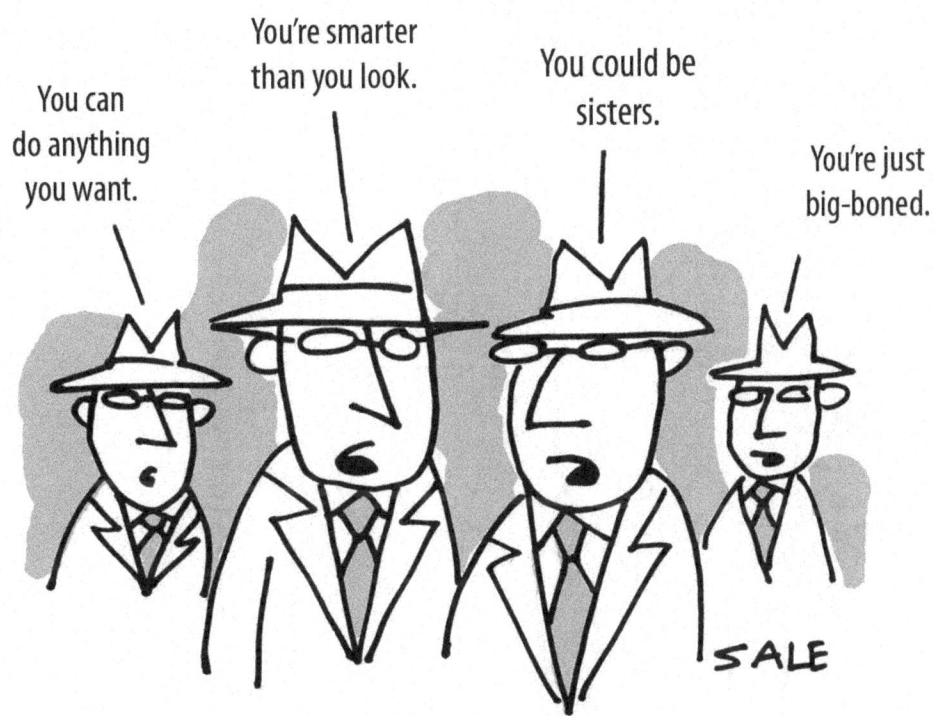

Liars Club. #102

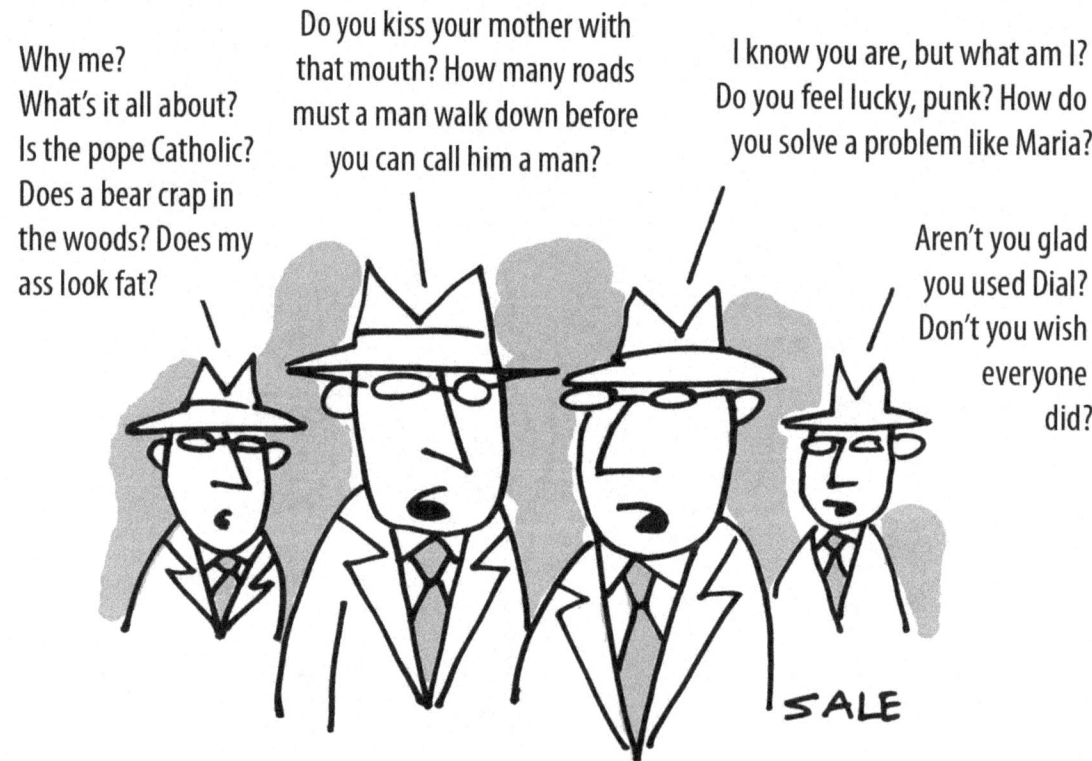

Board of Rhetorical Questions.

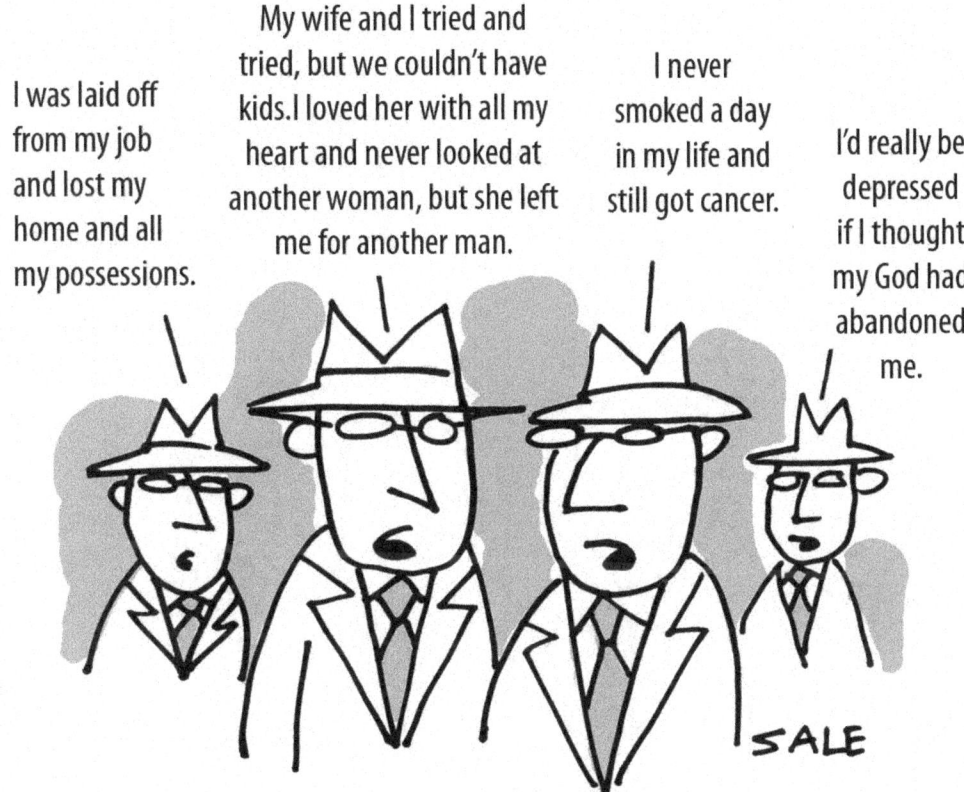

The bright side of Atheism.

Reality check: On 9/11 George Bush banned all air travel, but let two dozen bin Laden family members leave the U.S.A. without being questioned.

Six months later he said, "I don't know where (bin Laden) is, and I don't really care. It's not that important."

Instead, he invaded Iraq who had nothing to do with 9/11 or al-Quaeda.

The bin Ladens have had business ties with the Bushes for decades and invested in Dubya's oil companies.

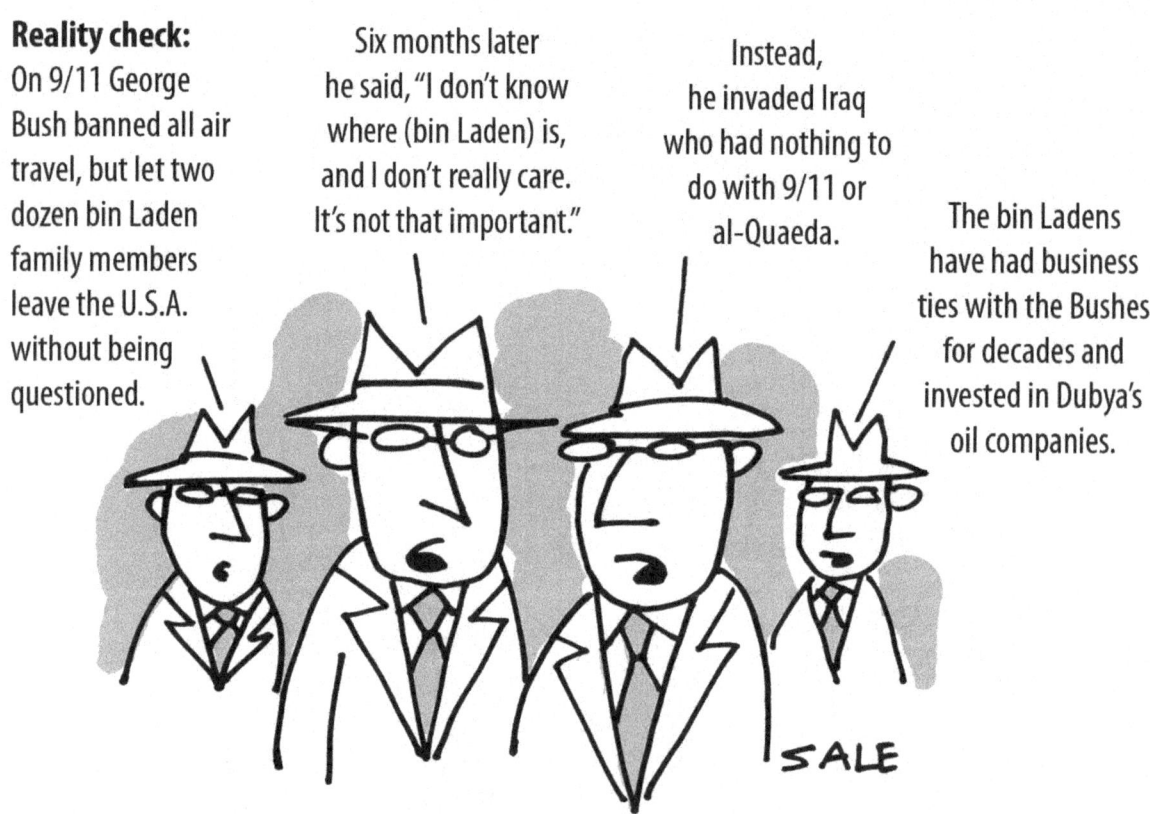

SALE

Blood is thicker than water, but nothing is thicker than oil.
This is what America should never forget.

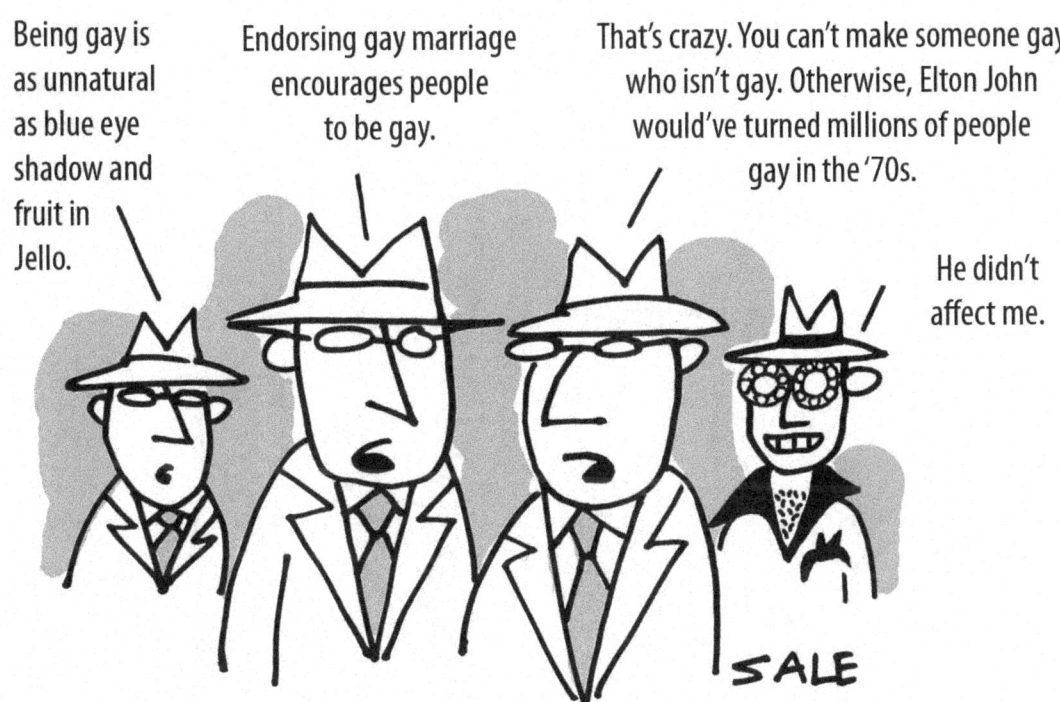

213

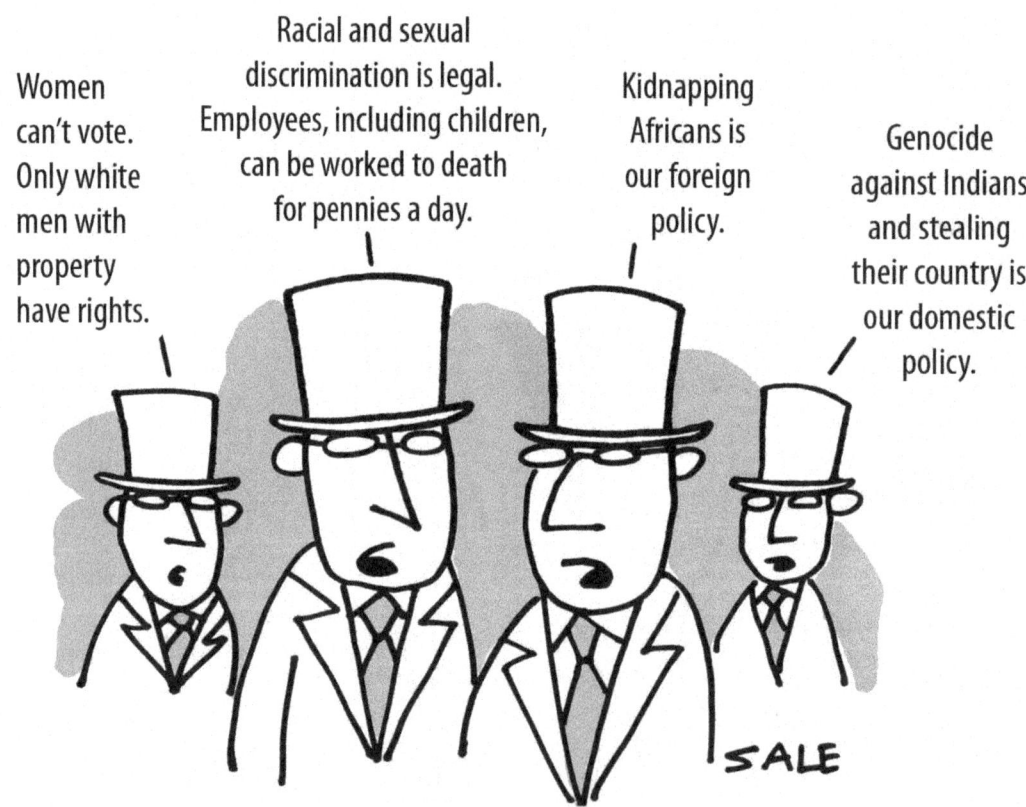

Traditional American values.
Which ones do you want to return to?

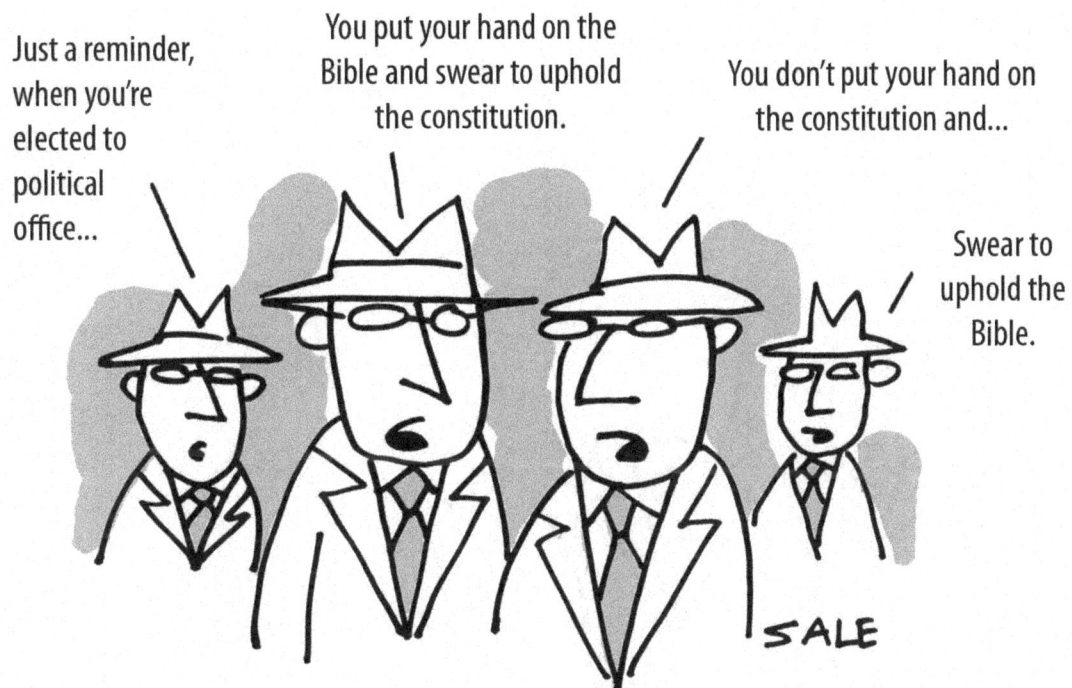

Some things aren't as self-evident as you'd think.

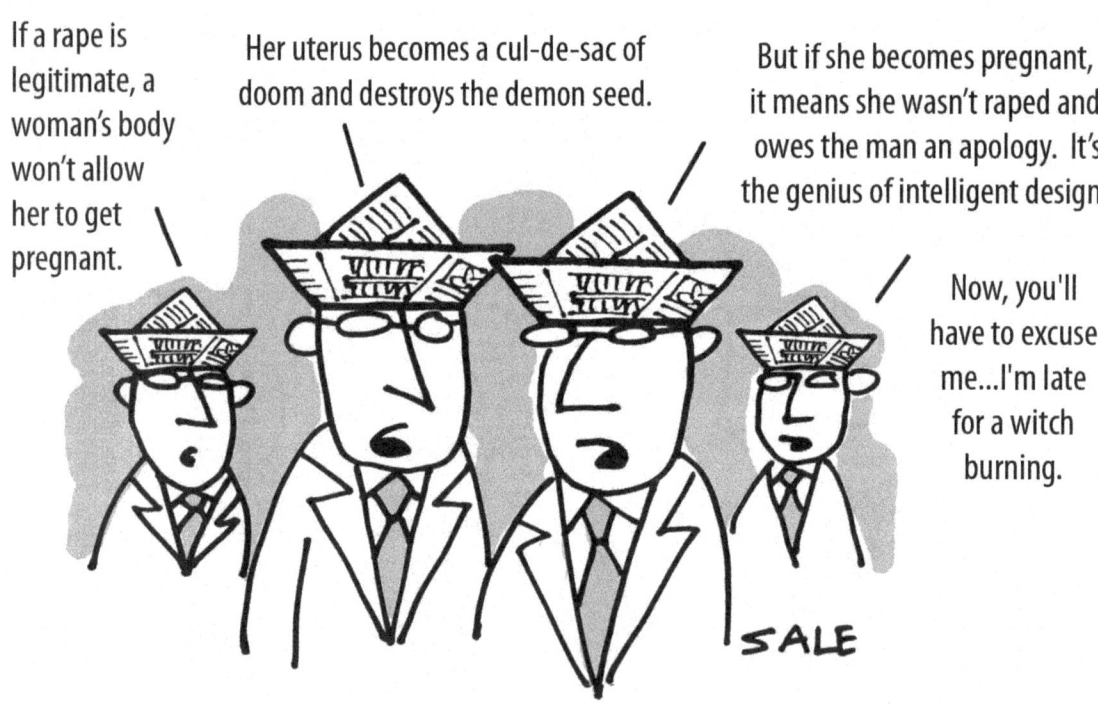

GOP: "A woman's body knows best."

About Graham

Graham is a prolific artist, writer and author best known for his cartoons and humorous illustrations that have appeared in advertisements, newspapers, books, on greeting cards, clothing and licensed products world-wide since the 1980's.

His clients have included, the *NY Times, NY Newsday, Funny Times, AT&T, Prudential, Allstate, Adweek, NY Magazine, Club Med, Absolut, Citibank, Forbes, Money, Scholastic,* various publishers, fortune 500 companies and many others. His political cartoons and his acclaimed series, "Men In Hats" was featured in *The Commercial Appeal* of Memphis, TN, one of the nation's oldest papers.

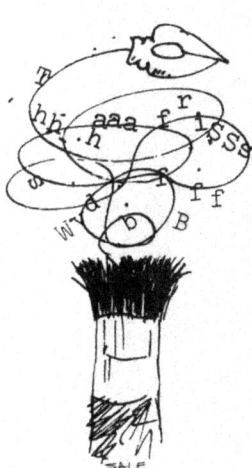

Graham was born in Detroit and grew up in Elmira, NY. He attended the College of Wooster and went to Parsons School of Design in NYC where he studied advertising. He began selling his art on the street and soon built a successful freelance business. His T-shirt company, 90 Degree Angle, produced and sold his work world wide. His famous "NY Gun" shirt is still a New York City icon.

Graham is the creator of Boneless Chuck the beloved character/toy loved around the world, and Club Crib the infant clothing. Graham is also the author of *What Women Want: A Gentleman's Guide to Romance* and the soon-to-be released, *Win at Work Without Losing at Love.*

After decades in New York and Los Angeles, Graham now lives in Memphis, TN.

This book is
dedicated to
Virginia Sale,
my mother, who
spent many long
nights at my bedside,
talking endlessly
with me about life
and helping me
to understand
the world and
the nincompoops
we're forced
to share
it with.

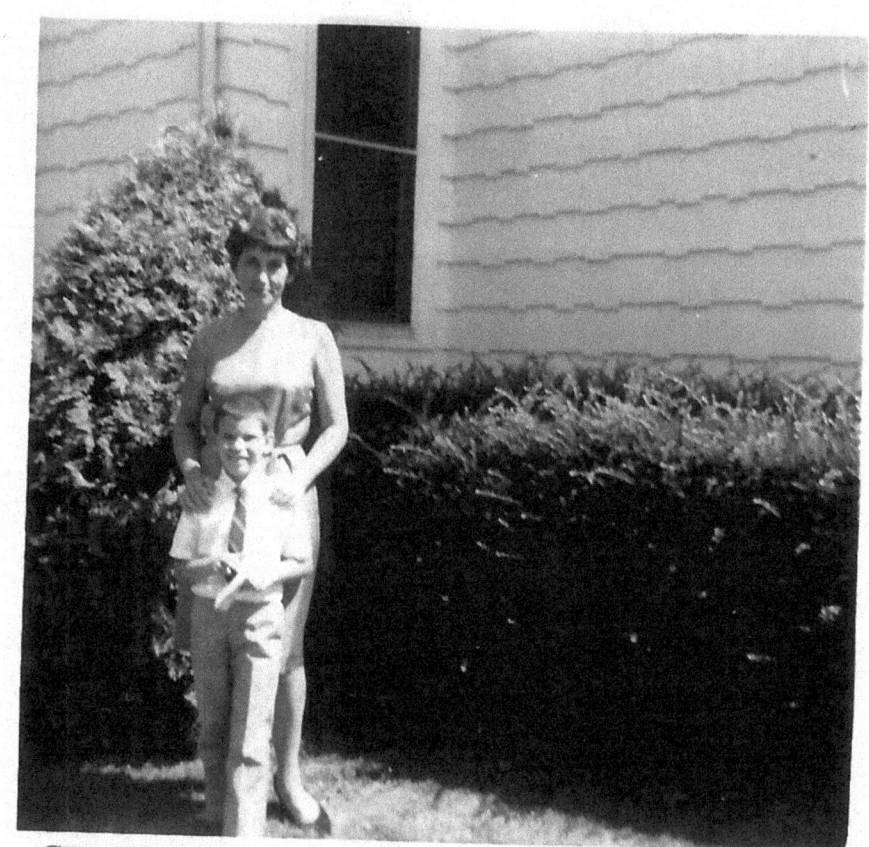

Circa 1965

Also by Graham Sale at:
WWW.GRAHAMSALE.COM

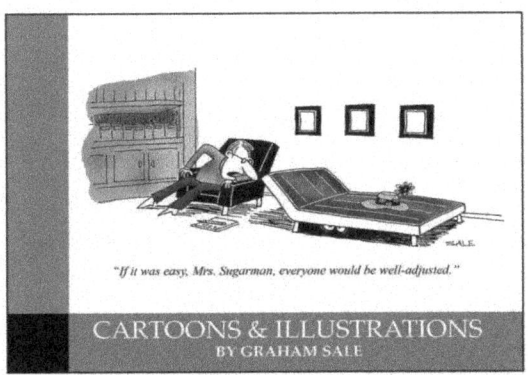

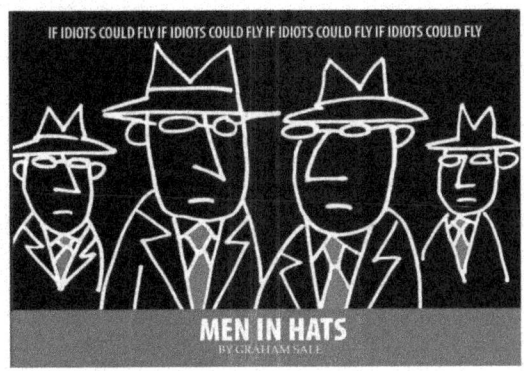

BONELESS CHUCK®

Boneless Chuck is Graham's proudest creation. Chuck is loved around the world. He is a friend to everyone - especially the sick and lonely. His journey and comeback story will amaze you.
Visit: Bonelesschuck.com

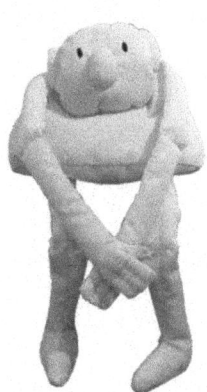

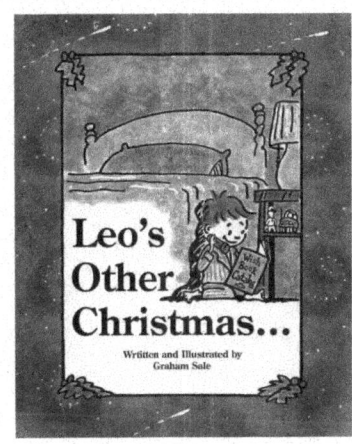

Made in USA - North Chelmsford, MA
1328826_9780967286556
08.23.2022 1643